Violence and the state

Edited by Matt Killingsworth, Matthew Sussex
and Jan Pakulski

Manchester University Press

Published by Manchester University Press
Altrincham Street, Manchester M1 7JA

www.manchesteruniversitypress.co.uk

British Library Cataloguing-in-Publication Data
A catalogue record for this book is available from the British Library

Library of Congress Cataloging-in-Publication Data applied for

ISBN 978 0 7190 9702 7 hardback

First published 2016

Typeset in Photina by
Servis Filmsetting Ltd, Stockport, Cheshire
Printed in Great Britain by
CPI Group (UK) Ltd, Croydon CR0 4YY

CONTENTS

NOTES ON CONTRIBUTORS

Jannika Brostrom is Associate Lecturer and PhD candidate in the Politics and International Relations Program at the University of Tasmania. She is currently writing her dissertation on the notion of morality in Australian foreign policy. Her research interests include international relations theory, approaches to aid and development, Australian foreign and security policy and political theory. She has published on the topics of moral realism, aid and development and cooperative security in Australia's foreign policy.

Gavin Daly is Senior Lecturer in Modern European History at the University of Tasmania, Australia. He has published widely on both Britain and France during the French Revolutionary-Napoleonic Wars. His most recent book is *The British Soldier in the Peninsular War: Encounters with Spain and Portugal, 1808–1814* (Palgrave Macmillan, 2013).

Graeme P. Herd is Professor of Transnational Security Studies at George C. Marshall European Center for Security Studies. He was previously Director of the School of Government, Plymouth University, and prior to this was Senior Programme Advisor and Senior Fellow, Leadership in Conflict Management Programme at the Geneva Center for Security Policy. His research focuses on diverse aspects of Russian foreign and security policy and Great Power relations. He is the co-editor (with John Kriendler) of *Understanding NATO in the 21st Century: Alliance Strategies, Security and Global Governance* (Routledge, 2013) and co-author (with Nayef Al-Rodhan and Lisa Watanabe) of *Critical Turning Points in the Middle East, 1915–2015* (Palgrave Macmillan, 2011).

Matt Killingsworth is Lecturer in International Relations at the University of Tasmania. His current research is concerned with the relationship between the laws of war and international order. He is the author of *Civil Society in Communist Eastern Europe: Opposition and Dissent in Totalitarian Regimes* (ECPR Press, 2012) and has published book chapters and journal articles on opposition and dissent in Communist Eastern Europe, justice in post-Communist Eastern Europe, the changing nature of war and the laws of war. In 2013 he was a Visiting Fellow at the University of Oxford's Institute for Ethics, Law and Armed Conflict.

Terry Narramore is Lecturer in International Relations at the University of Tasmania, where he specialises in the domestic and international politics of

China. His research interests include China's security strategy, Sino-Japanese relations, and the domestic challenges to China's authoritarian state, particularly minority resistance.

Jan Pakulski is Professor Emeritus at the University of Tasmania, Fellow of the Academy of the Social Sciences in Australia, Affiliate of the Stanford Centre for Poverty and Inequality, and Visiting Professor at Collegium Civitas, Warsaw. He is the (co-)author of 10 books and over 120 scholarly articles on elites, democratisation, multiculturalism, post-communism, social movements and social inequality. His most recent books include *Toward Leader Democracy* (with Andras Korosenyi) (Anthem, 2012) and *Declining Political Leadership in Australia* (with Bruce Tranter) (Palgrave, 2015).

Matthew Sussex is Head of Politics and International Relations at the School of Social Sciences, University of Tasmania. His research interests include strategic and security studies, Russian politics and foreign policy, and conflict in the international system. He has been awarded grants from bodies such as the Australian Research Council and the Fulbright Commission, amongst others. His recent books include *Conflict in the Former USSR* (Cambridge University Press, 2012). His numerous articles and book chapters focus on Russian foreign and security policy, the foreign policies of great powers, globalisation and contemporary war, and Australian security policy. He is a National Executive member of the Australian Institute of International Affairs and a founding member of the Australian Council for Strategic Studies.

Jasmine-Kim Westendorf is Lecturer in International Relations at La Trobe University. Her research interests lie in conflict and peace studies, negotiated peace settlements and peacebuilding, and the politics of international law. She has published her research in leading journals including the *Australian Journal of International Affairs*, and has conducted policy work for numerous development NGOs. She is the author of *Why Peace Processes Fail: Negotiating Insecurity After Civil Wars* (Lynne Rienner Publishers, 2015).

ACKNOWLEDGEMENTS

This book is the result of a collaborative effort that received generous financial support from the Faculty of Arts at the University of Tasmania. Funding for the 'War, Violence and State Elites' Research Group brought together a group with shared research interests in the nature and character of modern violence, and its relationship to the nation-state. We anticipate and look forward to more collaborative research projects with this group.

Further financial assistance was provided by the University of Tasmania's Institute for the Study of Social Change. The topics explored and analysed in this volume align with the goals and mission of the Institute, establishing a research nexus around understanding the causes of social change and addressing its consequences.

The editors are grateful to the team at Manchester University Press for their ongoing encouragement of this project. We are especially thankful to the 'New approaches to conflict analysis' series editor, Dr Peter Lawler, for his advice on our original proposal. We are similarly appreciative to the anonymous reviewer at MUP for their constructive feedback and informed recommendations.

Finally, we are grateful for the editing work of Rob Hortle, who, before taking up a Rhodes Scholarship, worked diligently and professionally to very tight deadlines.

ABBREVIATIONS

AB-Aktion	*Außerordentliche Befriedungsaktion* (Special Pacification Operations)
ASEAN	Association of Southeast Asian Nations
CIS	Commonwealth of Independent States
CPA	Comprehensive Peace Agreement
CPC	Communist Party of China (*Gongchandang*)
CPP	Cambodian People's Party
DDR	disarmament, demobilisation and reintegration
DRC	Democratic Republic of Congo
EG	*Einsatzgruppen*
ETIM	East Turkestan Islamic Movement
FUNCINPEC	National United Front for an Independent, Neutral, Peaceful and Cooperative Cambodia
GCS	global civil society
GOSS	Government of South Sudan
GPO	*Generalplan Ost* (Master Plan East)
GPU	*Gosudarstvennoye politicheskoye upravlenie* (State Political Directorate)
IA	*Intelligenzaktion*
ICC	International Criminal Court
ICG	International Crisis Group
ICISS	International Commission on Intervention and State Sovereignty
ICTR	International Criminal Tribunal for Rwanda
ICTY	International Criminal Tribunal for the Former Yugoslavia
IHL	International Humanitarian Law
IPN	*Instytut Pamięci Narodowej* (Institute of National Remembrance)
ISIS	Islamic State of Iraq and Syria
KPNLF	Khmer People's National Liberation Front
LNP	Liberian National Police
NATO	North Atlantic Treaty Organisation
NGO	non-governmental organisation
NKVD	*Narodnyy Komissariat Vnutrennikh Del* (People's Commissariat for Internal Affairs)
NTGL	National Transitional Government of Liberia
OSCE	Organization for Security and Cooperation in Europe

OTP	Office of the Prosecutor (International Criminal Court)
PDK	Party of Democratic Kampuchea
PLA	Palestine Liberation Army
PLA	People's Liberation Army
POW	Prisoner of War
PPA	Paris Peace Agreement
PRC	People's Republic of China
R2P	Responsibility to Protect
RPF	Rwandese Patriotic Front
RSHA	*Reichssicherheitshauptamt* (Reich Main Security Office)
SA	*Sonderaktion*
SPLA	Sudan People's Liberation Army
SPLM	Sudan People's Liberation Movement
SS	*Schutzstaffel*
SSR	Security Sector Reform
TAR	Tibetan Autonomous Region
UNDP	United Nations Development Programme
UNMIL	United Nations Mission in Liberia
UNSC	United Nations Security Council
UNTAC	United Nations Transitional Administration in Cambodia

Introduction:
understanding violence and the state

Matthew Sussex and Matt Killingsworth

THE CENTRAL OBJECTIVE of this book is to help unlock an intriguing interdisciplinary puzzle relating to violence. Put simply, we ask 'what is the relationship between the instrumental uses of violence, including its main forms, and the willingness of states to employ it?' To answer this question, the book combines social-political and historical analyses. Its span is from the birth of modern state violence in the French Revolution and Napoleonic campaigns, through the Stalinist and Nazi genocides, to the (sometimes) more selective and contained contemporary forms of state violence. We take as our starting point the assumption that violence cannot be completely divorced from 'traditional' political objectives, such as contests over resources. From this, we hypothesise that while *types* of violence might change, the main *purposes* of political violence largely do not. The structure of the volume also assumes that violence remains a central aspect of state conduct, whether viewed through the prism of international relations scholarship, diachronic or synchronic historical perspectives, or as an integral facet of sociological accounts. In this respect we share Hannah Arendt's view that 'no one engaged in thought about history and politics can remain unaware of the enormous role violence has played in human affairs'.[1]

While many scholars would broadly accept this particular observation, it is also important to note that the volume focuses on violence specifically as employed by the state. Following Max Weber (and later Charles Tilly), the contributors to this book all agree that states continue to seek to monopolise the legitimate use of violence.[2] This is not to say that other actors within, above and between states do not employ violence: quite the contrary, in fact. But whether justified in terms of various rights and obligations, pursued as a mechanism for internal cohesion, or out-sourced via proxies to private agencies or militias, there is little enthusiasm in the current international community for agents other than states to be seen as legitimate holders of the right to resort to violence. Naturally, this means that the purposes of violence are linked very much to notions of order, and hence they take on a dual character. In other words, violence can be employed by those who wish to challenge an existing order, but it can also be used those who seek to sustain it. On the internal, intra-state level, this helps to distinguish between governmental actors on the one hand, and revolutionaries, guerrillas, freedom fighters or champions of the people (broadly or narrowly defined) on the other. The former have tended to use violence to engender conditions necessary to the preservation of their authority, control and political longevity.[3] The latter seek to challenge that authority. And linking violence to order is also useful on the international level since it can help differentiate between those that are status quo actors, and those that are revisionist.

Violence as coercion, violence as war, and violence as force

What do we mean by 'violence' in this book? The literature on the topic is replete with definitions. Some of them are extremely broad, and aim to show that any unequal power relationship, whether overt or covert (or even conscious or unconscious) can be interpreted as coercion – and hence as violence.[4] Contributions from feminist scholars, critics of capitalism and liberal pluralism, environmentalist scholars and human rights advocates have all made this claim.[5] For an entire set of separate discourses that owe at least partial allegiance to the Frankfurt School, and which are reflected today in an array of critical theoretical approaches in the social sciences, such a characterisation of violence is accepted as customary.[6] Whether by thought, by deed or by speech, such scholars point out, violence is perpetrated by the powerful against the powerless.

At the other end of the spectrum, where one finds strategic thinkers and historians of major conflict, violence can simply be understood as war. In other words, war and violence in the modern state system are expressions of politics by other means.[7] And supplementing Clausewitzian approaches are the long-influential views of Carl Schmitt that the state exists as an agent of violence to maximise its power.[8] Those identified as 'defensive' realists in international relations theory would also see violence as more or less synonymous with armed conflict between like units in the international system.[9] In this case, those units are states, since it is only the state that has territory, borders and a central authority that controls the means of organised violence. And in normative and liberal international relations scholarship, states are the sole actors with international legal personality.

As a result, while non-state actors may – for various reasons – claim the 'right' to use force, states are the only agents for whom such behaviour is codified in international law. Moreover, non-state actors, whether ethnic groups, religious minority populations or socio-economically disadvantaged people, tend to seek protection from harm in material form. There are virtually no self-determination campaigns that have not had a territorial state as a central objective. This is true of contemporary struggles over territory and resources in 1970s Afghanistan, the former Yugoslavia, Chechnya and an array of decolonisation struggles after World War II. Even the Islamic State of Iraq and Syria (ISIS), as a contemporary expression of an amorphous set of fundamentalist values reminiscent of Al Qaeda, nonetheless seeks statehood through its conception of a broad Islamic Caliphate.

Since this book is concerned primarily with violence as practised by states, we adopt a definition closer to a more 'conventional' interpretation. Hence we define violence as the organised and systematic threat or use – primarily for political objectives linked to power – of state instruments that have the capacity to cause physical harm. In that context violence as practised by the state is synonymous with force when employed for a specific purpose, or under legal-normative mandates afforded by sources of international legitimacy like the United Nations. Violence, as we conceive of it here, is also synonymous with war as a broader manifestation of force that requires the state to mobilise considerably more national resources than it might otherwise have to when taking part in police operations or humanitarian interventions. Finally, violence is also synonymous with force when used as an internal mechanism of control for political purposes by pre-existing elites.

We certainly acknowledge that the nature of violence and the nature of statehood have both changed considerably in the modern era. So too have the laws and norms that govern them, both within states and between them. But we are less confident that those changes can be understood in a linear or evolutionary fashion. While some of the contributors offer a contrasting interpretation on the ideational aspects of violence, we are united in our argument about the continued centrality of the state in understanding violence. With this in mind, we now turn to examine in more detail the nature of statehood, the ways in which it has changed, and the various ways in which violence has been instrumentalised by states over time.

Violence and the formation of the modern state

At its most basic level, the state is an abstract entity comprising a government, people and territory. Historically, though, it has assumed a variety of forms, from cities to feudal orders, and most recently sovereign nation-states.[10] Thus, the state as a construction has over time assumed an increasing capacity as 'the principal institutional site of political experience'.[11] In this respect, definitions that focus on the coercive capacity of states remain illuminating. The most famous of these is Max Weber's characterisation of a state as 'a human community that (successfully) claims the monopoly on the legitimate use of physical force within a given territory'.[12] Likewise, Charles Tilly defines states as 'relatively centralised, differentiated organisations, the officials of which more or less successfully claim control over the chief concentrated means of violence within a population inhabiting a large, contiguous territory'.[13]

It is certainly the case that both these definitions focus on what the state *does*, rather than what it might *aim to do*. But such definitions nonetheless remain useful. Even if one were to focus on the aspirations of the state, one could not adequately do so without first appreciating that the ability to rule is sustained just as much by the state's capacity to coerce, as it is to persuade.[14] Central to this, too, is an appreciation of violence. As one of Weber's slightly lesser-known observations put it, 'the relation between the state and violence is an especially intimate one'.[15] And while Tilly's statement that 'war made the state, and the state made war' might be regarded as facile or tautological, it still encapsulates the fact that violence and statehood have historically been closely linked.[16] Across the early modern era, the growing demands of war assisted in state consolidation through the maintenance of large standing armies, the increasing professionalisation of the military classes, the integration of war materiel into industrialisation processes, and mass state taxation.[17] Prior to modernity, many agents may have made a legitimate claim to use violence, but the centralised state emerged as the dominant form of political organisation from the various overlapping authority types that were characteristic of pre-modern order.[18]

It did this in two interrelated ways. First, as the war making endeavours of European sovereigns expanded, and the cost of waging war dramatically increased, smaller decentralised units proved incapable of managing these new requirements. The military revolution of the seventeenth century was characterised by costly advances in technology and weaponry, and in military tactics. Once armies became permanent, peacetime became almost as expensive as times of war.[19] The increasingly centralised state proved itself adept at raising the capital required for this. Due to economies of scale it streamlined administrative capacities, and hence reduced transaction costs. The upshot was that it was able to monitor violence, to control it, and effectively monopolise it.[20]

Second, the modern state was able to successfully disarm competitors. As Janice Thomson notes, in the heteronomous system of the medieval period 'urban militias, private armies, fiscal agents, armies of regional lords and rival claimants to royal power, police forces and state armies all claimed the right to exercise violence'.[21] The emasculation of non-state actors was sometimes achieved through bargains struck between societal groups. But more often it was a long and bloody struggle. Hence violence moved from non-state, international economic and transnational authorities to a domestic political realm of authority. The result was a dual benefit to the state, which allowed it both to monopolise authority to use violence abroad, and to accept control over violence that came from within its own borders.[22] In this context Henryk Spruyt has correctly argued that while three organisational forms could be identified in the pre-modern order (city-states, city leagues and sovereign territorial states) only the last one was effective and efficient in controlling resources, external relations and delegitimising rival institutional forms.[23]

Violence and globalisation: constraining states and empowering others?

An equally important aspect of the modern state's claims on a monopoly over violence is that it has come to be understood as wielding its monopoly *legitimately*, both internally and externally.[24] The state's growth and global spread, as understood by Michael Mann, 'is explained primarily not in domestic terms but in terms of geopolitical relations to violence'.[25] Thus, while the assumption remains that the global structure of states ensures stability and hinders violence, that order ironically continues to be built on the state's perceived right to use coercion.

There are good reasons to see this arrangement as existing throughout modern history only as an ideal-type. Yet a significant proportion of the literature, especially since the end of the Cold War, has argued not just that the sovereign state has declined in relevance, but also that global transformations pose profound challenges to the state's continued claim to a monopoly on legitimate violence.[26] A number of arguments are made to this end. The first relates to the state's historical capacity as a war-fighting institution. While those who see the state's demise as looming do acknowledge the integral role that war fighting played in the development of the modern state, they also argue that the state's capacity for war fighting has been diminishing. As Martin van Creveld neatly put it:

> In law as well as in fact, as the twentieth century was approaching its end, interstate war appeared to be on the retreat. The right to wage it, far from being part and parcel of sovereignty, had been taken away except insofar as it was done in strict self-defence; even when states *did* wage war in strict self-defence (and precisely for that reason), they were no longer allowed to benefit by bringing about territorial change. Thus such war has lost its chief attraction.[27]

However, this does not automatically mean that war and violence has become altogether obsolete. Instead it is non-traditional expressions of violence, asymmetric warfare and intra-state war that have become much more significant. As a set of tactics distinct from modern mass war these have often resulted in success over what should on paper be far superior forces. As van Creveld argues, 'from France to the United States, there has scarcely been one "advanced" government ... whose armed forces have not suffered defeat' at the hands of those who were poorly trained, poorly equipped and poorly organised.[28]

While not necessarily part of the so-called 'new war' literature, van Creveld's thesis shares a number of similarities to the arguments put forward by Mary Kaldor and others associated with contemporary writing on war. Like many of the arguments about the decline of the state, Kaldor's views are anchored by the assumption that ideas and identity, facilitated by processes of globalisation, are fundamental in reshaping the nature of political authority. This, Kaldor and others have argued, has in turn transformed not only the nature of war, but also the capacity for states to use war as an instrument of statecraft. According to Kaldor, new wars occur when state authority erodes, and also when it fails entirely. In particular, 'they occur in the context of the erosion of the monopoly of legitimised organised violence'.[29] As an extension of this, and drawing links between the breakdown of the state and economic motives, Kalevi Holsti has suggested that the erosion of state authority might represent what he calls 'neo-medievalism'. Holsti's argument raises the possibility of an even more significant transformation than that offered by Kaldor, in the form of a return to a pre-modern order. Under this conception the state is merely one of a number of competing authority types:

> The new medievalism is demonstrated most dramatically in the nature of armed conflict in these states. War has become de-institutionalised in the sense of central controls, rules, regulations, etiquette and armaments. Armies are rag-tag groups frequently made up of teenagers paid in drugs, or not paid at all. In the absence of authority and discipline, but in keeping with the interests of the warlords, 'soldiers' discover opportunities for private enterprises of their own.[30]

A related claim about the decline of the modern state concerns the degree to which it remains the primary authority within a demarcated area. Also framed broadly within debates about globalisation, this view is of states increasingly beholden to forces from supra-state actors that compromise their capacity to act independently, or as an authority type. Here, the growing significance of international law and human rights norms are seen as imposing fundamental constraints upon what states can and cannot do in terms of resorting to force. For Christian Reus-Smit, this new international legal order is characterised by a 'movement away from a legal system in which states are the sole legal subjects, and in which the domestic is tightly quarantined from the international'. Instead, he argues, this movement is towards 'a transnational legal order that grants legal rights and agency to individuals and erodes the traditional boundary between inside and outside'.[31]

Critics of the state as the sole repository of legal violence are also found amongst advocates of the Responsibility to Protect (R2P) doctrine. They point in particular to the 2001 report of the International Commission on Intervention and State Sovereignty (ICISS) that saw states as having a diminished capacity with respect to the use of violence. The report argued that sovereignty, and thus the implied right of non-interference, was no longer an assumed right. Rather, 'sovereignty implies responsibility, and the primary responsibility for the protection of its people lies with the state itself'. A failure to uphold this responsibility would result in the principle of non-interference yielding to the international responsibility to protect.[32] In 2007, Martin Gilbert went as far as to proclaim that 'the ... concept of "responsibility to protect" proposed the most significant adjustment to national sovereignty in 360 years'.[33] One of R2P's most vocal proponents, Gareth Evans, writing on the tenth anniversary of the ICISS report, wrote that 'by any measurement, the achievement of the past decade – universal agreement that state sovereignty is not a license to kill – has been tremendous'.[34]

A third and final claim related to violence and globalisation concerns the development of law and norms associated with the protection of human rights. While human rights have arguably existed throughout history, the 1948 Universal Declaration marked a significant moment in attempts to define and protect those rights. Today it forms the foundation for a global framework of human rights, consisting of various instruments, declarations and treaties. The development of a global human rights regime has moved some to announce the existence of a cosmopolitan ethical order. Noting that 130 states had signed on to the International Bill of Human Rights by the mid-1990s, John Charvet argued that 'since most states have signed up ... it would seem that there already exists a world ethical consensus'.[35]

Contemporary violence and the continued centrality of the state

Yet the impact of globalisation, and the constraints that law and norms place upon the use of force by states, are open to question. First, as Anthony Langlois points out, glib references to a worldwide acceptance of international human rights law are premature. They belie 'the reality that this body of law is an interconnected patchwork of legal instrumentalities and institutions, each with their own (often competing) jurisdictions and interests'.[36] Second, and of even more relevance to the arguments being made in this volume, international human rights law cannot take effect if international agreements are not ratified and then consistently (rather than selectively) practised in local jurisdictions.[37] Most of the time this is a complex undertaking, since it asks states to cede authority to a malleable and loose set of international standards over what policy-makers see as vital national interests.

Third, globalisation remains an essentially slippery concept. As Susan Strange once argued, the term 'can refer to anything from the Internet to a hamburger'.[38] The conceptual and empirical shortcomings of approaches that link globalisation to cosmopolitanism, especially as the 'new wars' thesis seeks to do with the state, have been well documented. By understanding the behaviour of militias, criminal gangs and armed conflict through the prism of ideas and identity, any type of violence can be understood as a 'new' war. In the process of understanding everything, the result is that we actually understand nothing. Equally important is the fact that the apparently 'chaotic' nature of new conflicts – via looting; the trafficking of people; the targeting of civilians, a loose distinction between combatants and noncombatants; and violence seemingly for the sake of it – are all excellent descriptors of 'old' wars as well. And the prescription – for cosmopolitan international law and human security to ensure a just and fair order – ignores the fact that this relies on structures that are weakly developed, contested, routinely subject to cheating, and highly selective in their enforcement of compliance. Even in a post-9/11 world, in the absence of a formal overarching governing global authority, the sources of any responses to violence (and often the most effective users of it) are still states themselves.

The same is the case for premature proclamations about the victory of democracy, as witnessed by the so-called 'End of History' in Eastern Europe and the former Soviet geopolitical space, and in the messy Arab Spring. Rather than the inexorable spread of democracy, we are instead witnessing the erosion of democratic individualism as the sole normative narrative used to inform, shape and respond to international organisation. Part of this is due to changing power dynamics, with the gradual attenuation of US power prompting it to 'rebalance' its attention to Asia. Coupled to the relative military weakness of the European Union and the rapid rise of China (and to a lesser extent India), existing rationales for intervention on human rights grounds are likely to become more multifaceted and complex. Again, the state – and not a sense of enduring global community – is driving this process.

Further evidence of this can be seen in the rapid retreat by supporters of R2P, who initially hailed it as a new 'policy toolkit' to stop states from committing mass crimes against their own people.[39] Instead it has become clear that the doctrine is a highly convenient rationale for states seeking to justify instrumental policy agendas. The Russian invocation of R2P during its 2008 war with Georgia over South Ossetia set a precedent for China to refer to its 'responsibility to protect' Chinese citizens from groups among the Uighur population it chose to brand as terrorists. Even more worrying has been the inconsistent employment of R2P by the West. In Libya in 2011 an unseemly scramble by France and Germany to use violence resulted in the North Atlantic Treaty Organisation (NATO) being used as a *de facto* air arm for opponents of Muamar Qaddafi. However, once the alliance to unseat him fragmented, the country plunged rapidly into civil war. In Syria a strong case for intervention existed, but did not occur. And in 2014, proponents of R2P were strangely silent in the face of ISIS led violence in Iraq and Syria, even though thousands of civilians were facing execution in the most brutal and bloody ways.

This is not to say that contemporary violence, as practised by states, remains completely unconstrained by laws and norms. Indeed, the technological revolution has opened up myriad new ways for those seeking relief from state control to mobilise and express their opposition. The 2010 Arab Spring is an excellent example of ways in which contemporary states have struggled to adapt to new sources of challenge from their own populations. Instruments of dissent, and even violence, have to an extent been freed from the power structure of many states, especially those that are weak. But history is an excellent reminder that faith in wholesale change should be tempered by a longer view. The Napoleonic wars and the French Revolution certainly set the conditions for the emergence of the modern state, even though the scale of violence they utilised would seem impossible in the current global climate. However it would be a mistake to assume that globalisation alone, or globalisation in concert with a new form of ethical conscience, is in any way immutable. Likewise, the harsh eliticides practised by both Nazi Germany and the Soviet Union during WWII would seem unthinkable today. Yet many of the conditions that permit elites to conduct campaigns of decapitation still exist, and the few functional and consistent barriers to such conduct in future should temper any enthusiastic claims that they could never happen again.

Hence, violence has indeed become more fragmented, and should not be framed merely as solely the preserve of states. In fact, there are compelling arguments that this was never really the case. But it is equally the case that the diffusion of violence should not be interpreted as representing the demise of the state. As the contributors in this volume argue, the modern state (as a unit of political organisation) has lost neither its capacity nor desire for violence. At the same time, the state has proven itself remarkably resilient to forces – both external and internal – that attempt to restrain its evolved right to use coercive means.

Structure of the book

In order to understand contemporary violence it is arguably necessary to return to the past. Thus in the first main chapter of this volume Gavin Daly explores the period of the French Revolution and the Napoleonic Wars as a transformative moment in the quantitative and qualitative development of violence. Indeed, over the last decade or more, historians have increasingly debated the question of where the French Revolutionary period sits in terms of modern state violence. Much of this has focused on the themes of 'new' and 'total war' versus 'limited war'. Notwithstanding continuities with the past, this chapter focuses on both changing ideals and practices in the context of the French Revolution and its legacy. It considers the impact of revolutionary ideology and the Jacobin state on the 'totalisation' of war, both within and beyond French national borders, and the effects of mobilisation in the context of a 'nation-in-arms'.

Chapter 2 extends the book's examination of state violence as a tool of pacification. It focuses on the twin decapitations of Polish society by occupiers from Nazi Germany and the Soviet Union. During WWII Poland lost approximately 20 per cent of its citizens. But as Jan Pakulski argues, losses among the 'leading strata' – including political leaders and social activists – were much larger, ranging from 30 per cent to 60 per cent. This was due to the deliberate and systematic targeting of Polish elites and the sub-elite stratum, the intelligentsia, by the invading Soviet and German forces. Both Nazi and Soviet eliticides were carefully planned and executed in secrecy. As a result of the eliticide, Polish society emerged from the WWII socially and politically weakened, unable to resist a political takeover by the Soviet-backed communist regime.

From conquest and pacification, the book turns to an examination of violence as an important facet of national unification and state consolidation strategies. Terry Narramore examines the rationales and varieties of violence deployed by the state in modern China aimed at national unification and the consolidation of state power. His chapter demonstrates how state violence and coercion produce 'enemies' of the state in an attempt to reinforce a singular monopoly over both the 'nation' and the state. In the case of the People's Republic of China (PRC) this process remains significantly incomplete in areas that the ruling elite refers to as 'core interests': Taiwan, Tibet and Xinjiang. While the chapter draws on Tilly's ideas on collective violence, analysing the post-Maoist state as an 'exemplary high-capacity undemocratic regime', it argues that the 'minorities' of Tibet and Xinjiang represent a particular challenge to the PRC that go beyond state capacity and regime type.

Just as violence is a significant component of national unification strategies, so too are decisions to utilise violence externally. In contemporary world politics, maintaining plausible deniability in the face of international criticism requires new strategies for states seeking to use violence. This is especially the case for new illiberal and authoritarian states utilising a combination of nationalist and pro-Western rhetoric, coupled to new tactics, to achieve their aims. Thus, in the book's next chapter, Matthew Sussex examines Russia's use of violence in the geo-political space formally occupied by the Soviet Union. He demonstrates that elite decisions subsequently became potent domestic political instruments for the manipulation of identity. This in turn shows the extent to which Russian and other post-Soviet elites have managed to leverage identity for domestic political purposes indicates that – contrary to expectations about an increasing aversion to conflict in post-communist societies – violence remains a potent instrument for the mobilisation of popular support.

The book then moves to consider broader strategic questions about state violence in a similar geographical location. It examines the evolution of an important 'trilemma' that faces the West and Russia in their dealings with one another. In this chapter Graeme P. Herd traces the rationales, capacity and benefits – both domestic and international – from Russia's recent adventures in Crimea and Ukraine. From this he argues that although Russia's overt strategic agenda is to manage and contain regional instability, the tacit strategic agenda is to create ungovernable space and disorder. This deepens the 'trilemma' (understood as tensions between the theory and practice of sovereignty, stability and security) that provides a key organising dynamic of violence between East and West in the contemporary international system.

As the other chapters in the book demonstrate, history is replete with examples of state violence, state sanctioned violence and violence aimed at the overthrow or defeat of the state. Yet, as Jasmine-Kim Westendorf demonstrates in the next chapter, the proliferation of civil wars since the end of the Cold War, and the rise of peace settlements as the preferred way of ending them, has given rise to a new phenomenon in nascent post-civil war states, namely pervasive, low-level violence perpetrated by non-state actors. This ranges from criminality and lawlessness, to communal violence and electoral violence. Through examining the function and purpose of such violence in the aftermath of civil wars in Liberia, South Sudan and Cambodia, the chapter concludes by arguing that the cases investigated suggest that post-war violence remains shaped by conventional political ends.

A core question that has exercised specialists in contemporary world politics concerns the extent to which intervention on humanitarian grounds can be seen as a moral and legitimate form of state violence. To explore this, Jannika Brostrom examines the use of moral suasion in cases of violence justified as humanitarian intervention. She traces the evolution of a human security paradigm that grew in strength from its first tentative articulations in the UN's 1994 *Agenda for Peace* to the realisation of the R2P from 'word to deed' in 2005. She then examines practical examples of intervention – as well as non-intervention – to argue that humanitarian intervention strategies are in many respects hypocritical. After surveying a range of cases, including Kosovo, East Timor, Libya and Syria, she demonstrates that on each occasion, the core motivations for intervention were centrally tied to political objectives rather than normative concerns.

The final main chapter in this volume brings together the themes of violence as unification and pacification, violence and legitimacy, and violence for political as opposed to normative purposes. In the chapter Matt Killingsworth traces the evolution of international legal constraints on state violence. He explores how the post-1991 evolution of legal mechanisms to prosecute gross violations of international humanitarian law (IHL) challenged traditional understandings and interpretations of how actors might be restricted in their use of force. His chapter challenges the idea that the *ad hoc* Tribunals and the International Criminal Court (ICC) represent the 'progressive "cosmopolitanisation" of international law', and instead proffers two interrelated arguments: first, the extended reach of legality, as it concerns limitations on the use of force in the international system, remains restricted by factors explained by classic conceptions of state sovereignty and state interests; and second, while the instituting of legal mechanisms to punish individual violations of IHL challenges historically established norms regarding the way that states use force, constraints on the use of violence are best understood through 'pluralist' interpretations of the sovereign right to use force and the sovereign right of non-interference.

Drawing on all of the contributions in the volume, the book's conclusion highlights the significant historical continuity in patterns of violence from those of the French Revolutionary-Napoleonic epoch to more contemporary forms. This includes the continued centrality of the modern sovereign nation state as the main unit of violence, and the continued salience of resources and territory as the main variable. However, it also reveals patterns that are better understood by focusing on state capacity, the position of elites within it, and the dominant legal-normative conditions at each specific time. This helps account for the rapid acceleration of state violence in the first half of the twentieth century, followed by a relative decline in the Cold War period, followed again by an 'uptick' of violence in the immediate post-Cold War period. Despite various attempts to restrict both its regularity and severity, the state continues to reserve the right to resort to violence. Yet we conclude that – as elaborated upon in the volume – there are also signs that patterns of violence may be shifting into new arenas of power, amongst contemporary 'great powers' as well as second-tier actors.

NOTES

1   H. Arendt, *On Violence* (London: Allen Lane Press, 1970), p. 8.
2   M. Weber, 'Politics as a Vocation', in C. Besteman (ed.), *Violence: A Reader* (Houndmills: Palgrave, 2002), p. 13; C. Tilly, 'Western-State Making and Theories of Political Transformation', in C. Tilly (ed.), *The Formation of National States in Western Europe* (Princeton: Princeton University Press, 1975).
3   T. Skocpol, 'Bringing the State Back In: Current Research', in P. Evans, D. Rueschemeyer and T. Skocpol (eds), *Bringing the State Back In* (Cambridge: Cambridge University Press, 1985), p. 15.
4   J. Baudrillard, *Power Inferno* (Paris: Galilée, 2002).
5   For examples see M. Anglin, 'Feminist perspectives on structural violence', *Identities: Global Studies in Culture and Power*, 5:2 (1995), pp. 145–51; J. Derrida, *Of Grammatology*, trans. G. Chakravorty Spivak (Baltimore, MD: Johns Hopkins University Press, 1974), p. 110; J. Galtung, 'Cultural violence', *Journal of Peace Research*, 27:3 (1990), pp. 291–305; J. Kristeva, *Powers of Horror: An Essay on Abjection*, trans. L. S. Roudiez (New York: Columbia University Press, 1982), pp. 9–10; R. Nixon, *Slow Violence and the Environmentalism of the Poor* (Cambridge, MA: Harvard University Press, 2011).
6   H. Marcuse, *An Essay on Liberation* (Boston: Beacon Press, 1971); C. Peoples, 'Security after emancipation? Critical theory, violence and resistance', *Review of International Studies*, 37:3 (2011), p. 1123; J. Siebers, 'What cannot be said: Speech and violence', *Journal of Global Ethics*, 6:2 (2010), pp. 89–102.
7   Carl von Clausewitz, *Vom Krieg*, eds Michael Howard and Peter Paret (New Jersey: Princeton University Press, 1984), p. 87.
8   C. Schmitt, *The Concept of the Political: Expanded Edition*, trans. G. Schwab (Chicago: University of Chicago Press, 2007).

9   K. Waltz, *Theory of International Politics* (New York: Addison Wesley, 1976).
10 See C. Rues-Smit, *The Moral Purpose of the State: Culture, Social Identity, and Institutional Rationality in International Relations* (Princeton: Princeton University Press, 1996).
11 J. Dunn, *The Cunning of Unreason: Making Sense of Politics* (Harper Collins: New York, 2000), p. 60.
12 Weber, 'Politics as a Vocation', p. 13.
13 C. Tilly, 'War Making and State Making as Organized Crime', in Evans, Rueschemeyer and Skocpol (eds), *Bringing the State Back In*, p. 170.
14 See R. Devetak, 'The Modern State', in R. Devetak, A. Burke and J. George (eds), *An Introduction to International Relations* (Cambridge: Cambridge University Press, 2nd edn, 2012), pp. 135–6.
15 Weber, 'Politics as a Vocation', p. 13.
16 C. Tilly, 'Reflections on the History of European State Making', in C. Tilly (ed.), *The Formation of National States in Europe* (Princeton: Princeton University Press, 1975), p. 42.
17 Devetak, 'The Modern State', p. 142.
18 Tilly, 'War Making and State Making as Organized Crime', p. 173.
19 M. Mann, *The Sources of Social Power*, Vol. 1 (Cambridge: Cambridge University Press, 1986), pp. 452–3.
20 C. Tilly, *Coercion, Capital and European Sates, AD 990–1992* (Cambridge, MA: Blackwell, 1992), p. 68.
21 J. Thomson, *Mercenaries, Pirates and Sovereigns* (Princeton: Princeton University Press, 1994), p. 4.
22 Thomson, *Mercenaries, Pirates and Sovereigns*.
23 See H. Spruyt, *The Sovereign State and its Competitors* (Princeton: Princeton University Press, 1994).
24 As Tilly explains, 'the distinction between "legitimate" and "illegitimate" force ... makes no difference to the fact'. Tilly, 'War Making and State Making as Organised Crime', p. 171.
25 Mann, *The Sources of Social Power*, p. 490.
26 C. Besteman, 'Conclusion: Political Violence and the Contemporary World', in C. Besteman (ed.), *Violence: A Reader* (Houndmills: Palgrave, 2002), p. 300.
27 M. van Creveld, *The Rise and Decline of the State* (Cambridge: Cambridge University Press, 1999), pp. 353–4.
28 van Creveld, *The Rise and Decline of the State*, p. 395.
29 M. Kaldor, *New and Old Wars: Organised Violence in a Global Era* (Cambridge: Polity, 2nd edn, 2006), p. 5.
30 K. Holsti, 'The Coming Chaos? Armed Conflict in the World's Peripherary', in T. V. Paul and J. Hall (eds), *International Order and the Future of World Politics* (Cambridge: Cambridge University Press, 1999), p. 304.
31 C. Reus-Smit, 'Introduction', in C. Reus-Smit (ed.), *The Politics of International Law* (Cambridge: Cambridge University Press, 2004), p. 7.
32 'The Responsibility to Protect', Report of the International Commission on Intervention and State Sovereignty (2001), available at: http://responsibilitytoprotect.org/ICISS%20Report.pdf (accessed 10 March 2014), p. xi.
33 M. Gilbert, 'The Terrible 20th Century', *Globe and Mail* (31 January 2007).
34 G. Evans, 'End of the argument: How we won the debate over stopping genocide', *Foreign Policy* (28 November 2011), available at: www.foreignpolicy.com/articles/2011/11/28/gareth_evans_end_of_the_argument (accessed 5 March 2014).

35 J. Charvet, 'The possibility of a cosmopolitan ethical order based on the idea of universal human rights', *Millennium: Journal of International Studies*, 27:3 (1998), p. 523.

36 A. Langlois, 'Human Rights Universalism', in P. Hayden (ed.), *The Ashgate Research Companion to Ethics and International Relations* (Farnham: Ashgate, 2009), p. 209.

37 Langlois, 'Human Rights Universalism', pp. 210–11.

38 S. Strange, *The Retreat of the State* (Cambridge: Cambridge University Press, 1996), p. xiii.

39 For example, see L. Glasgow, 'Introductory Speech', *From Principle to Practice – Implementing the Responsibility to Protect*, Brussels (26 April 2007) available at: www. egmontinstitute.org/speechnotes/07/070426-L.Glasgow.html (accessed 17 August, 2014).

1

War in the Revolutionary-Napoleonic Age: the French experience, 1792–1815

Gavin Daly

O N 20 APRIL 1792, after months of intense debate, the deputies of the French National Assembly declared war on Austria. Over twenty-three years later, the defeat of Napoleon at Waterloo on 18 June 1815 finally brought an end to the French Revolutionary-Napoleonic Wars. Between these two dates lay over two decades of almost constant warfare, with Revolutionary and then Napoleonic France pitted against shifting coalitions of Europe's Great Powers – seven coalitions in all – broken only by the brief peace of Amiens (March 1802–May 1803) and the lull between Napoleon's first abdication in early 1814 and his return from exile on Elba in March 1815. For the British, until 1914, these wars were known simply as the 'Great War'.[1]

In recent decades, these wars have increasingly assumed a prominent and highly contested place in historical understandings of the development of European war. As Roger Chickering has identified, the French Revolutionary-Napoleonic Wars have been caught up in two 'master narratives', with each staking claims over the epoch.[2] On the one hand, the wars have fallen within the tail end of the narrative of the Early Modern European 'Military Revolution', a concept pioneered by Michael Howard and later modified and developed by Geoffrey Parker.[3] This holds that technological and tactical changes – gunpowder, musketry and artillery – lead to the creation of large standing armies and the growth of fiscal-military states over the course of the sixteenth and seventeenth centuries. The French Revolutionary-Napoleonic Wars are seen as a continuation and intensification of these early transformative changes in military affairs. On the other hand, the French Revolutionary-Napoleonic Wars have been seen as the crucial formative phase in a narrative of 'modern' or indeed 'total war'. Here, the epoch represents a fundamental break with the past: the 'limited' and 'restrained' dynastic or cabinet wars of eighteenth-century Europe giving way to an era of patriotic and ideologically charged nations-in-arms and 'peoples wars' that prefigured the greater transformative world wars of the twentieth century. The French Revolution is held as the crucible of this change, with its political, ideological and cultural dynamism transforming the nature of war, and the relationship between war, state and society.

The case for seeing in the French Revolutionary-Napoleonic epoch the seeds of modern 'total war' has recently been restated and refashioned by David A. Bell, who argues that the intellectual legacy of the Enlightenment on matters of war and peace, when combined with the radical politics of the early French Revolution, gave rise to a new 'culture of war'; one that 'drove the participants relentlessly towards a condition of total engagement and the abandonment of restraints'.[4] Bell's thesis has sparked considerable debate amongst historians about 'total war' and its appropriateness as a descriptor of war for this era.[5] The origins of the term 'total war' lie within this period, with Carl von Clausewitz's ideal of 'absolute war'; but 'total war' (*la guerre totale*) was first coined only in 1917 in the context of World War I.

There is no precise agreement on a definition of 'total war', but Peter H. Wilson's identification of three classic characteristics is as good a starting point as any: 'total mobilisation, the objective of the enemy's total destruction and the alleged fusion of soldiers and civilians'.[6] But as Wilson, among other historians, has pointed out, the term, concept and historical value of 'total war' remain problematic. In particular, there is the relationship between total war and modernity; dealing with a concept of 'totality'; and establishing 'thresholds' or 'tipping points' along a continuum from limited to total war.[7] In all of this, eighteenth-century specialists increasingly reject the claims of 'limited' war for their own epoch, with claims for total war in the Revolutionary-Napoleonic era predicated on establishing its limited nature beforehand. Twentieth-century specialists, on the other hand, remain largely sceptical of the appropriateness of labelling the French Revolutionary-Napoleonic Wars as an example of 'total war', arguing that the scale of mobilisation, battlefield destruction, and the impact of war on civilians is not meaningfully comparable to the twentieth-century world wars between modern industrial nations.[8]

In all of this, however, what is generally accepted within the scholarship is that war undoubtedly changed during the French Revolutionary-Napoleonic era. But what is at issue, as Chickering notes, is the 'nature, dimensions, and causes of the transformation'.[9] This chapter explores these broad issues by focusing on four interrelated themes, progressing from the origins of the wars to the battlefield itself. The focus is on France, as the epicentre of change, but also the impact of France across Europe. It begins with the role of ideology as a causal dynamic in the wars; it then addresses the role of the French state in mobilising a nation-in-arms; moves on to discuss the political and professional nature of the French armies; and finishes by examining the conduct of war and fighting. The conclusion is that the French Revolutionary-Napoleonic Wars were indeed a watershed in both French and European history. Notwithstanding continuities, there were both fundamental quantitative and qualitative changes in the nature of war. And the French Revolutionary-Napoleonic state was at the heart of this transformation.

Ideology and the origins of the wars

In January 1791, Edmund Burke wrote: 'no Monarchy limited or unlimited, nor any of the Old Republics, can possibly be safe as long as this strange, nameless, wild, enthusiastic thing is established in the Centre of Europe'.[10] The *thing* was the French Revolution, and Burke was the first contemporary to warn that the very existence of Revolutionary France was incompatible with international peace; that the Revolution would bring a war of ideas: 'It is with an *armed doctrine* that we are at war'.[11] The vexing issue of ideology remains central to debates over the nature of the Revolutionary-Napoleonic Wars and the extent to which they represented 'old' or 'new' wars within the broad currents of European history. Ideational factors are consistently addressed throughout this chapter, but firstly, from a French perspective, what role did ideology play in the origins of the Revolutionary Wars and as a contributing driver thereafter?

Long standing Republican and Marxist scholarly traditions in France have seen the Revolutionary Wars as an inevitable clash between two diametrically opposed ideological systems: in short, Revolutionary and Republican France versus Old Regime Europe.[12] These were not the traditional wars of European kings, it is argued, with limited royal armies and limited objectives, but rather wars fought by rival political and social systems, between popular sovereignty and royal absolutism, between the values of the Declaration of the Rights of Man and Citizen and the feudal Society of Orders. What was at stake for the French was the very existence of the Revolution and the Republic itself. War was a means to both defend the Revolution from internal and external threats, and to export revolutionary principles and reforms throughout Europe. The converse was European powers fighting for the restoration of the Bourbons and the Old Regime to France, and defending themselves against the contagion of revolution.

Since the 1980s, this interpretation has come under increasing scrutiny. In his study of eighteenth- and nineteenth-century European international relations, Paul Schroeder argues that the French Revolutionary-Napoleonic Wars were not a 'contest between the French Revolution and the old regime' but rather a 'conflict between three hegemonic powers [Britain, France and Russia] as to which or which combination of them would control and exploit the countries in between'.[13] In his now classic analysis of the origins of the French Revolutionary Wars, Tim Blanning put the case for *realpolitik* prevailing over ideological considerations, with the wars driven largely by traditional rivalries and power interests.[14] Blanning concedes that ideals certainly weighed more heavily with the French than with the Austrians, Prussians or British, but argues that the Girondin deputies ultimately pushed France to war in 1792 'chiefly for the purpose of obtaining political power'.[15]

Notwithstanding the continuation of eighteenth-century state rivalries based on power and security, the case for ideological factors as playing a key causal role in the Revolutionary Wars is unquestionably strongest for the case of France, and specifically between the years 1792 and 1794. This was both the most radical and ideologically fervent era of the French Revolution, culminating in the Jacobin dictatorship and Terror (1793–94); and the period when France was most vulnerable to foreign invasion and military defeat. While the French court and other French revolutionary leaders pursued war for their own reasons, it was the Girondin deputies led by Brissot who were ultimately responsible for winning over the French National Assembly between late 1791 and April 1792. Notwithstanding political self-interest, ideology mattered in this debate, and not simply as an emotive rhetorical device to close out the argument for war. As Alan Forrest has remarked of the Jacobin language of war in this era: 'there is no reason to doubt the reality of their underlying fear or the genuineness of their commitment to what they saw as a better society'.[16]

The French debates over war in 1791–92 arose amidst a mounting domestic crisis over the revolutionary settlement.[17] Amongst revolutionaries there were growing fears over the loyalty and designs of the French royal family, over domestic 'aristocratic plots', over the émigré army in Koblenz, and over the intentions of foreign powers, especially Austria. In the radical revolutionary mind-set, there was simply no distinction between domestic and international threats to the Revolution, both perceived as part of a broad counterrevolutionary concert. Girondin fears about foreign intervention in the internal political affairs of France certainly had a real basis: in the Declaration of Pillnitz (27 August 1791), the Holy Roman Emperor and the Prussian King appealed for a united front of Europe's sovereigns to ensure the liberty of the French royal family and the restoration of their political authority. Yet for the Girondins, this was a war not only of national survival and defence, but as Brissot declared to the Jacobin club: 'It will be a crusade for universal liberty'.[18] The French National Assembly had earlier, in May 1790, famously renounced wars of conquest. Now, the Girondins wanted a war of universal liberation, with war serving as a means to reshape Europe in the image of Revolutionary France. Yet further, in a point stressed by Bell, war was conceived here as something exceptional, not simply as part of Europe's recurring and natural cycle of war and peace, but a war that would bring about a final perpetual peace. As the Girondin general, Dumouriez, told the French Convention on 12 October 1792: 'This war will be the last war'.[19] Moreover, it is important not to forget that the calls for an ideological war against the enemies of the Revolution came not just from within the French National Assembly, but increasingly from the radical popular movement in Paris.[20] Against this seemingly inevitable tide of war, Robespierre was a voice in the wilderness, uttering his famous riposte to war as a revolutionary crusade: 'No one likes armed missionaries'.[21]

So the French went to war against Austria and Prussia in 1792. The following year, Britain, Spain and Holland joined the coalition, while France itself was torn asunder by civil war and political violence. Under the leadership and organisation of the Jacobins, the French finally prevailed against the First Coalition in the summer of 1794. Victory in the Low Countries against the Austrians at the Battle of Fleurus on 26 June 1794 proved a turning point. The following month, the execution of Robespierre brought an end to the Jacobin 'reign of terror'.

Robespierre's fall also brought an end to the ideological fervour of the Revolution. As the French Wars moved on from the years of the Jacobin Republic and passed into the Napoleonic era, the ideological dimensions of the conflict diminished. During the Directory (1795–99) – the centrist Republican regime created in the aftermath of the Terror – France's armies began to push outwards, far beyond France's 'natural frontiers': Belgium was annexed and 'sister republics' were created in Holland, Switzerland and northern Italy. Then came Bonaparte's seizure of power in 1799 and the creation of the Consulate (1800–4). Territorial expansion continued initially but there was also international peace with Austria (1801) and Britain (1802) – Bonaparte presenting himself as a peacemaker. The Consular years also brought political and social stability to France, healing the divisions of the revolutionary decade, and proving the most creative era of Napoleonic reform, with the Civil Code, Concordat and prefectoral administration.

Yet as Napoleon became more distant from his revolutionary and republican heritage on the domestic front, beginning with his coronation as Emperor in 1804, this was mirrored on the international stage. Over the years of the First French Empire (1804–14), Napoleon's armies increasingly became instruments of conquest and power, laying the foundations for almost a decade of French hegemony in Europe.[22] The defeat of the Austrians in 1805 and the Prussians in 1806, and the neutralisation of Russia in 1807, rendered Napoleon master of Europe, controlling a vast Empire and vassal states. From this moment on, if not before, Napoleon's primary motivation for war seemed to derive more and more from his own sense of personal destiny and military glory than other considerations. With Europe subdued, and at the height of his power, Napoleon invaded and occupied Spain in 1808, precipitating a six-year war that was to prove a military disaster for the French. Then came the invasion of Russia in 1812, the ensuing military catastrophe fatally wounding the Napoleonic Empire itself. And in 1810, Napoleon married Marie-Louise of Austria, linking himself to the Habsburgs, one of the oldest and most prestigious European royal lines.

On one level, the Napoleonic Wars (1803–15), like the preceding Revolutionary Wars, were a continuing part of the Great Power struggles of the eighteenth century. In this, they were part of what has been called the 'Second

Hundred Years War' (1688–1815) between Britain and France, a struggle played out within both Europe and the trade routes of the colonial world; and they were part of the ongoing tension amongst the Great Powers over the fate of Eastern Europe.

Yet there was also something very new here, too, relative to past conflicts. Firstly, Napoleon did not play by the diplomatic rules and balance of power restraints of the eighteenth century, with seemingly no end to his quest for territory, conquest, glory and 'universal monarchy'. Charles Esdaile, while arguing that it is helpful to understand the wars largely 'in terms of the dynastic wars of the eighteenth century', nevertheless concedes that Napoleon 'was never capable of setting the same limits on himself as the rulers and statesmen who had waged the conflicts of the eighteenth century'.[23]

Moreover, there was an important ideological dimension to the Napoleonic Wars, although it grew fainter with the years. This issue is part of the broader and timeless debate on the Napoleonic regime's relationship with the Revolution itself. At one level, the Empire can be likened to Napoleon dividing up the spoils of Europe amongst his 'Corsican clan', installing his siblings on both old and newly established kingdoms, and exploiting his newly acquired Imperial subjects – a plunder economy for both family and France. Yet this model masks the deeper complexities and contradictions of the Napoleonic Empire and the legacy of the French Revolution.[24] French armies brought both bayonets and law codes into the conquered territories. Moreover, this reformist agenda was not simply about improving the efficiency and capacity of the Napoleonic state to extract financial, economic and military resources from subject territories and states. As Stuart Woolf has cogently argued, there was a genuine commitment on the part of the Napoleonic state to 'modernise' and 'civilise' Europe, with a model that drew inspiration from the Enlightenment and the French Revolution: the civil code, rational administrative reforms, religious tolerance and secularisation.[25] Despite Napoleon's marriage to a Habsburg princess and concerns about securing his own dynasty he could show scant regard for Old Regime hereditary legitimacy, as demonstrated with his reorganisation of southern and western Germany, and overthrowing of the Bourbons in Spain and Naples. Between 1802 and 1803, 112 small German states disappeared under Napoleonic rationalisation; and Napoleon's creation of the Confederation of the Rhine in 1806 brought the formal end to the 1006-year-old Holy Roman Empire. Small wonder that Thomas Nipperdey began his history of modern Germany with the famous lines: 'In the beginning was Napoleon'.[26] Through the eyes of other European rulers, Napoleon was a revolutionary force and a fundamental threat to both the international order and to hereditary sovereignty – a self-made Emperor.[27]

Mobilising for war: the nation-in-arms

Historians who downplay the ideologisation of war in this epoch nevertheless acknowledge that what was transformative was the sheer scale of war making: the number of soldiers, the size of armies, and the mobilisation of human, financial and economic resources. This quantitative transformation in the waging of war occurred across all the major belligerent states, but was nowhere more pronounced than it was in France, which took the lead, with other states such as Prussia (following its defeat at Jena in 1806) subsequently reorganising and remodelling their war efforts on the French example.

The figures for troop mobilisation, army size and the number of combatants in battles during this era simply dwarf those across the greater eighteenth century. Louis XIV's army in the early eighteenth century, during the War of the Spanish Succession, was the giant of its time, amounting to 255,000 troops; yet the Jacobin Republic in 1794 fielded at least 750,000 soldiers.[28] The size of field armies and battles increased dramatically over the course of the French Revolutionary-Napoleonic Wars, reaching their height during the final years of the Empire. The over 200,000-strong force that Napoleon brought to Germany in 1805 was the largest ever single field army assembled in European history; yet this itself was soon rendered relatively minor compared to the 600,000-strong *Grande Armée* that Napoleon assembled for the invasion of Russia in 1812.[29] The greatest battles of eighteenth-century Europe involved on average 140,000 combatants.[30] Yet the battles of the late Napoleonic Wars were more than double this average with over 300,000 soldiers.[31] The greatest of all was the three-day Battle of Leipzig, or 'Battle of the Nations', in October 1813, involving some 520,000 combatants.[32] Nothing of the like had ever been seen before in Europe.

This transformation was made possible because of the French Revolutionary state and its Napoleonic successor. 'War made the state', so goes Charles Tilly's famous dictum, 'and the state made war'.[33] The relationship between war and state making in early modern Europe has a long historiographical lineage,[34] stretching from the foundational frameworks established by Max Weber and Otto Hintze,[35] to the work of later historical sociologists,[36] and to Perry Anderson's classic Marxist analysis of comparative absolutism.[37] This tradition has given rise to a rich and growing body of historical scholarship over the past thirty years, much of which has revised earlier assumptions about the early modern European state and its war making. With respect to France, there is a growing recognition of the extent to which the Bourbon absolutist state grew in partnership *with* rather than *against* prevailing *ancien régime* power dynamics. Guy Rowlands has highlighted the degree to which Louis XIV drew upon patronage, the dynastic interests of elites, and venality of office to develop the French army;[38] while David Parrott has shown the extent to which expanding state war making capabilities, both in France and elsewhere, relied upon public–private partnership, especially with private military contractors.[39] Nevertheless, the French state remained central to the business of war, and over the seventeenth and eighteenth centuries its power, authority and reach expanded as the pressures of war grew: recruitment, administration, taxation and logistics. Yet during the French Revolutionary-Napoleonic age, the sinews of war were taken to another level entirely.

The crucible of this transformation was, as Clausewitz identified, the year 1793:

> In 1793 a force appeared that beggared all imagination. Suddenly war again became the business of the people – a people of thirty millions, all of whom considered themselves to be citizens ... The people became a participant in war; instead of governments and armies as heretofore, the full weight of the nation was thrown into the balance. The resources and efforts now available for use surpassed all conventional limits; nothing now impeded the vigour with which war could be waged, and consequently the opponents of France faced the utmost peril.[40]

The 'nation-in-arms' had come into being. In this, the Jacobins certainly imagined and aspired towards 'total' mobilisation. Of course, in practice, the mobilisation was not 'total', but it was a long way removed from the previous Bourbon state's conception and organisation of war. Both quantitatively and qualitatively this mobilisation represented a fundamental rupture with the past, something never asked of, nor imposed upon, previous French generations. The Jacobins sought to break down the notion of war as a separate sphere between the military and civilians; instead seeking to militarise the entire French nation – with the exception of the internal enemies of the Republic. For the Jacobin 'totalisation' of war was inextricably linked to the Jacobin Terror more generally, of its internal war and political violence against counterrevolutionaries.[41] The same absolute commitment and mobilisation was required to meet all threats to the survival of the Republic. And the pressures for this all came not simply from above, but from below, with the militant *sans-culotte* movement wanting a 'people's war' and a mass revolutionary uprising.

Over the course of 1793–94, the Jacobin state assumed control over mobilisation, the army and military strategy.[42] Indeed the Jacobins imposed state-sanctioned terror to run and control the war effort. Supreme executive authority came to be invested in the Committee of Public Safety, charged with taking 'all measures necessary for the internal and external defence of the Republic'.[43] It became both a war cabinet and the organising instrument of the Reign of Terror. Of its eventual twelve members, Lazare Carnot – the 'organiser of victory' – was placed in charge of military affairs. Under the exigencies of war, the Committee came to preside over a vast and multi-layered bureaucratic machine with departments on the army, arms and gunpowder, transport, trade and supply, public works and hospitals. The Jacobin war economy relied on intervention, coercion and terror. The Jacobins took direct control over supplying the army, ending the eighteenth-century practice of private contractors. Factories and thousands of workshops were set up to produce arms and gunpowder, and labour was conscripted into the war industries. The Committee also asserted its authority over the Republic's generals, taking direct control of the overall war strategy. Deputies on mission from the National Convention, the most famous being Saint-Just, were dispatched to the war zones to oversee the supply and performance of the French armies. The centrepiece of total mobilisation was the famous *levée en masse*, announced on 23 August 1793:

> Henceforth, until the enemies have been driven from the territory of the Republic, the French people are in a permanent requisition for military service. The young shall go to battle, the married men shall forge arms and transport provisions, the women shall make tents and clothes, and shall serve in the hospitals, the children shall turn old linen into lint, the old men shall repair to the public spaces to stimulate the courage of the warriors and preach the unity of the republic and the hatred of kings.[44]

All these efforts converged on the French army, whose size grew in accord with the war crisis. In 1789, the old Royal army had numbered approximately 150,000 soldiers.[45] Over the course of 1791 and 1792, volunteer battalions were formed alongside the regular troops, totalling some 170,000 by the summer of 1792.[46] But as the international coalition against France grew in 1793, something fundamentally new was needed to raise the necessary numbers of troops. The solution was the introduction of conscription in 1793, a revolutionary development that was to have extraordinary consequences both in France and abroad. On 24 February 1793, a levy of 300,000 men was ordered by the Convention, with all single and widowed men without children between the ages of eighteen and forty eligible for the draft. The levy was strongly resisted in rural areas and indeed sparked off civil war in the Vendée. But still further troops were needed, prompting the *levée en masse*. All single men and widows without children between the ages of eighteen and twenty-five were eligible for conscription. Despite resistance, Jacobin conscription ultimately solved the manpower shortage, raising over 750,000 French effectives by 1794. This represented the peak of mobilising manpower during the Revolutionary Wars, with the army falling to over 400,000 soldiers the following year and numbering 380,000 by 1797.[47]

When conscription was first introduced in 1793, it was conceived as an emergency one-off measure to meet the prevailing military crisis; it was not intended to be an annual and regular levy. In order to ensure a regular supply of young men into the army, however, conscription was put on a sounder footing. The Jourdan Law of 5 September 1798 enshrined the principle of annual universal military service. All men between the ages of twenty and twenty-five were eligible to be called up for five years' military service; the exemptions were married men, widowers with dependents and priests.

This was the conscription system that Napoleon inherited, and, with only minor modification, remained the recruitment basis of the French armies throughout the Napoleonic Wars.[48] The Napoleonic prefectoral administration oversaw conscription, and meeting the regular drafts numbers for each department ultimately became each prefect's single most important priority. 'Conscription is', wrote one prefect, 'the first, the strongest of our modern institutions'.[49] Conscription was also the most contested site between the Napoleonic state and French village life, with initially great resistance manifesting in draft evasion and desertion, especially in southern and western departments.[50] Despite the principle of universal military service, it was the peasantry who bore the overwhelming burden of conscription, the wealthy able to avoid their obligation through purchasing a replacement. Ultimately, through a combination of coercive police and military tactics, fines and amnesties, the Napoleonic state broke down rural resistance to conscription, although it remained unpopular. Conscription became institutionalised and regularised, a rite of passage for more and more young Frenchmen. The annual conscription burdens varied over the years, rising and falling with the war needs of the state. Over the course of the Empire, the conscription levies grew progressively heavier, culminating in the crippling levies demanded after the Russian campaign, provoking widespread opposition. In total, somewhere between 3 and 3.5 million men served in the French army during the Revolutionary-Napoleonic Wars, with some two million conscripted during the Napoleonic years.[51]

Yet under Napoleon, the French war machine was also able to draw upon the vast resources of the Empire. French-style taxation and conscription were introduced throughout much of the inner Empire, although the levies and implementation varied across time and place.[52] Just as conscription had brought initial rebellion and long term resistance in France, so too did its introduction arouse resistance and hostility elsewhere: rebellion in Belgium in 1798 and the Austrian Tyrol in 1809; and draft evasion and desertion throughout rural Italy.[53] Nevertheless, conscription was introduced into Belgium in 1798, the Italian Republic in 1802, the Kingdom of Naples in 1806, the Grand Duchy of Berg and Westphalia in 1807, and in Holland in 1810.[54] In addition, military contingents were raised from the satellite kingdoms and states within the French sphere of influence. The end result was that by the late Empire, more foreign troops than French were fighting in Napoleon's armies. Of the 600,000 troops that Napoleon marshalled for the invasion of Russia in 1812, only 200,000 were French born: 100,000 were from foreign departments annexed to France, while the remaining 300,000 were foreign troops from across Europe, including Germans, Poles, Lithuanians, Italians and Illyrians.[55] Napoleon's grand army had come less to resemble the French 'nation-in-arms' than a 'European Union in arms'.

The army: politicisation and professionalisation

This raises the important issue: to what degree were the armies of Revolutionary and Napoleonic France politicised, imbued with a patriotic and revolutionary mind-set that set them apart from their eighteenth-century predecessors?

The early French revolutionaries, especially the Jacobins, were not satisfied with merely dramatically changing the size of the army; they wanted to revolutionise its very character to reflect the new France and its revolutionary and republican principles. Accordingly, the army's national and social composition changed. In the old Royal army, over 20 per cent of line regiments were 'foreign' mercenaries.[56] This was anathema to the idea of the 'nation-in-arms': by early 1793 the number of foreigners had fallen to only 4 per cent of the army.[57] Then there was the pressing issue of the aristocracy, which had dominated the old command structure. This near-monopoly was shattered by the French Revolution, which introduced the principle of merit-based promotion. As the Revolution became more radical, the defection of aristocratic officers became a flood, with 6000 officers emigrating by the end of 1791.[58] In September 1793, the Jacobins finally ordered the removal of every remaining aristocrat in the army; the following year, this ideal was tempered by the expediency of needing professionally trained officers, with some aristocrats reinstated.[59] But the officer corps had transformed, a meritocratic body now filled with men from bourgeois, peasant and artisan backgrounds.

As groundbreaking as these changes were, however, they were not enough. The revolutionaries set out to produce a new breed of soldier – the citizen-soldier. This was modelled on the ideal of the virtuous, heroic, self-sacrificing soldier of Republican Rome; an ideal earlier popularised by enlightened thinkers such as Diderot and Rousseau, and the influential military theorist and writer, the Comte de Guibert, and one boosted by the recent example of citizen militias and 'patriots' in the American War of Independence.[60] The volunteers of 1791 and 1792 enlisted amidst a climate of escalating revolutionary radicalism and calls to defend *la patrie*. The victory of the French army against the Prussians at Valmy was presented as a victory of the Revolution's citizen-soldiers, with the battle entering Republican mythology thereafter.[61] The high point of political indoctrination came during 1793–94, with soldiers subjected to both Jacobin propaganda and coercion. The army became a 'school of Jacobinism'.[62] Political newspapers were distributed to soldiers, and revolutionary songs became popular, most famously 'The Marseillaise'. National festivals and fetes were held to celebrate victories and to strengthen the bonds between soldiers and the French nation. At the same time, the representatives on mission scrutinised the morale, commitment and political consciousness of the armies, with accompanying purges and the dispensing of summary revolutionary justice for those military men who strayed. This was politicisation on strictly controlled Jacobin terms. As Forrest observes there was 'tension between the conflicting aims of ideological activism and political control, between the army as a revolutionary force and the army as an instrument of state'.[63]

Of course, there was a multiplicity of 'push' and 'pull' factors that drove French soldiers to enlist and fight, with conscription introduced in 1793. But the detailed research of many leading historians on the revolutionary army leaves little doubt that many soldiers of this era of the Revolutionary Wars carried a spirit of patriotism, citizenship and republican political consciousness.[64] One soldier wrote to his mother in December 1793: 'I, brought up in the liberty of conscience and thought, always republican in my soul even though forced to live in a monarchy, have the principles of love for the fatherland, liberty, and the Republic etched on my heart'.[65] In terms of political values and national ideals, this was a distinctly 'Revolutionary' and 'Republican' army, the likes of which had never been seen before in French, or indeed European, history.

The political consciousness of the army, however, changed over the course of the post-Jacobin years. In fact, it has become something of a historical ortho-doxy to stress the depoliticisation of the army under Napoleon and its increasing remoteness from the nation.[66] The citizen soldier became a professional sol-dier, and, in the words of John Lynn, the Jacobin 'army of virtue' transformed into a Napoleonic 'army of honour'.[67] Over the course of the Napoleonic Wars, the French army became more professional, filled with hardened veterans and careerists, motivated by military victories and glory, honours, rewards and plunder. Military men filled the ranks of both the Legion of Honour (1802) and the new Imperial nobility (1808). Identity was increasingly bound up with regimental esprit de corps; and in the affections and loyalties of his soldiers, Napoleon had displaced or subsumed the nation – or at least so it seemed. The French also now fought alongside soldiers from all over Europe. With all this in mind, the Napoleonic soldier seemed a long way removed from the patriotic and amateur volunteer of 1791 and 1792, or the conscript of 1793.

Nevertheless, Michael Hughes's recent study of the Napoleonic armies to 1808 has challenged this orthodoxy, offering a more nuanced view of the rela-tionship between the Napoleonic soldier and the French nation.[68] In Napoleon's proclamations and army bulletins, and during public celebrations and fetes within France, soldiers were reminded that they were indeed fighting for *la patrie* and that they were appreciated by the nation. Moreover, they were reminded that they were still fighting to finish off the old enemies of Revolutionary France, those powers that stood in the way of universal liberty and a final peace. These sentiments were clearly not as strong as in 1792–94, but they remained all the same, alongside a new military culture that celebrated the French nation's martial glories, victories and conquests. Hughes concludes: 'Napoleon combined revolutionary virtue with the traditional values of honour and glory to create a new synthesis that can best be described as Imperial virtue. The personal honour and glory of the individual were extended to the entire nation'.[69]

The conduct of war

So, the mentalities and self-identities of French soldiers over the course of the wars were shaped to a degree by new ideals of citizenship and patriotism, together with the coming of a new professional ethos and esprit de corps. Yet how did these French armies fight and conduct themselves on campaign, in battle, and during occupation? Horrified at the conduct of Napoleon's armies in Spain and Portugal during the Peninsular War, the Duke of Wellington was convinced this 'new French system of war is the greatest evil that ever fell on the civilized world'.[70] Wellington was far from alone amongst contemporaries in believing there had been a major transformation in how the French conducted and fought wars.

The conduct of eighteenth-century European warfare was not subjected to international laws of war in the modern sense of the term.[71] Nevertheless, the conduct of war *(jus in bello)* was conditioned and regulated by the military codes and laws of individual states; by customary practices that had evolved over the centuries, drawing on the enduring legacies of Roman and medieval Christian traditions; and especially the honour codes of a pan-European cohort of aristocratic-gentlemen officers. Moreover, the eighteenth century saw enlightened military theorists, jurists and *philosophes* (most famously Emer de Vattel) setting out ethical and rational guidelines for war-time practices, including limits and restraints on violence towards non-combatants. All of this helped shape both how rival armies fought and interacted with one another, and the relationship between armies and civilian populations. It informed the supply systems for armies; the treatment of prisoners and the wounded; the conduct of sieges and surrender rituals; and the treatment of civilians. Of course, in practice, as studies of eighteenth-century warfare have shown, the 'laws of war' were not always adhered to amongst combatants, and war impacted upon the lives of civilians.[72] In particular, laws of war were often not respected when soldiers fought 'rebels', those deemed 'uncivilised', or civilians who took up arms.[73] Nevertheless, broadly speaking, warfare across the eighteenth century was much more 'limited' and restrained relative to the seventeenth century, which witnessed the Thirty Years War (1618–48), and also Louis XIV's devastation of the Palatinate (1688–89).

Without question, eighteenth-century restraints and customary practices of war were put under great stress during the French Revolutionary-Napoleonic Wars. Yet in assessing the extent to which the French conduct of war changed during this epoch we need to be sensitive to shifts over time, differences between and within particular theatres of war, differences between particular sets of belligerents, and between soldiers and civilians.[74]

One of the greatest changes was in the feeding of French armies – one that had enormous consequences for civilian populations. Over the course of the eighteenth century, the feeding of armies in occupied territories had been regulated by a system of paid requisitions, which both minimised unregulated troop plunder of the local inhabitants, and also sought to produce a more stable military–civil relationship. Moreover, French armies from the time of Louis XIV had relied on a magazine or depot system of supply – whereby food and forage stations were established along the planned routes of armies. Twenty years before the French Revolution, Guibert had proposed the abandonment of this very system. In order to facilitate much greater strategic flexibility and mobility for armies, he had advocated that they should live off the land, whereby, famously, 'war could feed off war'.[75]

This did indeed become the reality from 1794, with ever-larger French armies advancing across Europe.[76] It was one thing to raise an army of 750,000 soldiers; it was another to feed it. In 1793, the solution domestically was to put France in a permanent state of requisition, a product of both expediency and new thinking on the relationship between war and society. But once the Republic was saved, the French then exported this model throughout Europe, with Republican armies from 1794 living off the lands of occupied territories. The French simply took what they wanted, with dire consequences for civilian populations. This was the system that Napoleon inherited and extended across Europe. It was never taken to more extremes than in Spain and Portugal during the Peninsular War. When Napoleon's troops crossed the Pyrenees in 1808, in the words of Esdaile, they 'fell upon the Peninsula like wolves'.[77] Harvests were requisitioned, contributions levied, churches and monasteries destroyed, and there was mass French pillage and plunder from the humblest French private taking church gold to the Bonapartes, and their marshals looting royal art treasures. Of course, such practices only undermined the relationship between the occupiers and occupied. By 1810–11, there were some 350,000 Imperial soldiers in Spain.[78] Wellington knew only too well that this great mass of troops survived 'by authorized and regulated plunder of the country and its inhabitants'.[79] This was the 'new French system of war' and he astutely traced it back to the 1793 *levée en masse*, highlighting its inherent accumulative radical dynamic:

> In the early days of the revolutionary war, the French, at the recommendation, I believe of Brissot, adopted a measure which they called a *levée en masse*; and put every man, animal, and article in their own country in requisition for the service of the armies ... It is not astonishing that a nation among whom such a system was

established should have been anxious to carry the war beyond their own frontiers. This system both created the desire and afforded the means of success; and with the war they carried, wherever they went, the system of requisitions.[80]

There were also significant changes in this epoch to French army organisation and battle tactics, and to campaign strategies and goals.[81] These were born out of quantitative shifts in the size of armies and battles, and from changes in the culture of war itself. The sheer size of French armies relative to the past required reorganising them into smaller units – divisions and corps – which also gave greater operational flexibility and speed. How French armies engaged in battle also altered. Prior to the French Revolutionary Wars, infantry were organised into linear formation, normally three rows deep, to enhance firepower. Yet the French Revolutionaries adopted a new tactic, born partly out of the initial inexperience of volunteer troops and the idea of mass warfare. This was to attack the enemy lines through a column formation, an offensive strategy of 'shock and awe' very different to eighteenth-century style tactics. The column was almost a miniature *levée en masse* in battle, capturing the 1792–94 patriotic ideal of masses of French soldiers armed with bayonets – the weapon of the true *sans-culotte* revolutionary and republican – storming and overcoming the enemy.

The use of columns at a tactical level also pointed to a broader strategic and cultural shift – the idea of the 'decisive battle' and the complete destruction of the enemy's army, at least in terms of fighting and capture. The relatively small size of eighteenth-century armies encouraged commanders to preserve their trained professionals, to focus on manoeuvre and to avoid battle for as long as they could. Ensuing battles, devoid of 'shock tactics', rarely ended with one army crushing the other. Yet with such numbers of men now at the disposal of the French state, French armies actively sought to engage the enemy in battle, with the result that many more battles were fought, with greater numbers of combatants and greater casualties. Of course, this all operated within the technological restraints of the age. For like their eighteenth-century predecessors, the armies of the Revolutionary-Napoleonic epoch were captive to musket, cannon and horse.[82] Nevertheless, and despite the increased frequency of battles, there was now a new focus on decisively destroying the enemy's military force – not simply winning on the day and then beginning peace negotiations, but pursuing the enemy army beyond the battle to ensure its complete capture. The case par excellence of this newfound relentlessness in crushing the entire enemy army was Napoleon's actions after the Battle of Jena, where the French continued to pursue the defeated and retreating Prussian forces, ultimately killing, wounding or capturing (largely the latter) 96 per cent of the 171,000 strong Prussian forces sent against Napoleon.[83]

But with this, did French soldiers also carry a new hatred of their enemies that manifested in an intensification of wartime combat and violence, one that cast aside eighteenth-century protocols and restraints? This very issue is one of the central pillars of Bell's thesis of total war, seeing in the conduct of the French Revolutionary-Napoleonic Wars something akin to Carl Schmitt's notion of 'absolute enmity' between adversaries.[84] For Michael Broers, this is one of the more compelling dimensions to Bell's argument.[85] Certainly, during 1792–94 one can speak of a 'Jacobin way of war' that encapsulates this intense hatred and dehumanisation of the enemy; and so too did counterrevolutionary forces view Republicans in this way. Within both the language and policies of the Jacobin political elite was the aspiration at least to realise a 'war of annihilation' against both the external and internal enemies of the Republic. This was a Jacobin imagining of war that fused classical stories of heroic self-sacrifice (the Spartans at Thermopylae) and the absolute destruction of the enemy (Rome's obliteration of Carthage) with Revolutionary ideology and politics.[86] This was a war of intense ferocity and hatred; conceived as a war without mercy, a war to the death. Carnot instructed military commanders to 'exterminate to the bitter end'.[87] In June 1794, the Jacobins notoriously ordered that no British or Hanoverian prisoners of war be taken alive, later extending this to Spanish troops.[88]

This type of war did indeed materialise with respect to the Vendée. In March 1793 the region of the Vendée in Brittany rose up against the Republican government, the rebellion triggered by the conscription levy but a product of deeper and long seated grievances. Republican armies were sent into the Vendée to wage a war against Royalist-Catholic forces. The conflict descended into barbarism, with dehumanisation of the enemy, mass atrocities committed by both sides, guerrilla warfare against Republican soldiers, and a blurring of the distinctions between combatants and civilians. For Republican troops, every 'Vendean' was a potential rebel despite the complexity of political allegiances throughout the wider region. After the Royalist army was destroyed, General Turreau's infamous 'hell columns' finished off the job in 1794, cleansing the Vendée of remaining rebels and rebel villages, destroying the very landscape itself. In December 1793, after defeating the royalists at Savenay, General Westermann wrote to the Committee of Public Safety:

> There is no more Vendée, citizens. It has died under our free sword, with its women and children. I have just buried it in the marshes and woods of Savenay. Following the orders you gave me, I have crushed children under the hooves of horses, and massacred women who, these at least, will give birth to no more brigands. I do not have a single prisoner with which to reproach myself. I have exterminated everyone.[89]

But, of course, the Vendée was not a war between foreign armies, but a civil war involving republican armies and counter-revolutionary forces. Republican generals and their forces operated within the broader legal framework and discourse of the Terror, carrying out the punitive will of the Jacobin government against the 'enemy within'. And it involved guerrillas and civilians. The 'enemy' was not a regular army or soldier, but in some senses a whole people, and this point is crucial in exploring the question of 'absolute enmity'. For over the course of the French Revolutionary-Napoleonic Wars, atrocities, massacres and breaches of customary laws of war were much more likely to occur in regions involving guerrilla and partisan warfare, where the notion of a 'people's war' broke down the traditional distinctions between soldiers and civilians.[90] This was precisely the case in the Vendée; and beyond France, especially so during the French occupation of Calabria (1806–10), during the revolt in the Tyrol (1809), during the Grand Army's retreat through Russia (1812), and most infamously during the Peninsular War (1808–14). While civilians had been caught up in the fighting of eighteenth-century wars, never before in their history had French armies faced armed numbers of civilians and guerrillas on this scale and across multiple theatres of war. As Esdaile, a leading specialist on the Spanish guerrillas, suggests, although this type of warfare was not new, 'it is possible to argue that it was the Napoleonic Wars that formalized the concept of asymmetrical warfare'.[91]

This was never truer than in the Peninsular War, which popularised the Spanish word, *guerrilla*. As graphically captured in Francisco Goya's *Disasters of War*, this was a conflict involving extraordinary violence. The French pillaged, plundered and committed atrocities against local inhabitants; civilians were caught up in horrific sieges and urban street fighting; guerrillas and armed peasants waged a 'little war' behind the conventional battles and front lines, killing and mutilating French soldiers; there were cycles of insurgency and counter-insurgency, atrocities begetting counter-atrocities; and French and Spanish soldiers themselves all too often gave one another no quarter. The brutality of the war sprung from many factors, of which the guerrillas were but one: the lengthy period of French occupation; the size of Napoleon's armies and their exploitative practices; the cultural and ideological clash between the Napoleonic state's attempts to revolutionise and 'civilise' the Iberian world versus the local peoples, their customs and the Catholic Church; guerrillas and popular insurgency; and the size and geography of Spain all combined to produce a maelstrom of violence and destruction.[92]

Importantly, though, the Peninsular War was not representative of the general character of fighting and violence during the Napoleonic Wars. Its brutality and lack of restraint was at the extreme end of the spectrum. Moreover, a different picture emerges when we consider the general conduct of French soldiers towards enemy regular soldiers. During the Revolutionary-Napoleonic Wars, we can find numerous examples and incidents of professional soldiers failing to adhere to eighteenth-century restraints: showing no quarter on the battlefield, or killing the wounded or prisoners of war.[93] This was especially so in the brutalising campaigns of Spain and Russia, and there is the notorious case of Napoleon ordering the execution of 4,000 Ottoman prisoners at Jaffa in 1799. But, generally speaking, eighteenth-century customary conventions and humanitarian restraints survived and persisted between the major belligerent armies, especially in Western Europe.[94] A case in point is the notorious 1794 Jacobin demand for no British, Hanoverian or Spanish prisoners to be taken – French soldiers in the field largely disobeyed this command, although some 8,000 Spanish soldiers were killed.[95]

Prisoner of war conventions regarding parole and regular exchange, however, did break down in this period. In the eighteenth century, prisoners were regularly exchanged in cartels, and officers were released on 'parole', giving their oath as gentlemen not to return to fighting until the cessation of hostilities or upon exchange. Under parole, officers could return to their home countries. Yet the Jacobins in 1793 ordered that French officers no longer honour parole but return to the war, an order driven by necessity and the ideological assault on aristocratic privilege and honour. This was to have a lasting impact. While the Napoleonic regime and its field commanders granted parole to captured officers, they were generally not allowed to return home. Moreover, the release or exchange of prisoners of war became much less common. Indeed, during the Napoleonic Wars the French and British states kept each other's respective prisoners for the entire war, meaning some 16,000 British prisoners were held in France and over 100,000 Frenchmen in Britain. The modern prisoner of war had come into being.[96]

But eighteenth-century customary practices and honour codes amongst French military men proved remarkably enduring.[97] Despite the barbarisation of war in the Iberian Peninsula, French and British martial and cultural interaction was unmistakeably grounded in eighteenth-century customs and civility. While the British consistently condemned the violence and destruction that the French wrought on the Iberian peoples, they could find no fault in French conduct towards themselves; indeed, French and British soldiers considered one another as 'civilised' nations who fought and behaved accordingly. As one British officer wrote: 'The French are a brave and generous enemy, and their humanity to the English prisoners is generosity to the extreme'.[98] As such, this highlights a crucial point: French soldiers' adherence to customary restraints was shaped not only as to whether the enemy was an armed civilian, but the degree to which they perceived the enemy as 'civilised'.[99]

Conclusion

In the end, the French experience of war in the Revolutionary-Napoleonic era was transformative, with a dynamic of change prevailing over continuities with the past. The degree of change, however, varied across time and place.

Continuities remained: eighteenth-century technologies of war; and much of the eighteenth century's customary practices and honour codes among 'regular' combatants, especially officers. Indeed, the Peninsular War demonstrates the co-existence of the old and the new: British and French soldiers behaving like their eighteenth-century predecessors, while all around them were traumascapes of total war. The aristocratic way of war, as an honour code, far from vanished in this era; indeed, one has only to look at the ideals and behaviour of young officers on the Western Front between 1914 and 1916 to see its survival as an ethos – it was the Somme and Verdun that destroyed its vestiges.

Yet alongside these important continuities stood profound changes in how the French now perceived and waged war. Napoleon was not Louis XIV incarnate, and nor was the Revolutionary-Napoleonic state's war making, notwithstanding the development of a French fiscal-military state over several previous centuries, akin to its Bourbon predecessors. There was both quantitative and qualitative change: the ideologisation of war, the extraordinary growth of the state's claims and control over its citizens for the purpose of waging war, and the nation-in-arms. The *levée en masse* was truly revolutionary and it was to cast a shadow over the entire period. This was an age of mass warfare, where war became the business of the nation and of 'citizens', despite resistance to conscription and the professionalisation of soldiers under Napoleon. On this last count, this chapter has sought to highlight the links between the Revolutionary and Napoleonic Wars, notwithstanding noticeable changes. Napoleon, in a sense, inherited and tamed the *levée en masse*, bringing order, discipline and professionalisation to the army, and taking it across Europe. The army was no longer a hot bed of the 'radical' revolution, but in its victorious and conquering march across Europe came revolutionary changes nonetheless.

On the specific question of 'total war', the concept has brought its own challenges and difficulties, with historians measuring the Revolutionary-Napoleonic Wars against the litmus test of various characteristics of total war, generally from the perspective of the twentieth century. In the end, though, like all grand historical theses, Bell's work has encouraged only greater historical scrutiny and rethinking on the nature of war in this epoch, especially its long neglected cultural dimensions. This chapter has argued that some periods and theatres of war in the Revolutionary-Napoleonic epoch do approximate to something like total war: the Jacobin era and the Peninsular War are the two stand out candidates. The French Revolutionary leaders of 1792–94 imagined total war; they articulated it; and they 'tried' to realise it. Arguably, they came about as close to realising it as a French state and people could in a still largely agrarian, pre-industrial society, convulsed in political and social revolution.

Of course, France was the epicentre of changes to the nature of war in this epoch. As Broers has argued, the French revolutionary leadership's vision of total war was not shared by other European elites.[100] Certainly, the coalition powers did not share this radical reimagining of war to nearly the same degree as the French. But there were variations within Europe, and states were forced out of necessity to adapt and transform. Neither Britain nor Austria introduced conscription, but their scale of mobilisation was unprecedented nevertheless. Since John Brewer's ground-breaking study of the development of a British 'fiscal-military state' over the course of the eighteenth century,[101] there has been a growing interest in the ways in which the British state marshalled financial, commercial and human resources, including a heavy reliance on private contractors, to support its expanding navy and army.[102] This mobilisation was taken to another level during the Napoleonic Wars.[103] The army, for example, numbered 250,000 effectives by 1813 (more than double its size during the American War of Independence), many of whom fought in the most barbaric and 'total' of all campaigns – the Peninsular War.[104] Moreover, Britain was confronted with an economic war on a monumental scale – Napoleon's Continental Blockade. Unlike its neighbour Austria, Prussia – following its 1806 defeat, humiliation and occupation – looked explicitly to the French model to survive and rebuild: universal conscription and the ideal of the nation-in-arms followed.[105] Prussia would fight its own 'War of Liberation' against the French occupier in 1813, although the patriotic sentiment of official propaganda and of nationalist poets struggled to find a great deal of traction with the population at large.[106]

Still, fundamental changes had occurred. All across Europe, civilians found their lives increasingly affected by war to a degree unknown to previous generations of eighteenth-century Europeans: through conscription and recruitment, requisition, occupation, and taking up arms themselves. Overall, an estimated five million Europeans died during the Revolutionary-Napoleonic Wars, proportionally comparable to the losses of WWI, albeit over a much longer period of time.[107]

The French Revolutionary-Napoleonic Wars ultimately hold a unique place in the history of modern European war, neither simply a repeat performance of eighteenth-century conflicts, nor akin to the industrial wars of the twentieth century. They did, in the end, represent a watershed between the old Europe and the new. Indeed, with the benefit of hindsight, they were a tipping point, laying down a footprint of what was later to come. Seen in this light, it can be argued that Waterloo was the end of the beginning.

NOTES

1   C. Esdaile, *The Wars of Napoleon* (London and New York: Longman, 1995), p. 143.
2   R. Chickering, 'Introduction: A Tale of Two Tales: Grand Narratives of War in the Age of Revolution', in R. Chickering and S. Förster (eds), *War in an Age of Revolution, 1775–1815* (New York: Cambridge University Press, 2010), pp. 1–17.
3   For an overview of the works of Howard and Parker and the debates they engendered,

see C. J. Rogers (ed.), *The Military Revolution Debate: Readings on the Military Transformation of Early Modern Europe* (Boulder, Col: West View Press, 1995).

4   D. A. Bell, *The First Total War. Napoleon's Europe and the Birth of Warfare as We Know It* (Boston: Houghton Mifflin, 2007), p. 8.

5   See for instance *H-France Forum*, 2:3 (Summer 2007), no. 1; M. Broers, 'The concept of "Total War" in the Revolutionary-Napoleonic period', *War in History*, 15:3 (2008), pp. 247–68.

6   P. H. Wilson, 'Was the Thirty Years War a "Total War"?', in E. Charters, E. Rosenhaft, and H. Smith (eds), *Civilians and War in Europe, 1618–1815* (Liverpool: Liverpool University Press, 2012), p. 24.

7   Wilson, 'Was the Thirty Years War a "Total War"?', pp. 21–4.

8   See for example, R. Chickering, 'Total War: Use and Abuse of a Concept', in M. Boemeke, R. Chickering, and S. Förster (eds), *Anticipating Total War: The German and American Experiences, 1871–1914* (Cambridge: Cambridge University Press, 1999), pp. 13–28; J. Black, *The Age of Total War, 1860–1945* (Lanham, ML: Rowman & Littlefield, 2010), pp. 1–11.

9   Chickering, 'Introduction: A Tale of Two Tales', p. 10.

10   Quoted in E. V. Macleod, *A War of Ideas: British Attitudes to the Wars Against Revolutionary France 1792–1802* (Aldershot: Ashgate, 1998), p. 12.

11   Quoted in Macleod, *A War of Ideas*, p. 18.

12   For an overview of this tradition, see A. Forrest, *Soldiers of the French Revolution* (Durham and London: Duke University Press, 1990), pp. 5–11.

13   P. W. Schroeder, *The Transformation of European Politics 1763–1848* (Oxford: Clarendon Press, 1994), p. 309.

14   T.C.W. Blanning, *The Origins of the French Revolutionary Wars* (London: Longman, 1986).

15   Blanning, *The Origins of the French Revolutionary Wars*, p. 123.

16   Forrest, *Soldiers of the French Revolution*, p. 11.

17   For a recent discussion, see Bell, *First Total War*, pp. 111–19.

18   Quoted in Bell, *First Total War*, p. 115.

19   Quoted in Bell, *First Total War*, p. 115.

20   Forrest, *Soldiers of the French Revolution*, p. 12.

21   Quoted in P. McPhee, *Robespierre: A Revolutionary Life* (New Haven, Conn: Yale University Press, 2012), p. 114.

22   For an overview of the Napoleonic Wars, see D. Gates, *The Napoleonic Wars, 1803–1815* (London: Arnold, 1997); C. Esdaile, *Napoleon's Wars: An International History, 1803–1815* (London: Penguin, 2008).

23   Esdaile, *Napoleon's Wars*, pp. 6, 13.

24   Among the many histories addressing the nature of the Napoleonic Empire, see G. Ellis, *The Napoleonic Empire* (Basingstoke: Macmillan, 1991); S. Woolf, *Napoleon's Integration of Europe* (London and New York: Routledge, 1991); M. Lyons, *Napoleon Bonaparte and the Legacy of the French Revolution* (Basingstoke: Macmillan, 1994); M. Broers, *Europe under Napoleon, 1799–1815* (London: Arnold, 1996); Esdaile, *Napoleon's Wars*.

25   Woolf, *Napoleon's Integration of Europe*.

26   T. Nipperdey, *Germany from Napoleon to Bismarck* (Princeton: Princeton University Press, 1996).

27   On this last point see for instance, D. P. Jordan, 'Napoleon as Revolutionary', in P. G. Dwyer and A. Forrest (eds), *Napoleon and His Empire: Europe, 1804–1814* (Basingstoke: Palgrave Macmillan, 2007), p. 40.

28   J. A. Lynn, 'Recalculating French Army growth during the Grand Siecle, 1610–1715', *French Historical Studies*, 18:4 (1994), p. 904.

29   D. Gates, *Warfare in the Nineteenth Century* (Basingstoke: Palgrave, 2001), p. 32.

30   Gates, *Warfare in the Nineteenth Century*, p. 38.

31   Esdaile, *Napoleon's Wars*, p. 9.

32   Gates, *Warfare in the Nineteenth Century*, p. 33.

33   C. Tilly, 'Reflections on the History of European State-Making', in C. Tilly (ed.), *The Formation of National States in Western Europe* (Princeton: Princeton University Press, 1975), p. 42.

34   For an overview, see T. Ertman, 'The Sinews of Power and European-State Building Theory', in L. Stone (ed.), *An Imperial State at War: Britain from 1689 to 1815* (London: Routledge, 1994), pp. 33–51.

35   M. Weber, *Economy and Society: An Outline of Interpretive Sociology*, eds. G. Roth and C. Wittich (New York: Bedminster Press, 1968); O. Hintze, *The Historical Essays of Otto Hintze*, ed. F. Gilbert (New York: Oxford University Press, 1975).

36   C. Tilly, 'War Making and State Making as Organised Crime', in P. Evans, D. Rueschemeyer and T. Skocpol (eds), *Bringing the State Back In* (Cambridge: Cambridge University Press, 1985), pp. 169–86; C. Tilly, *Coercion, Capital, and European States, AD 990–1992* (Cambridge MA: Blackwell, 1992).

37   P. Anderson, *Lineages of the Absolutist State* (London: NLB, 1974).

38   G. Rowlands, *The Dynastic State and the Army under Louis XIV: Royal Service and Private Interest 1661–1701* (Cambridge: Cambridge University Press, 2010).

39   D. Parrott, *The Business of War: Military Enterprise and Military Revolution in Early Modern Europe* (Cambridge: Cambridge University Press, 2012).

40   C. von Clausewitz, *On War*, ed. M. Howard and P. Paret (London: Everyman's Library, 1993), pp. 716–17.

41   See for example, W. Kruse, 'Revolutionary France and the Meanings of the Levée en Masse', in Chickering and Förster (eds), *War in an Age of Revolution*, pp. 299–312.

42   On the Jacobin mobilisation for war, and the accompanying extraordinary growth in state bureaucracy, see H. G. Brown, *War, Revolution, and the Bureaucratic State: Politics and Army Administration in France, 1791–1799* (Oxford: Clarendon Press, 1995), especially pp. 98–134; A. Forrest, 'The Logistics of Revolutionary War in France', in Chickering and Förster (eds), *War in an Age of Revolution*, pp. 177–95.

43   D. Andress, *The Terror: Civil War in the French Revolution* (London: Abacus, 2005), p. 164.

44   Quoted in Andress, *The Terror*, p. 201.

45   S. F. Scott, *The Response of the Royal Army to the French Revolution: The Role and Development of the Line Army, 1787–1794* (Oxford: Clarendon Press, 1978), p. 5.

46   M. Lyons, *France under the Directory* (Cambridge: Cambridge University Press, 1975), p. 149.

47   J. Bertaud, *The Army of the French Revolution: From Citizen Soldiers to Instruments of Power* (Princeton: Princeton University Press, 1988), p. 272.

48   For an overview, see Isser Woloch, 'Napoleonic Conscription: State Power and Civil Society', *Past and Present*, 111:1 (May 1986), pp. 101–29.

49   Quoted in G. Daly, *Inside Napoleonic France: State and Society in Rouen, 1800–1815* (Aldershot: Ashgate, 2001), p. 220.

50   See especially A. Forrest, *Conscripts and Deserters: The Army and French Society During the Revolution and Empire* (New York: Oxford University Press, 1989).

51   Lyons, *Napoleon Bonaparte*, p. 155.

52   For an overview see Lyons, *Napoleon Bonaparte*, pp. 240–3.

53   For Italy, see A. Grab, 'Conscription and Desertion in Napoleonic Italy, 1802–1814', in D. Stoker, F. C. Scheid and H. D. Blanton (eds), *Conscription in the Napoleonic Era: A Revolution in Military Affairs?* (Abingdon, Oxon: Routledge, 2009), pp. 122–33.

54   Grab, 'Conscription and Desertion in Napoleonic Italy, 1802–1814', p. 122.

55   O. Connelly, *The Wars of the French Revolution and Napoleon 1792–1815* (New York: Routledge, 2006), p. 170.

56   Bertaud, *The Army of the French Revolution*, p. 16.

57   Scott, *The Response of the Royal Army to the French Revolution*, p. 185.

58   Scott, *The Response of the Royal Army to the French Revolution*, p. 106.

59   Connelly, *Wars of the French Revolution and Napoleon*, p. 43.

60   Bell, *First Total War*, pp. 78–81.

61   Connelly, *Wars of the French Revolution and Napoleon*, p. 31.

62   Bertaud, *The Army of the French Revolution*, p. 99.

63   Forrest, *Soldiers of the French Revolution*, p. 194.

64   See especially J. A. Lynn, *Bayonets of the Republic: Motivation and Tactics in the Army of Revolutionary France, 1791–1794* (Urbana, IL: University of Illinois Press, 1984); Bertaud, *The Army of the French Revolution*; Forrest, *Soldiers of the French Revolution*.

65   Quoted in M. Thoral, *From Valmy to Waterloo: France at War, 1792–1815* (Basingstoke: Palgrave Macmillan, 2011), p. 110.

66   See for instance, A. Forrest, 'The Nation in Arms I: The French Wars', in C. Townshend (ed.), *The Oxford History of Modern War* (Oxford: Oxford University Press, 2000), pp. 62–4; Esdaile, *The Wars of Napoleon*, pp. 54–7.

67   J. A. Lynn, 'Toward an army of honor: The moral evolution of the French Army, 1769–1815', *French Historical Studies*, 16:1 (1989), pp. 152–73.

68   M. J. Hughes, *Forging Napoleon's Grand Armée: Motivation, Military Culture, and Masculinity in the French Army, 1800–1808* (New York: New York University Press, 2012), pp. 79–107.

69   Hughes, *Forging Napoleon's Grand Armée*, p. 106.

70   Duke of Wellington, *The Dispatches of Field Marshal the Duke of Wellington*, ed. J Gurwood, 8 vols (London, 1852), vol. 5, Wellington to Baron Constant, 31 January 1812, pp. 494–5.

71   For an overview of the 'laws of war' in the eighteenth century see G. Best, *Humanity in Warfare: The Modern History of the International Law of Armed Conflicts* (London: Weidenfeld and Nicolson, 1980), pp. 32–70.

72   See for example, J. Black, *European Warfare, 1660–1815* (London: UCL Press, 1994).

73   Bell, *First Total War*, p. 49.

74   For an overview of how the 'laws of war' fared during the Revolutionary-Napoleonic Wars, see Best, *Humanity in Warfare*, pp. 89–127; G. Rothenberg, 'The Age of Napoleon', in M. Howard, G. J. Andreopoulos, and M. R. Shulman (eds), *The Laws of War: Constraints on Warfare in the Western World* (New Haven and London: Yale University Press, 1994), pp. 86–97.

75   *Diaries and Letters of G. T. W. B Boyes*, ed. Peter Chapman (Melbourne: Oxford University Press, 1985), vol. 1, p. 50.

76   Best, *Humanity in Warfare*, pp. 89–95.

77   Esdaile, *Peninsular War*, p. 242.

78   R. Muir, 'Wellington and the Peninsular War: The Ingredients of Victory', in R. Muir, R. Burnham, H Muir and R. McGuigan (eds), *Inside Wellington's Peninsular Army, 1808–1814* (Barnsley: Pen & Sword, 2006), p. 20.

79 Wellington, *Dispatches*, vol. 4, Wellington to Marquis Wellesley, 26 January 1811, pp. 555–6.

80 Wellington, *Dispatches*, vol. 5, Wellington to Baron Constant, 31 January 1812, p. 494.

81 See Esdaile, *Wars of Napoleon*, pp. 42–8; Thoral, *From Valmy to Waterloo*, pp. 14–18.

82 Michael Broers stresses the technological limitations of the wars as a key factor acting against the realisation of total war in this epoch; Broers, 'The concept of Total War', pp. 258–60.

83 Bell, *First Total War*, p. 239.

84 Bell, *First Total War*, pp. 14–15.

85 Broers, 'The concept of Total War', pp. 253–5.

86 On the influence of classical role models, see Bell, *First Total War*, pp. 79–80; Broers, 'The concept of Total War', p. 256.

87 Quoted in Rothenberg, *Age of Napoleon*, p. 88.

88 Rothenberg, *Age of Napoleon*.

89 Quoted in Bell, *First Total War*, p. 173.

90 On massacres and atrocities during the Napoleonic Wars, see P. G. Dwyer, 'It still makes me shudder: Memories of massacres and atrocities during the Revolutionary and Napoleonic Wars', *War in History*, 16 (2009), pp. 381–405.

91 Esdaile, *Napoleon's Wars*, p. 11.

92 On violence in the Peninsular War, see Bell, *First Total War*, pp. 275–93.

93 See Dwyer, 'It still makes me shudder'.

94 Rothenberg, *Age of Napoleon*, pp. 87–9, 97; Best, *Humanity in Warfare*, pp. 121–5; Thoral, *From Valmy to Waterloo*, p. 39.

95 Rothenberg, *Age of Napoleon*, p. 88.

96 On prisoners of war conventions between France and Britain, see M. Lewis, *Napoleon and his British Captives* (London: Allen & Unwin, 1962); G. Daly, 'Napoleon's lost legions: French prisoners of war in Britain, 1803–1814', *History*, 89:3 (July 2004), pp. 361–80.

97 This is nowhere more dramatically demonstrated than in the behaviour of French and British soldiers towards one another in the Peninsular War, see G. Daly, *The British Soldier in the Peninsular War: Encounters with Spain and Portugal, 1808–1814* (Basingstoke, Palgrave Macmillan, 2013), pp. 153–4; L. Montroussier-Favre, 'Remembering the Other: The Peninsular War in the Autobiographical Accounts of British and French soldiers', in A. Forrest, É. François, and K. Hagemann (eds), *War Memories: The Revolutionary and Napoleonic Wars in Modern European Culture* (Basingstoke: Palgrave Macmillan, 2012), pp. 66–71.

98 G. Simmons, *A British Rifleman*, ed. W. Verner (London: A. & C. Black, 1899), p. 33.

99 On notions of 'civilised' and 'barbaric' war, see W. E. Lee, *Barbarians and Brothers: Anglo-American Warfare, 1500–1865* (Oxford: Oxford University Press, 2011).

100 Broers, 'The concept of 'Total War', pp. 264–8.

101 J. Brewer, *The Sinews of War: War, Money and the English State 1688–1783* (London: Unwin Hyman, 1989).

102 For a recent synthesis, see A. Page, *Britain and the Seventy Years War 1744–1815* (Basingstoke: Palgrave Macmillan, 2015).

103 See especially R. Knight, *Britain Against Napoleon: The Organization of Victory, 1793–1815* (London: Penguin, 2013).

104 On the raising of the British army, see K. Linch, *Britain and Wellington's Army: Recruitment, Society and Tradition, 1807–15* (Basingstoke: Palgrave Macmillan, 2011).

105 On these transformations see for example, D. Walter, 'Reluctant Reformers, Observant

Disciples: The Prussian Military Reforms, 1807–1814', in Chickering and Förster (eds), *War in an Age of Revolution*, pp. 85–99.

106 See for example, L. S. James, *Witnessing the Revolutionary and Napoleonic Wars in German Central Europe* (Basingstoke: Palgrave Macmillan, 2013), pp. 172–7.

107 Gates, *Napoleonic Wars*, p. 272.

2

State violence and the eliticide in Poland, 1935–49

Jan Pakulski

> Let us suppose that all of a sudden France loses fifty each of its leading scientists, artists, engineers, bankers, businessmen, farmers, manufacturers and professionals of all kinds ... making in all the three thousand best scientists, artist and producers in France ... The nation would become a lifeless corpse as soon as it lost them. It would immediately fall into a state of inferiority *vis-à-vis* its present rivals, and it would remain their subordinate as long as it was waiting for a new head to emerge. It would take France at least one whole generation to make up for this disaster.[1]

Henri de Saint-Simon, an eccentric French aristocrat and founding father of sociology, uses the now-famous parable of 'decapitation' to illustrate the importance, in fact the social indispensability, of what he called 'leading members' of the ascendant 'industrialist class' – which closely approximates Vilfredo Pareto's 1935 national 'elite' and Gaetano Mosca's concept of the 'ruling class'. Such an elite, as Mosca notes, consists of two strata: the actual 'governing class' composed of those who are not only the best in their field of endeavour, but also enjoy the most wealth, prestige, power and influence, and the adjacent stratum from which the ranks of elites are replenished. National decapitations or 'eliticides', suggested Saint-Simon (as well as Pareto, Mosca and their followers),[2] always target both elite strata. National decapitations, as Robert Conquest, Timothy Snyder, the Memorial Group of historians in Russia, and the *Instytut Pamięci Narodowej* (IPN, Institute of National Remembrance) historians in Poland argue, destroy whole societies and nations. An eliticide, when prolonged and ruthless, endangers social, political and moral order and undermines the capacity of the nation to maintain its statehood.

Such a prolonged and ruthless eliticide was committed in Poland in 1939–45. It was a case of state-perpetrated violence at its worst, planned and conducted by Hitler's and then Stalin's occupying forces. The massive assault on the Polish leading strata, lasting for the entire period of war, proved tragically effective. While the national decapitation did not break the spirit of resistance – as clearly demonstrated by the 1944 Warsaw Uprising and the long-lasting political opposition – it significantly weakened the anti-occupation forces. This led to spreading social pathologies, and fatally affected the post-war reconstruction of Poland. The immediate effects of the 1939–41 coordinated German-Soviet assault on the Polish leading strata indeed resembled Saint-Simon's and Mosca's frightening scenarios. The national decapitation left Poland not only vulnerable to political subjugation by Nazi and Soviet forces, but also caused a power vacuum that was filled by a socially deracinated, mediocre, opportunistic (and therefore politically ineffective) 'quasi-elite'.

The reasons for overlooking the eliticide in Poland are obvious, but so are the gains from bringing it to light. First, it helps us understand little-known forms of state violence. The concepts of elites and eliticide are useful to identify its deliberate and rational aspects. Second, bringing to light the eliticidal design is an important correction to the portrayal of war crimes predominantly in terms of irrational or insane ideological motivations. The eliticide conducted by the Nazi and Soviet occupiers in Poland highlights the importance of strategic elite designs, such as Stalin's construction of the 'socialist bloc' and the Nazi *Generalplan Ost* (GPO, Master Plan East), both frequently ignored by historians and social scientists. The elite focus, in turn, helps in seeing these deliberate strategic plans as a part of the large-scale strategic-ideological visions underlying the war. Third, the proposed interpretation helps to solve a number of puzzles, especially concerning the consequences of national decapitation, such as the relatively swift Soviet political takeover of Poland in 1945–47 and the failures of the Soviet-controlled 'quasi-elite' in rebuilding the nation.

With this in mind, this chapter will proceed in five parts. The first introduces and provides a definition of eliticide, highlighting its distinctiveness as a form of state-initiated violence. Part two offers an insight into the perpetrators of the Polish eliticide and part three, through describing the prelude to the Polish eliticide, again reinforces the distinctiveness of this particular form of organised violence. The fourth part focuses on the eliticide, explaining the different methods used by the Nazis and Soviets to achieve somewhat similar results. The chapter concludes by arguing that the violence that was brought upon Polish elites served to severely hamstring Poland's post-war recovery.

Elites and eliticides

The word 'elite' applied initially to high-quality or exclusive goods, and only later became a synonym for those distinguished persons who form ruling minorities. Thus one of the founding fathers of elite theory, Pareto (1935), defined elites as individuals superior in any aspect of human endeavour – intellectual, martial, moral, artistic, political and so on – and as those who occupy the top positions in the hierarchies of power and wealth. These two hierarchies, as he insisted, always overlapped producing irresistible (because of their superior status, wealth, authority and organisation) 'ruling classes'. It was Mosca (1939), Pareto's major intellectual partner and theoretical rival, who clarified the distinction between power-holding political elites and the influential and prestigious upper circles, and who studied the complex relations between the power-wielders and their immediate social bases. These classical studies were supplemented by more detailed analyses of modern (and increasingly complex) elites by a whole generation of researchers from Max Weber to C. W. Mills (1956).[3]

In pre-industrial and developing societies, such elites were socially entrenched, closed and ascriptive, closely coinciding with traditional aristocracies and nobilities. In modernised and democratised societies, as noted by Mosca, Weber and contemporary 'democratic elitists', the ruling minorities tended to be more open and meritocratic (reproduced through achievement), as well as functionally differentiated and internally stratified.[4] They included the top land- and wealth-holders, the most influential intellectuals (sometimes referred to as the 'cultural elite'), as well as executives of the largest organisations, political parties, and the top echelons of the largest business corporations. Modern elites, in other words, are embedded not only in the 'second stratum' of their immediate successors, but also in a broader educated and well-off strata often described in Central and Eastern Europe as the intelligentsia. This complex social anchoring enhances social distinction and authority, as well as national identity and democratic legitimacy.[5] In democratised national political elites 'openness' – understood as broad social basis and meritocratic recruitment – as well as strong anchoring in national culture, are as important for elite legitimacy as electoral mandate-authorisation. Only socially 'open', 'distinguished', nationally committed and democratically mandated ruling minorities have been seen as 'authentic' elites.[6]

The Nazi and Soviet eliticide in Poland from 1939–45 targeted such authentic elites. The objective was to eliminate the national leading strata (the term used by the German occupiers to designate their target was 'the Polish elite'). Such a broad target encompassed not just immediate rulers, but also the upper ranks of the Polish intelligentsia, whose members were seen as the key repositories of national identity. The blacklists prepared by both the Soviet *Narodnyy Komissariat Vnutrennikh Del* (NKVD, People's Commissariat for Internal Affairs) and the Nazi Gestapo included office holders in state bureaucracies, the officer corps of the army, the professions, as well as top personnel in agricultural, industrial and commercial organisations. These people were recognised as potential resistance organisers, as well as pillars of the social and political order. The German and Soviet occupiers, one should stress, aimed not only at political conquest and subjugation of Poland, but also – and primarily – at the destruction of the Polish nation. This design made the broad national leading strata the main target for decapitation. Such a broad 'nation-killing' – and therefore 'eliticidal'

– design was masked, but it clearly transpired in the often confidential statements of political leaders, the conquest plans (such as the infamous GPO), and in the instructions issued to the occupying forces. This was especially the case for secret police and special command groups.

The national decapitation was exceptionally brutal, partly because it targeted civilians and non-combatants together with the actual resistance fighters, and partly because it utilised the most violent means. It involved systematic mass killing – usually executions without trials or with pseudo-trials, as well as deportation, expulsion and/or long term imprisonment of all actual and suspected members of the broadly defined elite, as well as their closest kin. Such targeting created a climate of terror in which no Pole could feel safe, and from which there was practically no escape.

National decapitations like those conducted by the Nazi and Soviet occupiers in Poland should be distinguished from well-known and understood 'genocides', 'politicides' and 'class cleansing'.[7] Genocides involve more or less indiscriminate killing of persons belonging to certain ethno-racial, ethnonational or ethno-religious categories. They target the entire population as a category, without stratifying potential victims. Similarly, politicides involve systematic mass extermination of political opponents (real or suspected) inside and outside the elite, while class cleansing targets people from certain backgrounds (usually those seen as inferior, hostile or undesirable). Eliticides differ from genocides in their stratified (or vertical) targeting of victims, as well as categorical (or horizontal) targeting. They share with genocides the ascriptive nature of victimisation. Hence victims are targeted and killed for what they are or what they represent, rather than for what they have done. This makes victimisation both involuntary and inescapable. Eliticides can therefore be identified when this two-dimensional targeting takes place. Their important features include the ethno-hierarchical social profiles of victims; the stated intentions, goals and strategic plans of the perpetrators (typically other elites); and ultimately the social-political outcomes. All eliticides result in the 'law of reversed disproportion' whereby the most affected – that is, the most likely to be killed – are those members of a targeted national community who are in the highest positions of status and power.

Eliticides have profound social and political effects, some of which are discussed in the second part of the chapter. They weaken the social, political and moral order, make nations vulnerable to conquest and domination, and – ultimately – may lead to the destruction of entire national communities. Yet, unlike genocides, they have not been recognised by law as criminal acts, and they have typically been confused with politicides (the targeting of just political opponents) – with which they often coincide and overlap. And while mass atrocities committed by German and Soviet occupiers in wartime Poland are widely known, specific evidence of eliticide has only come to light recently. This is partly because the Nazi and Soviet perpetrators masked their plans and accomplishments, and partly because popular and academic victimology had seldom focused on the hierarchical dimension of mass crimes.

Hence the overwhelming concern of historians has been with ethnic genocides, rather than eliticides, such as the Jewish Holocaust and the Ukrainian *Holodomor*. The awareness of elite targeting emerges alongside studies of planned and designed state violence, particularly Hitler's and Stalin's strategic plans for national decapitations alongside both *de jure* and *de facto* territorial aggrandisement. With operational plans like the Katyń Massacre and *Intelligenzaktion* coming to light, the unique and distinctive nature of eliticides becomes more apparent.

Large-scale national decapitations that target elites are comparatively rare in modern times. Traditional warfare and conquest, especially involving takeovers of racially and religiously divergent societies, typically involved *some* acts of extermination of the vanquished aristocracies (perhaps the best known being the Norman conquest of Britain, during which the local (English) aristocrats were systematically executed, dispossessed and/or banished).[8] Modern warfare limited the targeting of civilians and non-combatants. Civilians, particularly those in the upper strata who submitted to the new rulers, were increasingly spared. This has been considered a part of limiting and 'civilising' organised and state-sponsored warfare.

Yet, suddenly and unexpectedly, eliticides and genocides intensified in the early twentieth century, accompanied by ideologies justifying 'cleansing', whether as a result of ethno-racial campaigns or class struggles. There were mass war atrocities in 1914–18, involving brutal ethnic cleansing, as well as 'revolutionary' assaults on so-called ruling classes, but they tended to be limited to politicides and Jacobin-style revenge rather than systematic eliticides. Stalin and Hitler, and their power elites in particular, were the first organisers of systematic, deliberate, and state-organised violent assaults that targeted the elites amongst conquered peoples. Their aim reflected what Conquest labelled as 'killing of nations'. Such assaults involved planned and coordinated mass extermination of the 'upper strata' conducted by military and state security apparatus, often in secret. The national decapitations involved waves of mass executions, deportations, long imprisonment. The result was to silence organised dissent and achieve the moral annihilation of victims on the individual level.

The official secrecy under which eliticides are generally conducted deserves additional comment. There is little doubt that maintaining secrecy is important to avoid a negative backlash that would be generated from publicising them. It is also functionally important: targeted elites command some social-political resources that they can mobilise if forewarned. Secrecy, especially when combined with misleading propaganda that targets traitors, saboteurs, and other opponents of the regime pre-empts defensive mobilisation. The result is that a false illusion of choice is developed: a hope of survival through submission and compromise. Such fear-based complacency, in turn, fragments elites into small groups, thus destroying their internal loyalties and solidarities. It also encourages (largely futile) deal-making and informing behaviour on behalf of those seeking personal salvation and/or advancement.

The eliticide in Poland perpetrated by the Nazis and Soviets neatly illustrates this strategy of secrecy, masking and denial. The plans and designs for the national decapitation, as well as parts of its execution, were shrouded in secrecy and distorted by propaganda as legitimate pacifications or punishment of saboteurs, with details of the operations and acts of extermination carefully masked, denied and censored. Naturally they were highly embarrassing as war crimes and broken undertakings. While the Germans faced the 'months of reckoning' at the Nuremberg trials, Stalin emerged from World War II as the victor – a 'liberator of Europe', adulated at home and admired in the West, so much so that he was nominated twice for the Nobel Peace Prize.[9] His collaboration with German occupiers contradicted the official version of history promoted by the Soviet regime, reluctantly accepted by the West, and imposed by the communist authorities in post-war Poland, as well as the entire Soviet-dominated Warsaw Pact space.

The perpetrators

One of the tragic ironies is that eliticides are conducted by elites – but quite specific elites. The decapitation of Polish society was perpetrated by two crisis-spawned 'power elites' that were highly specific in their origin, structure and outlook. The Soviet and Nazi 'power elites' emerged from radical revolutionary movements under conditions of deep social and political crises. Moreover, these were 'leonine' (as Pareto labelled them) elites: aggressive, violent and brutal in their orientation. Their leadership resembled criminal gangs that consisted of a hierarchy of political mobsters and were led by a feared and respected *cappo di capi*.[10]

Stalin, the feared *Vozhd* (Leader), was a Georgian bandit-turned-revolutionary, a brutal and shrewd individual characterised by Lenin as 'crude and narrow-minded'. He destroyed his political rivals – including nearly all the old Bolsheviks – swiftly and without remorse, and he emerged in the 1930s as not only the unchallenged Soviet dictator but also as the sole leader of the international communist movement. Stalin, unlike Hitler, was a poor speaker but an effective political manipulator who ran the Soviet *Politburo* by terrorising critics, eliminating all challengers, stacking the top positions with his loyal (often sycophantic) supporters, and subjecting the highest ranks to regular purges. Hitler, on the other hand, was a nationalistic and anti-Semitic extremist with a gift for demagogy. He also displayed many of the characteristics of a shrewd mobster, a Bertolt Brecht's Arturo Ui, but it was his rhetorical skills that helped him to dominate the national socialist movement. His speeches were filled with manic delusions of Germany's greatness, racial fantasies of Aryan superiority, and paranoid visions of vile and hostile global conspiracies, primarily from the forces of international Jewry.[11]

Both Stalin and Hitler's leadership groups formed through political usurpations that were masked as revolutionary takeovers. They thoroughly replaced the old elites, who were accused of treason and plotting against the new regime. They discarded and condemned liberal and democratic principles in the name of socialism, class justice, national pride, racial superiority, upturned laws, norms and political conventions, and destroyed rivals in opposition. The new rulers of Germany and the Soviet Union used violence more than persuasion, and they combined terror with propaganda. Both formed ultra-centralised and radical regimes with a single power apex combining the economic, cultural, political, and military hierarchies. At the top of this single party-state structure stood the Leader (*Führer*, and *Vozhd*) surrounded by a cult of personality. Both leaders promised a radical reconstruction of the national and world orders. The core leadership groups around Hitler and Stalin (the *Politischen Leiter* and the *Politburo*) were handpicked by the leaders and subjected to surveillance. They were united by the 'ruling formula', by their shared loyalty to the leader and by 'blood pacts', where it was insisted that all member of the so-called inner circle 'bloody their hands' by signing death warrants and/or ordering and implementing purges. Significantly, both Hitler and Stalin harboured paranoid suspicions of conspiracies by enemies and traitors, and their closest collaborators (especially Himmler and Beria) reinforced those suspicions. Finally, both leaders believed in the effectiveness of force, and freely utilised violence when dealing with enemies and traitors, either real or imaginary.

One corollary of this commitment to violence and paranoid suspicions was regular purging of the higher echelons of power. A second was targeting of elites of other nations, where the most dangerous enemies were seen to reside. Another was a heavy reliance on state security apparatus (*Gosudarstvennoye politicheskoye upravlenie* (GPU, State Political Directorate), Gestapo), party-controlled security forces and 'elite bodyguard units' (NKVD, *Schutzstaffel* (SS)). The latter operated as the most reliable executioners of enemies and traitors.

The two leaders' suspicion of conspiracies 'at the top' was combined with a strong belief in their special historical mission. Both made Hitler and Stalin particularly receptive to the idea that eliticides were the best means for realising those missions. Hence eliticide was regarded as a natural and appropriate method of securing power. This explains why Stalin's early campaign against 'Polish spies' targeted the leaders of the Communist Party of Poland, as well as state leaders, and why his plan to 'expand the socialist camp' focused on eliminating national leaders, including the top intellectuals. Hitler's GPO also embraced eliticide as a principal means of social reconstruction and the best method of 'eliminating' the Polish nation. Both were foreshadowed in *Mein Kampf* (first published in 1926), considered as the first outline of the Nazi vision. The body responsible for the drafting of the GPO was the *Reichssicherheitshauptamt* (RSHA, Reich Main Security Office), the security arm of the SS responsible for protecting the Nazi elite. The GPO was confidential and only Hitler and his closest confidantes knew its contents. The initial version was outlined under Hitler's direction in 1938–39 in consultation with the Nazi elite. The more detailed final version was drafted in early 1940. The GPO originally envisaged, first, a conquest with elite decapitation of Eastern Europe, followed by a systematic cleansing of ethno-racial undesirables: Jews (100 per cent), Poles and Lithuanians (85 per cent), Byelorussians (75 per cent), Ukrainians (65 per cent) and Czechs (50 per cent), thus clearing the East European *Lebensraum* for German colonisation. Furthermore, according to the GPO, forty five million 'non-Germanisable' people were to be removed through extermination and/or deportation to west Siberia. About fourteen million were initially to remain as slaves working for German colonists, and to be ultimately assimilated, deported or killed. The GPO was further revised in 1941. The Polish nation was to be destroyed through extermination of its leaders and elites, forcible Germanisation of children, the wholesale destruction of Polish culture, and a ban on education beyond basic literacy.[12]

The main objective for Stalin was first to construct 'socialism in one country', and then to overcome what he saw as the capitalist enclosure by expanding the Soviet Union westward. Both objectives involved pitching Nazi Germany against the Western capitalist/imperialist system and expanding the Soviet system over new territories and new populations. We know more about Stalin's early plans and strategies than about his later designs. In preparation for the second Five Year Plan, the *Vozhd* announced a new vision of a 'more acute class struggle' requiring more repressive measures both at home and internationally. It served as an ideological justification for forced collectivisation, the campaign against the *kulaks* (affluent farmers) and the Ukrainian *Holodomor* – a punishment for persisting nationalism and delays in collectivisation. In 1936, the plan was adjusted. A new law on 'terrorist organisations and terrorist acts' prompted the security organs to investigate hostile plots, especially involving state organs, the army and party-political leadership. In 1937–38 Stalin personally signed 357 proscription lists ordering the executions of over 40,000 persons. About 90 per cent of victims were promptly shot. Externally, he sent fighters to the Spanish Civil War and contemplated the 'neutralisation' of Poland.[13]

While we know less about Stalin's designs concerning Poland, since some Soviet archives are still closed, we can make some informed guesses. Poland – hated by Stalin for defeating the Soviet forces in the 1920–21 war, checking the westward Soviet expansion, and accused of fomenting anti-Soviet agitation – was to be eliminated as a sovereign nation-state. This was intended to be accomplished not through genocidal extermination but through a decapitation and absorption as a politically neutered 'Soviet nationality'. Such a design was revealed in the secret Annex to the Nazi-Soviet Pact of 1939. Polish territories were to be partitioned between Germany and the Soviet Union, and their inhabitants were to be absorbed into the Soviet state. Hence the objective was to absorb Poland as a seventeenth republic. This was a plan feared and resented by Poles no less than forced Germanisation.

The Soviet design changed between late 1941 and early 1943. After the German invasion of the Soviet Union in June 1941, Poles were reluctantly recognised (though never trusted) as Soviet allies and 'hostages' in negotiations with the Allies. At the end of 1942, when the Red Army started its westward push and the negotiations with the Allies intensified, Poland was 'redesigned' (or 're-assigned') as a future semi-autonomous member of the socialist camp. The scope of autonomy of the nation was treated as an important bargaining chip in negotiations with both the Allies and the surviving Polish communists, the latter gradually drafted by Stalin as potentially loyal and compliant rulers of a 'People's Poland'.

Consequently, the two parts of the eliticide – the Nazi and the Soviet – were quite different. The Nazi eliticide was most intense in 1939–40, and continued throughout the war with varying intensity, peaking again in 1944. The Soviet eliticide, by contrast, reached its peak between November 1939 and June 1941, and then subsided, turning into an intense politicide – a systematic elimination of political opponents. Thus while the officer corps of the Polish prisoners of war (POWs) were executed in a wholesale manner in 1940, after the Soviet-Polish pact of July–August 1941 those surviving members of the Polish elite who declared their willingness to collaborate with the Soviets were spared. Those suspected of disloyalty but considered useful (like the Polish Army formed in the USSR under the command of General Anders) were allowed to leave Soviet territory. If they engaged in opposition, they were persecuted: arrested, tortured, deported or killed. If they declared loyalty to the Soviet-dominated regime, they were left alone or even offered positions of responsibility, influence and privilege in the new Soviet-controlled administration.

The preludes

The prelude to these eliticides – and most probably the first political 'road test' of national decapitation – was Stalin's notorious Great Purge of 1936–38. Unlike campaigns against conquered peoples, Stalin victimised his own society, with the aim of politically weakening it. Yet although it was markedly different to the events that were to follow, the Great Purge nonetheless also reflected the key trademarks of eliticide. It was semi-secret (officially denied and masked as politicide); it aimed at the 'top' officials (suspected of disloyalty and nationalism); and the social profile of its victims followed the 'law of inverse disproportion'. The scope and brutality of this prelude was surpassed only by Hitler's eliticides conducted during the ethno-racial cleansing of the East European *Lebensraum*.

The Great Purge cemented Stalin's power by pre-emptively eliminating all potential rivals. Those who replaced them knew well that they enjoyed power and privilege only as long as the *Vozhd* trusted them. You could exit the Kremlin, as they used to say, only in one of two ways: through the main gate in a limousine, or through the side door in a coffin. Over a period of about two years, Stalin's henchmen executed or deported to the Gulag over 800,000 persons. This included most members of the *Politburo*, about 50 per cent of the Central Committee, the highest party echelons, and the high officer corps in the army and security services, including 44,000 high-ranking military officers. It coincided with the massive expansion of the Gulag, now treated as an essential part of the Soviet forced labour force.[14]

The Nazi 'prelude' was smaller. The brutal execution of the *Sturmabteilung* leaders in June 1934 (in the infamous 'Night of the Long Knives') paralleled – though on a much smaller scale – Stalin's Great Purge. The subsequent sacking of top officials had more to do with their perceived ineffectiveness than their loyalty to the *Führer*, though the two reasons were typically fused into one.

The purges considerably strengthened Stalin's and Hitler's power, reputation and security. By decapitating the *Sturmabteilung* leadership Hitler not only got rid of dangerous rivals, but also terrorised the rest of the elite – and the population at large. Stalin not only eliminated in 1937–38 his (mainly imaginary) opponents and instilled fear in the remaining staff, he also brought to power people whose careers depended entirely on his political patronage. Such people were attached to him by personal loyalty and fear. These initial 'successes' paved the way for the full-scale eliticide undertaken – this time in coordination with Nazi Germany – in Poland.

The plans for decapitation were kept secret. Only the Nazi elite knew the GPO, and the Annex to the Communazi Pact was strictly confidential and concealed by the Soviets until 1992. Both documents set not only the goals, but also a framework for collaboration; the two powers promised to cooperate in suppressing any 'agitation' against the partition. Indeed, according to the secret Additional Protocol of the Communazi Pact, 'Neither party will allow on its territory any Polish agitation which affects the territories of the other country. Both shall suppress in their territories all beginnings of such agitation and inform each other concerning suitable measures for this purpose'.[15] Publicly, this collaboration necessitated a political U-turn, especially for the Soviet Union. In preparation for this, one week after the German invasion of Poland, Stalin summoned Georgi Dimitrov, the General Secretary of the *Comintern*. In the presence of Molotov and Zhdanov he dictated to him directives concerning the new political goals of the USSR. These were to become the official 'line' adopted by all communists worldwide. The anti-fascist Popular Front was wound down. The expressions of sympathy for invaded Poland were to cease immediately; pre-war Poland was to be described as a 'fascist state'; and the Polish ordeal was now to be described as deserved and self-inflicted. Nazi Germany was to be portrayed as an ally.[16]

The Soviets never declared war on Poland, and never justified their invasion of eastern Poland on 17 September 1939. Instead, they called the military annexation of eastern Poland a 'protection of the inhabitants' in the face of a collapsing Polish state. This proved to be particularly violent. On 21 September, People's Commissar for Defence, Klement Voroshilov, was ordered by Stalin to assist the *Wehrmacht* in 'crushing Polish units and bands' and 'give, if necessary, to [German] disposal the necessary force to destroy nests of resistance on the way of the march'. Mass arrests and internments of alleged opponents began throughout the entire Soviet-occupied territory. On the same day, the Soviets and Germans signed a further agreement coordinating actions against Polish 'agitation' and 'saboteurs'.[17]

While the decision about the 'elimination' of the Polish state was made much earlier, more specific decisions about the methods of annexation were made by the German and Soviet commanders during a series of coordinating meetings starting in late September 1939.[18] On 19 September 1939 Hitler proudly announced in Gdansk (Danzig) that 'Poland will never reappear in the shape given by the Treaty of Versailles! In the end, it is guaranteed not only by Germany, but also by Russia'.[19] Following that, the Germans introduced the death penalty for disobedience to the German rulers of the occupied territories.[20] At the same time, the Soviets started mass arrests and the systematic wiping out of Polish culture in the annexed eastern half of Poland. Polish currency was banned, land and factories were confiscated. Ominously, any activity construed as aiming at sustaining Polish statehood was declared 'treason', and thus carried the death penalty. This was a prelude to national decapitation.

The eliticide

Poles can only have one master, and that is the German; two masters cannot and must not exist side by side; therefore all representatives of the Polish intelligentsia should be eliminated (*umbringen*).[21]

Who remembers the names now of the *boyars* Ivan the Terrible got rid of? No one.[22]

The decapitation of the Polish nation started with the German invasion on 1 September 1939. It involved 1.8 million soldiers, 2,800 tanks, 3,000 planes and 10,000 guns. The Soviets joined the invasion on 17 September with about

470,000 soldiers, 3,700 tanks, 380 armoured cars, and 2,000 aircraft. The much weaker Polish army was overwhelmed in six weeks, losing 66,000 dead and 134,000 wounded. About 400,000 Polish soldiers ended up in the German detention camps, and about 250,000 were taken prisoner by the Soviets. Almost all of Poland's top political leaders and government officials, and some military commanders, escaped through Hungary and Romania to France, where they formed a Polish Government-in-Exile and the embryo of a Polish Army in the West. Most local government officials and middle-level military commanders stayed behind. These individuals and their families were the primary targets of the eliticide.

The Nazi eliticide

The German decapitation of Polish society progressed in two stages. The first stage started with the invasion of Poland on 1 September 1939, and consisted of a well-planned and prepared *Außerordentliche Befriedungsaktion* (*AB-Aktion*, Special Pacification Operations), especially the *Intelligenzaktion* (IA) and *Sonderaktion* (SA). In preparation for this stage, on 7 September 1939 Heydrich announced that all Polish nobles, clergy, state officials, and all Polish Jews were to be arrested, and on 12 September Wilhelm Keitel added to this black list 'all members of the intelligentsia'. In his speech to the SS corps in late 1939, Himmler outlined the strategic task with equal clarity: 'you should hear this but also forget again – to shoot thousands of leading Poles'. On 15 March 1940, Himmler announced that 'All Polish specialists will be exploited in our military-industrial complex. Later, all Poles will disappear from this world'.[23]

The IA and SA operations lasted till spring 1940 on the territories annexed by Germany, and they were extended until late summer 1940 on the German-occupied territories of General Government (south-eastern Poland). Both parts of the *AB-Aktion* involved death lists extended on the basis of seized Polish documents, and on confessions extracted from the victims of the initial terror. Officially the IA was disguised as a 'security mop-up' directed against the 'enemies of the Reich'. Its scope and brutality were carefully masked. The executions were conducted in forests, the graves were unmarked, and the families of victims were sent letters with false dates and causes of death. And while the IA was relatively small in terms of the absolute number of people killed (about 100,000), it was specifically targeted at the core of Polish elite. This incorporated the surviving politicians, landowners, noblemen, priests, lawyers, judges, teachers, entrepreneurs, social activists, war veterans, and, in particular, ex-political activists and state officials. These people were not only the key organisers of national resistance, but also the main local leaders, and the principal carriers of Polish culture and traditions.[24]

All German military units were involved in the execution of the *AB Aktion*.

The troops entering Poland on 1 September 1939, especially the infamous *Einsatzgruppen* (EG), carried with them proscription lists (*Sonderfahndungsbuch Polen*) of around 80,000 officials. They were regarded as the backbone of the Polish intelligentsia, the key members of the Polish 'leading strata'. They were to be captured – with the help of the local German militias and spies – and then interrogated, killed or sent to the concentration camps.[25]

The IA operations were quite precise in the targeting of elite victims. Initially, over 60,000 persons were killed in these operations in the annexed territories. Later about 30,000 victims were killed in the German protectorate of the General Government. The death lists were gradually extended to cover community leaders, as well as entrepreneurs, businesses leaders, landowners, university professors, government officials, artists and even top sportspeople. In sum, these were everyone who held a position of authority and/or enjoyed high social standing. They were continuously updated and expanded by the RSHA on the basis of confiscated Polish archives and incoming reports by the Gestapo, as well as locally recruited German volunteers (*Selbstschutz*). Both agencies collaborated closely with the army and the SS in hunting down the blacklisted Poles, in interrogations, detention in concentration camps and increasingly in mass executions. In the first nine weeks of the war, the Germans conducted 764 such executions of Polish civilians, killing over 24,000 prominent and educated Poles.[26]

The key role in the Nazi eliticide was played by the EG, the SS paramilitary death squads, and by *Selbstschutz* volunteers. EG, the security police special detachments of the advancing German troops, operated under the direction of Reinhardt Heydrich and the top Higher SS and Police Leaders. Heydrich explicitly instructed his commanders to 'liquidate all leading elements in Poland' as a first step in the implementation of the GPO.[27] As Snyder notes:

> It was in Poland that the *Einsatzgruppen* were to fulfil their mission as 'ideological soldiers' by eliminating the educated classes of a defeated enemy. They were in some sense killing their peers: fifteen of the twenty-five *Einsatzgruppen* and *Einsatzkommando* commanders had doctorates. In Operation Tannenberg, Heydrich wanted the *Einsatzgruppen* to render 'the upper levels of society' harmless by murdering 61,000 Polish citizens. As Hitler put it, 'only a nation whose upper levels are destroyed can be pushed into the ranks of slavery'. The ultimate goal of this decapitation project was to 'destroy Poland' as a functioning society. By killing the most accomplished Poles, the *Einsatzgruppen* were to make Poland resemble the German racist fantasy of the enslaved country, and leave the society incapable of resisting German rule.[28]

In summer 1940 the eliticide gradually subsided and transformed into routinised political terror, to be re-ignited in June 1941, following the German invasion of the Soviet Union. This was the second stage of the Nazi eliticide, this time targeting the remnants of the Polish elite who had survived the Soviet invasion and occupation in eastern Poland. It was combined with the extermination of the key 'ideological enemies', the Jews, especially those suspected of pro-Bolshevik sympathies. The operations in this stage were less systematic but more brutal than the first one. Arrests and executions had the same pattern as the earlier *AB Aktion*, though they were more spontaneous and random. In one such action, forty-five professors of the Lwów University, together with their families and guests, were arrested and immediately shot without any formal procedure. The targets involved also the Polish-Jewish intelligentsia (whom were quite numerous in eastern Poland), as well as Polish and Jewish political leaders, activists and intellectuals – together about 20,000 victims. The majority of these victims were murdered in and around Wilno (Vilnius), especially in Ponary. As before, the crimes were carefully hidden. In one of the most gruesome attempts to cover up mass murder, the Germans ordered special *Sonderaction 1005* to use Polish and Russian prisoners to exhume and burn the bodies of previously murdered victims. After that, the prisoners themselves were executed and their bodies burned.

The second stage of the eliticide coincided with the extermination of Polish Jews, many of whom had become assimilated and shared Polish ethnic identity. A large proportion of Polish Jews in eastern Poland were successful in industry and worked in key professions (especially law and medicine). And while the Nazi eliticide continued at a slower pace throughout 1942 and till 1944, the bloody suppression of the Warsaw Uprising in autumn 1944 provided the Germans with another opportunity to target Polish elites. These were the leaders of the resistance Home Army who confronted the well-armed German troops. The Uprising, initially planned for a week, lasted sixty-three days and cost over 200,000 lives. To some observers, this was the final act of eliticide in Poland, conducted by Germans (as well as their Ukrainian, Lithuanian and Latvian auxiliaries) with a passive Soviet complicity. Stalin condemned the Uprising and refused to allow the Allies to aid it from the Soviet-controlled eastern bank of the Vistula River. Those resistance soldiers who survived the German revenge killings soon faced persecution by their new Soviet political masters.

The Soviet eliticide

The Soviet elite decapitation was short, simple and brutal. About 250,000 Polish soldiers and officers, taken prisoner by the Red Army in September–October 1939, were initially held in Soviet POW camps. They were constructed by the newly formed NKVD Directorate for Prisoners of War Affairs, responsible to Beria and Stalin. Inmates were promised prompt release. But on 2 October 1939 the Soviet *Politburo* passed a resolution concerning the selection and separation of officers, including volunteer non-commissioned officers, from the rank-and-file. According to the instructions, 'generals, colonels and lieutenant-colonels, as well as high state and military officials' were to be housed separately, together with 'members of the secret services and counter-espionage, gendarmes, police-men, prison wardens'. This was broadened to include 'prisoners resident in the German [occupied] part of Poland' and all non-commissioned officers who held professional jobs, especially as lawyers, and who were activists of politi-cal organisations.[29] The exchange of prisoners between the German and Soviet occupiers also started in October 1939: 42,000 Polish POWs were transferred to German hands and promptly arrested, and 13,000 Polish POWs were handed to the Soviets – all of whom were sent to the POW camps.[30]

These moves, together with the declaration that opposition to Sovietisation constituted 'treason', clearly suggested some nefarious designs by the Soviets, but they did not raise suspicion among the POWs. In the event the selection process was thorough, and was conducted according to social backgrounds rather than political intentions. The NKVD picked all volunteers and drafted members of the intelligentsia, including landowners, entrepreneurs, leading professionals, gov-ernment officials, as well as priests, artists and intellectuals. The victims included some sworn opponents of the Soviet Union, as well as Soviet 'sympathisers' who were critical of the Polish government and ready to collaborate. The selected officers were kept detained, while rank-and-file POWs were gradually released.

Officers were not the only Poles subjected to a hierarchical selection. On 4 December 1939, in the middle of an unusually cold winter, the NKVD started carefully targeted mass arrests and deportations of entire families of higher officers and military veterans, civil servants, political activists, prison wardens, landowners, entrepreneurs, foresters (with good knowledge of local woods), policemen, priests, and members of the gentry and aristocracy. While the *Politburo* directive to the NKVD estimated the number of elite families to be deported at 22,000–25,000, the actual number was much higher. More than 100,000 Poles were rounded up in February 1940 alone.[31] They were loaded at gunpoint into freight trains, often in temperatures as low as minus twenty degrees Celsius, and sent for what became known as 'death rides' to Siberia or eastern Kazakhstan. Some 5,000 people – first the aged, then the children and finally the adults – died during these winter deportations, most frozen to death. The survivors were unloaded in the taiga or the Kazakh steppes, dispersed among the bewildered and often hostile locals (many suffering from starvation), and ordered to fend for themselves. Only about half of them survived to return to Poland.[32]

These surviving deportees, as it turned out, were the lucky ones. At the beginning of 1940 the 'selected' officer corps of the Polish POWs were interro-gated by the NKVD and then moved to camps around Smolensk awaiting the decision of the leaders. According to Soviet sources, 97 per cent of the selected officers declared Polish nationality. According to various estimates, between 3 and 8 per cent of the Katyń victims were Jewish (though a precise ethnic categorisation is, of course, impossible because of the victims' multiple national identities).[33] As it was subsequently revealed, on 5 March 1940 the top members of the Soviet *Politburo* – Stalin, Beria, Molotov, Kaganovich, Voroshilov, Kalinin and Mikoyan – signed a secret order to the NKVD ordering mass 'special proceedings', with the 'maximum prescribed penalty' for 'traitors and enemies of the Soviet state' being 'death by shooting'.[34] About 22,000 were swiftly sentenced and secretly executed in March–April 1940 in the forests around the camps. They were shot in the back of the head and their bodies buried in unmarked mass graves. These mass executions of Polish officers were subsequently referred to as the Katyń Massacre. While they were being killed, their closest relatives – about 61,000 of them – were arrested between mid-April and May 1940 and deported to Kazakhstan.[35]

Like the Nazi IA operations, the Katyń Massacre was to remain a state secret. The orders were confidential, the executions took place in isolated forests, the graves were unmarked, and the Soviet executioners used German ammunition. Witnesses were either killed or terrorised into silence. When the invading German troops discovered the graves of the victims in April 1943, Stalin blamed the Germans. The Soviet version, initially accepted by the Allies, was then ruthlessly imposed by Soviet propaganda in the Soviet Union and Eastern Europe.[36]

The Katyń Massacre cannot be seen as a mere 'politicide' or 'class cleansing'. It is quite clear that the selection of the victims, and the arrests that followed them, targeted Polish elites, not just opponents of the new regime.[37] The instructions given to the NKVD, and the criteria according to which the victims were selected also point to eliticide. The victims were the 'leading' industrialists and landowners (expropriated), professionals, government officials and intellectuals, some of whom were actually sympathetic to the Soviet political cause. Yet, even those declaring pro-Soviet views were killed. This is clearly incompatible with an interpretation of politicide.[38] Nor was the selection consistent with a 'class cleansing' interpretation. The victims represented a broad spectrum of backgrounds, and the fact that most of the Soviet 'sentences' (as revealed in 1991) referred to the class backgrounds of the victims simply reflected the official 'politically correct' language of prosecution – the language of ideological rationalisation, rather than reason. Finally, Stalin's intentions signalled in the earlier pronouncements and in the Communazi Pact also point to eliticidal design. The massacre and the accompanying deportations were parts of a preemptive decapitation of Polish society in preparation for the initially planned 'absorption' of Poland as a 'de-nationalised' Soviet republic.

The Katyń Massacre, it must be stressed again, was just a part in the Soviet decapitation of Poland. As Snyder noted

in the background, the NKVD entered the [occupied] country in force. In the twenty-one months to come it made more arrests in occupied eastern Poland than in the entire Soviet Union, seizing some 109,400 Polish citizens. The typical sentence was eight years in [the] Gulag; about 8,513 were sentenced to death.[39]

The Soviet persecution of Polish intelligentsia lasted throughout 1940 and into the first half of 1941. According to the estimates of Russian historians working for the Memorial Society, in about twenty months of terror in the Soviet-occupied territories of Poland, about 4 per cent of the population of eastern Poland – about 400,000 people – were shot, imprisoned, or deported to Siberia.[40] Among them were almost all members of the 'leading strata' of Polish society, especially those formerly engaged in politics and state administration. The majority of the victims were educated members of the local intelligentsia accused of treason and/or 'agitation'.

The Soviet eliticide eased with the German invasion of the Soviet Union on 22 June 1941 and ceased around 1943. For Stalin, the Poles became valuable military allies and important bargaining chips in his negotiations with the Allies. The Polish prisoners were released from the Gulag camps and Siberian detention, though the numbers did not add up to the lists of POWs and detainees. The First Polish Army, formed from the released prisoners, was allowed to leave Soviet territory. Those who missed the departure of the First Army were incorporated into the communist-controlled 'Kosciuszko Army'.

While the Soviet eliticide ceased (or at least slowed down), the mass killings of political 'enemies' continued in preparation for the planned revival of Poland as a vassal member of the expanding 'socialist camp'. The émigré elite groups outside Poland, especially in the UK, did not bother Stalin much, perhaps with the exception of General Wladyslaw Sikorski, the only military leader who had defeated Stalin (in 1920). The members of the Government-in-Exile in London, politically divided and losing influence, were subjected to vicious propaganda attacks aimed at discrediting them politically and morally. Sikorski himself died in a plane crash in 1943.

The Soviet annexation of eastern Poland was accepted by the Allies in Tehran, then Yalta, and finally at Potsdam. Stalin then turned his attention to neutralising surviving political opponents, especially the leaders of a still active underground resistance movement in the Polish territories. This started a long wave of terror. Starting in mid-1943, Stalin also started the formation of a pro-Soviet government, a pro-Soviet 'quasi-elite' that was to be installed in soon-to-be Soviet-liberated Poland. For these roles the Soviets handpicked the most reliable 'Soviet Poles', mainly Polish war refugees living in the Soviet Union. In the meantime, the Soviet offensive stopped on the outskirts of Warsaw, thus allowing the Germans to supress the Warsaw Uprising. In mid-1945 the NKVD abducted the surviving leaders of the Polish Underground State and show-tried them in Moscow later that year – as if to demonstrate that all of the political trump cards were now in Stalin's hand.

Conclusion: the aftermath of the eliticide and the post-war 'quasi-elite'

The war-time elite casualties in Poland were staggering. The IPN historians estimate the number of victims belonging to the Polish 'intellectual elite' alone at 50,000–70,000, more than half of its pre-war number.[41] The most affected, though, was the very apex of the pre-war Polish political elite. Out of 360 Senators and ex-Senators of the second Polish Republic who were alive on 1 September 1939, only 205 (57 per cent) were alive on 8 May 1945, and only 105 (30 per cent) survived on the territories of postwar Poland. The remaining survivors were either in exile in Great Britain and Western Europe, or in the Soviet Union, or, finally, dispersed in Asia and Africa. Thus the physical loses at the apex of the Polish political hierarchy amounted to a staggering 70 per cent. Some of the surviving prewar Senators escaped from Poland in the face of communist persecution, and some returned from exile.[42]

One should stress again that these were just the physical losses. In practical-political terms, of course, the entire Polish pre-war political elite was wiped out, because not a single member of this elite, not a single parliamentarian, retained power beyond 1947, and the Senate itself was closed by the communists in 1946.

The figures illustrate well the 'law of inverse disproportion' – which is a trademark of eliticide. While Poland lost about 18–20 per cent of its pre-war population, almost all of its pre-war and war-time political leaders were gone: most of them killed, and the remainder imprisoned, deported, and a handful of lucky survivors forced to flee the country. Also gone were almost all of Poland's leading industrialists and landowners, the victims of both persecution and creeping nationalisation. Among the victims were 70 per cent of Senators, over 60 per cent of the top public intellectuals and journalists, 58 per cent of barristers, 40–45 per cent of medical doctors, 40 per cent of top academics (professors), 33 per cent of teachers, 30 per cent of scientists, technicians and academics, 28 per cent of priests, 26 per cent of all lawyers.[43] To this list must also be added the most prominent artists, artisans and sportspeople – all killed or forced into exile in much larger proportion than the general population. The eastern provinces, incorporated into the Soviet Union in 1939, were virtually cleared of the Polish intelligentsia. Some educated refugees from eastern Poland moved to the western 'recovered territories', especially to Wrocław, but they were too dispersed and socially fragmented to re-create the pre-war civil society.

The decapitation made Polish society vulnerable not only to political takeover, but also to all sorts of social pathologies. Society was atomised, traumatised and demoralised, facing a wave of lawlessness. 'Banditism' was widespread, especially in rural areas and in the 'recovered' western territories. It was now directed against any target that promised quick gains: old landowners, remaining German Protestants, returning migrants, new settlers, or – most tragically

– Jewish survivors. In a decapitated society few people were able to contain such criminality, to safeguard social norms, and to defend law and order. In the absence of indigenous local elites, the authorities were weak, devoid of social legitimacy and frequently corrupt. The remnants of Poland's intelligentsia at home were atomised, terrorised and/or corrupted. At any rate, their ranks were so depleted that they lost their influence as pillars of the social and moral order.

The violence continued long after the war, though on a lesser scale, and with ups and downs. Most of this violence was dished out by the newly resurrected state security apparatus to political opponents of the new regime. It involved mass arrests, imprisonments, threats and harassment against opposition and mere critics, as well as the draconian enforcement of 'the new order'. About 20,000 Polish underground fighters (and this number rapidly dwindled throughout the late 1940s) continued their resistance well into the 1950s. Between 1945 and 1955 the Stalinist authorities in Poland sentenced to death and executed 4,500 political opponents, most of them anti-Nazi resistance fighters from the upper echelons of the Polish intelligentsia.[44] Scores more were imprisoned, tortured, deported, blackmailed and blacklisted. While some opponents of the communist regime continued their tragic quest, the political takeover was already completed by 1948. The opposition was intimidated, the media muzzled, and the new Stalin-picked replacement elite were introduced to the political scene as the governors of 'socialist Poland'.

The new government was gradually installed during the Soviet 'liberation' of Poland in 1944–45. It was initially inclusive of the remnants of the pre-war intelligentsia, regardless of their political sentiments. In 1947–48 the ranks of the communist 'quasi-elite' were filled by new local recruits who benefited from a communist-sponsored 'social-political elevation'. These new recruits lacked the key elite characteristics: social anchoring, recognition and distinction. They also lacked authority, trust, social legitimacy and political autonomy. They formed a Soviet-dependent and 'quasi-elite' consisting of communist operatives who came from Moscow, as well as a number of political opportunists and idealists. Thus, Poland acquired a new ruling minority. But it was mediocre, socially deracinated, dependent on Moscow and reliant on Soviet force. The new rulers of People's Poland enjoyed little public trust and support, and compensated for the lack of these qualities with coercion and propaganda. Consequently, they lived in constant fear of Soviet 'recall' and Polish revenge. This permanent insecurity resulted, in turn, in internal splits and factional struggles, both reflected in regular crises and in social upheavals.

For the same reasons – to do with the quality of the 'quasi-elite' – Polish economic and social progress was slow, and the country lagged behind not only the rapidly developing West, but also her Eastern neighbours. The 'quasi-elite' had gradually evolved and established its 'social roots', especially after a wave of de-Stalinisation in 1955–56. In the 1960s and 1970s it gradually turned into a more self-confident communist party-state *nomenklatura*.

There was a happy end to this the story, though. During the 1960s and 1970s an embryo of a new Polish 'challenger-elite' had begun to grow beyond the ranks of the decaying *nomenklatura*. It was an embryo of Polish oppositional critical intelligentsia, first appearing in small social enclaves (like the Catholic Church, dissident groups, trade unions and reformist factions), gradually gaining strength, public trust and popular support. As predicted by Saint-Simon, this re-growth of a socially anchored elite took more than one generation. The new 'authentic' elite acquired its social distinction and political skills during years of dissident activism, often at the cost of harassment and persecution. It appeared on the political stage with the ascendant post-Stalinist generation in the late 1970s and early 1980s, and entered the political scene by heading the powerful Solidarity movement. When Gorbachev's window of opportunity opened unexpectedly in 1989, this new 'Solidarity elite' led the first non-violent revolution that swept from power the communist *nomenklatura* not only in Poland, but also throughout Central and Eastern Europe.

The Soviet-German eliticide represents and illustrates a specific form of state violence. National decapitations aim at destroying the strategically important part of the 'political class' – the national elite – and therefore undermining the social order and national identity that those elites sustain. Eliticides can destroy or politically weaken societies for many decades. Yet they are not recognised as a distinctive form of mass violence or a specific type of war crime, and they are seldom analysed in depth. The attention of historians and political scientists, as well as the public at large, is focused on genocides: the mass but 'vertically circumscribed' mass killings. Studies of 'national decapitations' – mass murders selective in the hierarchical sense – presupposes hierarchical ranking of victims, and such ranking may look 'undemocratic' to those who see all victims as equals. Even so, a neglect of the social-hierarchical dimension in 'mass victimology' risks ignoring a real aspect of social damage.

A second observation can be made concerning the long-term consequences of eliticides. The Polish nation was the main victim of the Soviet-Nazi decapitations, but certainly not the only one. Ukraine and Belarus suffered similar fates, and their recovery was slower and less successful than the Polish one. The decapitation in all the 'bloodland' nations nearly succeeded in destroying national organisation, culture, identity, and the capacity to survive as independent nation-states. In Poland, the eliticide did result in decades of (poor and oppressive) administration by a Soviet-backed 'quasi-elite'– a group of socially deracinated power-holders whose capacity to rule effectively was seriously compromised. But the decapitated elites were successfully 're-grown' in Poland, and this confirms not only Mosca's warning, but also what one may call the 'Saint-Simon law of elite recovery'.

Notes

1 Henri de Saint-Simon, *Selected Writings on Science, Industry and Social Organisation*, ed. K. Taylor (London: Croom Helm, 1975), p. 194.
2 The classical elite theorists include Vilfredo Pareto, Gaetano Mosca and Robert Michels, as well as Max Weber, Joseph Schumpeter and Jose Ortega y Gasset.
3 See M. Weber, *Economy and Society* (Berkley: University of California Press, 1978); J. Ortega y Gasset, *The Revolt of the Masses* (authorised translation from the Spanish) (New York: W. W. Norton, 1994); J. Schumpeter, *Capitalism, Socialism and Democracy* (London: Allen and Unwin, 1942); C. Wright Mills, *The Power Elite* (Oxford: Oxford University Press, 1956). The concept of the 'power elite' introduced by Charles Wright Mills rests upon the coincidence of interests among economic, political and military organisations. It also rests upon the similarity of origin and outlooks, and the social and personal intermingling of the top circles from each of these hierarchies. Mills, *The Power Elite*, p. 292.
4 See G. Satori, *The Theory of Democracy Revisited* (Chatham: Chatham House, 1987); J. Higley and M. Burton, *Elite Foundations of Liberal Democracy* (Lanham: Rowman and Littlefield, 2006). See also S. Keller, *Beyond the Ruling Class* (New York: Arno Press, 1963); M. Useem, *The Inner Circle* (Oxford: Oxford University Press, 1984).
5 See J-P. Daloz, 'How political representatives earn legitimacy: A symbolic approach', *International Social Science Journal*, 60:196 (2009), pp. 285–96. This social embedding secures high social status and the accompanying 'social distinction' and social authority.
6 While the classical elite theorists, especially Pareto, circumscribed national 'elites' in terms of their social status *and* ruling functions, Marxist scholars, such as Antonio Gramsci, described the most active members of such elites as 'organic intellectuals': those who secure cultural and social hegemony, shape public opinion and, most critically, secure mass consent.
7 'Politicide' refers to systematic exterminations of political opponents; 'classicide' or 'class cleansing' refers to eliminations (removals) of certain classes through mass killing, deportation, and re-settlement. See B. Harff and T. Gurr, 'Towards an empirical theory of genocides and politicides', *International Studies Quarterly*, 32 (1988); M. Mann, *The Dark Side of Democracy* (Cambridge: Cambridge University Press, 2004), p. 17; V. Zaslavski, *Class Cleansing: The Massacre of Katyń* (New York: Telos, 2008), pp. 10–12; N. Naimark, *Stalin's Genocide* (Princeton: Princeton University Press, 2010), p. 20.
8 See A. Williams, *The English and the Norman Conquest* (Ipswich: Boydell Press, 2000).
9 See the 'Nobel Prize Nomination Database', available at: www.nobelprize.org/nomina tion/archive/show_people.php?id=8722 (accessed 1 October, 2014).
10 See Bertolt Brecht's play 'The Resistible Career of Arturo Ui'.
11 See A. Bullock, *Hitler: A Study in Tyranny* (London: Penguin, 1990); A. Bullock, *Hitler and Stalin: Parallel Lives* (London: Vintage Books, 1993); L. Snyder, *Hitler's Elite* (Berkeley: University of California Press, 1990); T. Snyder, *Bloodlands: Europe Between Hitler and Stalin* (New York: Basic Books, 2010).
12 See Instytut Pamięci Narodowej, *The Destruction of the Polish Elite: Operation AB – Katyń* (Warsaw: Instytut Pamięci Narodowej, 2009); J. Connelly, 'Nazis and Slavs: From racial theory to racist practise', *Central European History*, 31:1 (1999), pp. 1–33; A. Szcześniak, *Plan zagłady Słowian: Generalplan Ost* (Radom: Polskie Wydawnictwo Encyklopedyczne, 2001); M. Wardzyńska '"Intelligenzaktion" na Warmii, Mazurach oraz Północnym Mazowszu', Główna Komisja Ścigania Zbrodni Przeciwko Narodowi Polskiemu, Biuletyn Instytutu Pamięci Narodowej nr. 12/1, 2003/04, pp. 38–42; and M. Wardzyńska, *Był*

    rok 1939: Operacja niemieckiej policji bezpieczeństwa w Polsce. Intelligenzaktion (Warsaw: Instytut Pamięci Narodowej, 2009).

13 R. Conquest, *The Great Terror: A Reassessment* (Oxford: Oxford University Press, 2008); R. Conquest, *Stalin: Breaker of Nations* (Oxford: Oxford University Press, 1991); M. Ellmann, 'Stalin and the Soviet famine of 1932–3 revisited', *Europe-Asia Studies*, 59:4 (2005), pp. 663–93; Instytut Pamięci Narodowej, *The Destruction of the Polish Elite*.

14 Snyder, *Bloodlands*, pp. 86–7.

15 Instytut Pamięci Narodowej, *The Destruction of the Polish Elite*, pp. 9, 27.

16 'It would not be bad if Germany were to destabilise the position of the richest capitalist countries (especially England). Hitler, without understanding or intending it, is smashing and undermining the capitalist system ... Poland is a fascist country that oppresses Ukrainians, Byelorussians and other nationalities. Under present conditions, its destruction would mean one less fascist state. What would be wrong if, following the defeat of Poland, we were to expand the Soviet system over new territories and new populations?' Cited in Zaslavski, *Class Cleansing*, pp. 8–9.

17 Instytut Pamięci Narodowej, *The Destruction of the Polish Elite*, p. 8–29.

18 Instytut Pamięci Narodowej, *The Destruction of the Polish Elite*, p. 8–29.

19 Cited in Instytut Pamięci Narodowej, *The Destruction of the Polish Elite*, p. 9.

20 See also W. Anders, *Bez Ostatniego Rozdziału* (Lublin: Test, 1995); G. Herling-Grudzinski, *A World Apart: Imprisonment in a Soviet Labor Camp During World War II* (Basingstoke: Penguin, 1996); A. Nekrich and G. L. Freeze, *Pariahs, Partners, Predators: German–Soviet Relations, 1922–1941* (New York: Columbia University Press, 1997); and J. T. Gross, *Revolution from Abroad* (Princeton: Princeton University Press, 2003).

21 Cited in W. Shirer, *The Rise and Fall of the Third Reich: A History of Nazi Germany* (London: Book Club Associates, 1960), p. 938.

22 Cited in D. Volkogonov, *Stalin: Triumph and Tragedy* (New York: Grove Widenfeld, 1991), p. 210.

23 Piotrowski cited in Instytut Pamięci Narodowej, *The Destruction of the Polish Elite*, pp. 57–72.

24 Wardzyńska, *Był rok 1939*.

25 Wardzyńska, '"Intelligenzaktion" na Warmii, Mazurach oraz Północnym Mazowszu', p. 1; Wardzyńska, *Był rok 1939*.

26 See Wardzynska, *Był rok 1939*.

27 It was Wilhelm Keitel who added people to the list of 'prime targets' (Polish nobles, clergy and Jews), also the broader social category 'the leading strata' and 'intelligentsia'. See Instytut Pamięci Narodowej, *The Destruction of the Polish Elite*; and Wardzyńska, *Był rok 1939*.

28 Snyder, *Bloodlands*, p. 126.

29 Cited in Zaslavski, *Class Cleansing*, pp. 13–16, 20.

30 Instytut Pamięci Narodowej, *The Destruction of the Polish Elite*, p. 10.

31 See Snyder, *Bloodlands*.

32 See A. Cienciała, N. Lebedeva and W. Materski (eds), *Katyń: A Crime Without Punishment* (New Haven: Yale University Press, 2007); Instytut Pamięci Narodowej, *The Destruction of the Polish Elite*, pp. 33–48; Snyder, *Bloodlands*, pp. 124–38; Zaslavski, *Class Cleansing*.

33 Cited in Zaslavski, *Class Cleansing*, p. 32.

34 Zaslavski, *Class Cleansing*, pp. 31–2.

35 Instytut Pamięci Narodowej, *The Destruction of the Polish Elite*; Cienciała et al., *Katyń*.

36 The Soviet version was also supported by elaborate forgeries, as well as 'expert advice' and confessions of 'eyewitnesses' procured by the NKVD. Although the subsequent

Nuremberg trials cleared the Germans of this war crime, and President Yeltsin formally confirmed the identity of the perpetrators, no one has yet pursued those responsible for the Massacre.

37 A more detailed list of the targeted categories can be found in the 'Directive of the NKVD of the SU on the Deportation of Socially Alien Elements'. It includes the following categories: 'Members of counterrevolutionary parties and nationalist, anti-Soviet organisations, gendarmes, border police, high-ranking officials of the police forces and prisons, policemen, prison guards, land owners, merchants, entrepreneurs, high-ranking officials of the bourgeois state, army officers and former members of the White Guard – and their relatives'.

38 According to the IPN historians and Zaslavski, only twenty-four Polish POWs were spared after declaring their willingness to join the Soviet army. Zaslavski, *Class Cleansing*, p. 35.

39 Snyder, *Bloodlands*, pp. 125–6.

40 Instytut Pamięci Narodowej, *The Destruction of the Polish Elite*, pp. 48–9; Zaslavski, *Class Cleansing*, p. 36.

41 Instytut Pamięci Narodowej, *The Destruction of the Polish Elite*, p. 81.

42 J. M. Zawadzki, *Senatorowie: losy wojenne i powojenne* (Warsaw: Kancelaria Senatu, 2013), pp. 4–17.

43 These estimates are based on W. Materski and T. Szarota, *Polska 1939–45: Straty osobowe i ofiary represji pod dwiema okupacjami* (Warsaw: Instytut Pamięci Narodowej, 2009); R. Lukas, *Forgotten Holocaust: The Poles Under German Occupation, 1939–44* (New York: Hippocrene Books, 2nd edn, 2001); Instytut Pamięci Narodowej, *The Destruction of the Polish Elite*.

44 See Snyder, *Bloodlands*.

3

State violence and China's unfinished national unification: conflict with minorities

Terry Narramore

Introduction

The path to statehood for the People's Republic of China (PRC) surely stands as one of the most violent and traumatic in modern history. The political arithmetic of lives lost through imperial conquests, interstate and civil wars, revolution, violent 'struggle sessions' (*pidou*) and horrific famine recalls the kind of grim, impersonal 'statistics' reputedly calculated by Stalin.[1] In important ways, this trajectory of relentless upheaval made China's state different from Charles Tilly's capital-intensive, coercive European states.[2] Apart from a significant imperialist expansion under the final dynasty – the Manchu Qing dynasty (1644–1911) – in the eighteenth century, China was a case of profound state disintegration. The post-imperial state therefore not only lacked the capacity to enforce a monopoly over legitimate violence, it also failed to overcome the challenges of establishing a stable nation among its culturally diverse population. Although the PRC recognised itself as a multi-ethnic state of fifty-six 'nationalities' (*minzu*), including the Han or Chinese, pledged to support minority rights and established so-called 'autonomous' (*zizhi*) minority government, its policies of national unification became a conspicuous failure among key non-Han peoples. Failure during the Maoist period was notable for the conjunction of a divided political elite and the mobilisation of widespread collective violence. But the 'minority nationalities' (*shaoshu minzu*) of Tibet and Xinjiang in particular have continued a consistent resistance to integrationist policies down to the present. National unification remains an unfinished project and continuing challenge for the state.[3] This is despite the PRC's rapid transition in the post-Mao reform era to what Tilly refers to as an 'exemplary high-capacity undemocratic regime'.[4] Indeed, being subject to the state's most intensive campaigns of national unification has in recent years increased state-minority violence and provoked serious Han-minority communal violence in Tibet and Xinjiang. The greatly enhanced state capacity of the PRC has only made the goals of national unification in these regions less secure and more remote.

China's nationalities policy has in practice 'imposed sometimes severe and sometimes less severe restrictions on the autonomy of the minorities',[5] but there is a common thread of expectation, running from the Qing through to the present, that minorities would eventually integrate into one form or other of the dominant Chinese culture. This expectation has 'proved to be erroneous', and remains the central political problem of national unification today.[6] Minorities are subordinate to the state's arbitration of the limits of autonomy or integration, with their political loyalty to the Chinese state being paramount. Genuine autonomy risks separatism or what the state calls 'splittism' (*fenliezhuyi*), while intensive integration risks undermining the legitimacy of the state and reinforcing minority-Han boundary conflict.[7] Along with Taiwan, Tibet and Xinjiang constitute what the state now routinely refers to as 'core interests' (*hexin liyi*), meaning they are non-negotiable sovereign territories that will be defended with military force if necessary.[8] Since China joined the 'war on terror' after the 9/11 attacks on the United States, minority policy in Tibet and Xinjiang has shifted towards a more intensive integrationist strategy. Indeed, the state's decision to 'securitise' separatism as an international threat appears to have contributed to increased Han-minority communal violence. The phenomenal rise of China in international affairs has not resolved these profound problems, and the central state goal of 'integrating China with a changing international arena while completing the project of unifying a multi-national state built upon the remains of the Qing Empire' reveals serious policy failure.[9] The state's coercive crackdown on suspected terrorism and separatism indicates that it is prepared to deploy minority resistance as the enemy of the national unification of the greater 'Chinese people' (*Zhonghua minzu*) and 'China's national rejuvenation'. The distressing conclusion is that the PRC state is still not secure enough to move beyond the use of violence in the name of national unification.[10] Continual reliance upon coercion to ensure compliance with state policy is 'not only an inefficient and expensive strategy, but probably ultimately a self-defeating one'.[11]

State disintegration, violence and national unification

The sovereign territories and peoples claimed by the PRC today are based upon the boundaries of the Qing Empire, the most extensive in Chinese history. The ruling Communist Party of China (CPC, *Gongchandang*) has developed a national narrative or ideology of continuous historical possession or control of its current territory.[12] This, of course, includes the reclaimed territories of Hong Kong, Macau and Taiwan – the last of which the PRC still does not exercise direct jurisdiction over – as well as disputed islands in the East China Sea and South China Sea. Although current state policy appears to be more actively pressing the PRC's claims to disputed islands, official rhetoric refers only to Taiwan, Tibet and Xinjiang as 'core interests'.[13]

It is no historical accident that these territories are accorded the highest priority within the PRC's sovereign statehood. They are central to the CPC's historic mission of national restitution of the privations of foreign imperialism. That Tibet and Xinjiang in particular encompass minority peoples in territories that are the legacy of Qing imperial conquests is an irony not readily conceded by the CPC. Minority populations are estimated to be around 8.4 per cent of the total, residing in 'autonomous regions' (*zizhi qu*) constituting 64 per cent of China's territory.[14] These regions are not only of value to China's wider economy, offering resources and energy of their own as well as transit to those of Central Asia. Given the history of imperialist rivalry, they are also a 'strategic hinterland' vital to the Han heartland, the CPC regime, and state security.[15] Yet they are core interests precisely because centuries of 'state building through mobilisation of culture, commerce and violence' have not succeeded in making them stable parts of the Chinese nation.[16] Although the state remains in overall control of Tibet and Xinjiang, with their independence not a realistic prospect, there is widespread recognition among state policy-makers that what are euphemistically called 'nationality problems' remain among the 'key social issues' for the state.[17]

The diversity of peoples in China's hinterland of the west and northwest have long proven stubbornly resistant to projects of a centralising state and national unification. The Qing conquests of these regions left a significant legacy of at times brutal rule and only partial integration of minorities into the wider Chinese empire, which shaped minority-Han relations down to the present. To begin with, the Manchu Qing state did not hesitate to use their full capacity for violence in exterminating enemies and pacifying rebellions against their rule.[18] It achieved a 'final solution' over the western Mongols (or Zunghars), subdued the Turkic Muslims of present day Xinjiang, and constructed a loose 'patron-priest' relationship with the Buddhist theocracy of Tibet.[19] Second, the Manchus dominated conquered populations by preserving a 'superstratified elite that avoided assimilation' with the Han.[20] This segregated ruling elite effectively operated as a superior shadow to the traditional Han bureaucracy, and this system was later adapted by the Communist Party elite in governing minorities. The Qing also revived an ancient policy of stabilising conquered regions, particularly the northwest, through military garrisons, penal colonies and coerced migration, practices also adapted to the PRC during the Maoist period.[21] Third, the profound disintegration of the Chinese state began with the decline and eventual collapse of the Qing by 1911. Besieged from within by frequent popular rebellions and from without by Western and Japanese imperialism, a long period of weak state capacity with divided elites created opportunities for violent political struggles and local collective violence. Control of Republican China (1912–49) was divided between local warlords, foreign powers, and two rival representatives of national revolution, the Nationalist Party (*Guomindang*) and the Communist Party. This disintegration allowed some minorities, inspired by their own newly acquired nationality claims, to press for greater autonomy. Tibet 'unquestionably controlled its own internal and external affairs during the period from 1913 to 1951 and repeatedly attempted to secure recognition and validation of its de facto autonomy/independence', although the Chinese state never renounced its claims to the territory.[22] Uyghurs and other Turkic Muslims in Xinjiang sought independence and, after an aborted attempt in 1933, established an East Turkestan Republic (1944–49).[23] These experiences, however limited, provided inspiration to later calls for independence from the PRC state.[24]

Although the fractured Republican period allowed Tibet and Xinjiang greater scope to develop nationality claims, neither of the major parties contending for state power gave concessions to independence in their nationalities policy. Both the Nationalist and Communist parties were influenced by Soviet nationalities policy, and each found a way of superseding minority claims for self-determination. The Nationalists acknowledged five races or 'stocks' – Han, Mongols, Tibetans, Manchus and the Hui (a catch-all category for Muslims) – but saw China as composed of 'not only one nation, but one blood'.[25] This idea of a greater Chinese nation embracing Han and minorities as one has returned, minus the racist cast, in the post-Mao era formulation of the Chinese nation/people (*Zhonghua minzu*) as being all the peoples of the PRC. The Communists, particularly Mao, sought to 'enfold minority nationalities within the revolutionary people of China', subsuming their 'struggle' within the general struggle against oppression. Despite warning against both 'Han chauvinism' (*dahanzu zhuyi*) and the 'local chauvinism' (*difang minzu zhuyi*) of minorities, Mao and the Communists saw that socialism would eventually erase nationality problems.[26] Both of the major parties had moved towards their own vision of one party and one nation within one organic state.[27] Both developed a military capacity and deployed it as their primary means of achieving political goals, cooperating to fight warlordism and Japanese militarism.[28] But this marriage of a singular political vision with coercive power did not bode well for the formation of a genuine multi-ethnic state. Many millions of people in China have been victims of state and collective violence.[29] None more so than those minority nationalities who inhabit the difficult terrain between autonomy and integration.

Nation-building, violence and 'minority nationalities' in the PRC

Tibet and Xinjiang have long been regarded as outlying (*waidi*), border (*bianjiang*) or hinterland regions in China.[30] The key political challenge they represent is to prevent their minority nationalities developing separatist movements that threaten the CPC state's direct monopoly rule. Comparative studies of separatist conflict place Tibet and Xinjiang within a category where 'military victory by the state' is 'successful but inconclusive' and there is 'ongoing or intermittent armed violence'.[31] Similarly, Tilly's classification of the PRC as a 'high capacity undemocratic regime' helps explain the persistence and the scale of state-minority conflict. Such regimes allow only a narrow range of claim-making performances and forbid 'many (if not most) technically possible performances'. The surveillance and repressive capacity of the state pushes most contentious politics into the 'forbidden range' and thus towards 'encounters likely to have violent outcomes'. There is a 'medium' level of violence, usually involving agents of the state, with 'great variability' in frequency, but which demonstrates the 'high political stakes of contention'.[32] In neither Tibet nor Xinjiang has separatist conflict moved beyond the ambiguous 'inconclusive' category. Whereas the exiled Central Tibetan Administration's movement for 'genuine autonomy' (without territorial independence) enjoys a high international profile and won a period of regular, if fruitless, dialogue with the state, Uyghur separatism is less prominent, lacks unity and the leadership of a Dalai Lama-like figure, and has not won any concessions to its cause.[33] Overall, despite the state's security capacity never being higher than at present, violent conflict has only grown and Han-minority communal violence has become a more serious political problem.

The Communist state moved quickly to reclaim the Qing borders, their troops pushing into the hinterland provinces throughout 1949–50. When the Communists under Mao came into power, like the Qing Empire they recognised that the strategic importance and sensitivity of these regions required a different approach to governing them. But nationalities policy was to swing violently between a loose rein of limited local autonomy – captured in the ancient technique of 'using the barbarian to rule the barbarian' (*yi yi zhi yi*)[34] – and the imposition of radical economic, social and cultural change on a nation-wide scale. Tibet and Xinjiang were initially 'liberated' through a combination of occupying People's Liberation Army (PLA) troops and negotiation with local leaders. Despite signalling that Tibet would resist the loss of *de facto* independence, with no international support and hopelessly outnumbered by PLA troops, by mid-1951 the Tibetans accepted China's Seventeen-Point Agreement for 'the return to the big family of the Motherland – the People's Republic of China'.[35] Similarly, in Xinjiang the presence of PLA troops with Soviet support was sufficient to establish Communist control over the province.[36] In both cases the new regime did not rush to radical reform and gave some latitude to the pre-existing governing structures and local leaders.[37] Mao himself urged cautious change in Tibet and warned against 'Han chauvinism' (*da Hanzhuyi*) in dealing with 'minority nationalities'.[38]

This relatively soft approach did not last long. Resistance to Communist rule emerged in the early 1950s and has persisted at a low level ever since. In Xinjiang small insurgent groups seeking independence continued into the mid-1950s, underground parties existed into the post-Mao era, and demonstrations and sporadic violence have regularly occurred since the 1980s.[39] Although of low capacity, these were the more obvious manifestations of a broader resistance to the PRC's state-building project in Xinjiang.[40] In Tibet the Dalai Lama and his coterie, based in Lhasa, were initially cooperative and hopeful about the modernising effects of the Communist regime. The former Kham and Amdo regions to the east were, however, seen as part of the provinces of Sichuan, Qinghai, Gansu and Yunnan, and subject to the same central planning and re-education campaigns as the Chinese heartland. Resistance emerged in eastern regions precisely because from 1953 it was expected to implement a Five-Year Plan for agriculture in which the ancient landlord–peasant relations were to be forced into socialist 'collectives'. From 1955 the well-armed people of Kham began to attack and kill Chinese officials. When the PLA was sent in to restore order, the Sampeling monastery sheltered the rebels and became a kind of fortress of resistance. After failing to extract a surrender, in February 1956 the military bombed the monastery, destroying it and killing many monks and rebels inside. The PRC's policies towards Tibet went tragically awry from this point as resistance grew into an organised force. Many Tibetans believed that the Chinese authorities intended to destroy Tibetan Buddhism. From 1958 the Central Intelligence Agency (CIA) began training and supplying weapons to some of the rebels, who engaged in a form of guerrilla war against the Chinese up to 1962.[41] At the time of the Dalai Lama's flight into India in March 1959, an armed popular uprising calling for independence was in train in Lhasa. The PLA militarily engaged the rebels over three days, with possibly over 80,000 deaths.[42] In the aftermath of the uprising, Beijing ushered in a harsh crackdown, rounding up suspected supporters and instituting military rule: a 'de facto police state'.[43] It quickly dismantled the manorial landlord–peasant relationship, re-distributed land according to socialist policy, and almost completely undermined the monasteries and power of monks within them.[44] A 1960 report by the International Commission of Jurists – a non-governmental organisation (NGO), not an international government organisation – concluded that 'acts of genocide had been committed in Tibet in an attempt to destroy the Tibetans as a religious group', but it did not find sufficient proof of genocide according to the conventions of international law.[45] This appeared to confirm the fears of the Tibetans themselves without suggesting a clear legal remedy. From this point on, however, the PRC state unequivocally treated Tibet as a separatist problem with the primary policy objective being to prevent 'reactionary rebellion to separate Tibet from the Motherland'.[46]

Resistance to the new PRC state in Tibet and Xinjiang was not only a nationalities problem involving a clash of cultures, values and local power structures. It was also a rejection of the broader Communist agenda for radical economic, social, and political change. Mao's more pragmatic building of class coalitions that helped bring the Communist Party into power gave way to a more cynical manipulation of 'contradictions among the people' and mass mobilisation to root out 'enemies' of the state and his own political power. What at times amounted to an incitement of local violence was accompanied by coercion, threats and intimidation against Mao's critics. A lack of economic growth, widespread resistance to change, and external threats such as the Korean War also fed a siege mentality in Mao and the senior Party leaders. As early as mid-1950 Mao had declared that general policy was to 'eliminate the remnant Nationalist forces, the secret agents and the bandits, overthrow the landlord class, liberate Taiwan and Tibet and fight imperialism to the end'.[47] Ambitious land reform programmes aimed to redistribute both economic and political resources to the peasantry by eliminating what Mao saw as the 'landlord class'. 'People's justice' unleashed widespread violence and summary executions. An estimated 40 per cent of land was redistributed, while possibly 1.5 to 2 million people were killed between 1947 and 1952.[48] Such killings have been seen as 'revolutionary politicides' – mass murders of class or political enemies.[49] Although the result of anarchic 'mass' violence, they became a particularly grisly feature of Mao's mobilisation campaigns.

As economic development continued to fail to meet expectations, state policies lurched to an extreme left position. Mao's campaigns attempted to coerce communist society into being: herding people into communes, accelerating industrialisation to absurd targets, erasing differences of class, religion or 'nationality', and replacing 'feudal' cultural practices with modern materialism. The horrific famine of the Great Leap Forward (1958–62) – an attempt to force progress in China's industrialisation – cost an estimated thirty-five million premature or unnecessary deaths, including those killed for opposing its policies, and left Mao's political credibility in ruins.[50] In what proved to be a final attempt to resurrect his leadership, Mao promoted and sought to direct the Cultural Revolution (1966–76), a nation-wide unleashing of collective violence against the purported enemies of the revolution 'taking the capitalist road'. The violence was unusual in being directed against parts of the state – Mao's calls that 'to rebel is justified' (*zaofan you li*) and to 'bomb the headquarters'[51] – and in the relative autonomy of perpetrators at the local level. Although the battles between factions of educated youth in the Red Guards, frustrated by their lack of opportunity, were the focus of Mao's mobilisation, collective violence at the local village level accounted for the bulk of the killing, estimated to be around 1.5 million deaths in total. The violence was reactionary in the sense that it broke down into conflicts between rival kinship lineages, was unsophisticated, perpetrated in public by known members of the community, and often passed unpunished. There were also a high number of casualties inflicted in attempts by the PLA and revolutionary committees to impose order.[52]

The minority nationalities of Tibet and Xinjiang certainly suffered through all of these mobilisation campaigns. The imposition of PLA rule in Tibet coincided with the worst period of the Great Leap Forward. In Xinjiang the push to form communes went hand in hand with greater Han migration, closer moni-toring and control of economic development from Beijing, and crackdowns on perceived 'local nationalism'. The Sino-Soviet split was also a factor in possibly more than 100,000 Kazaks and Uyghurs deciding to cross over into the Soviet Union, with Soviet encouragement.[53] Xinjiang was divided by violent conflict between rival factions of provincial rulers.[54] But the Tibetans and Turkic people of Xinjiang were particularly vulnerable to the Cultural Revolution's ideological targeting of the 'four olds': old ideas, old culture, old customs and old habits. Monasteries and mosques, religious and cultural practices and artefacts were vandalised, destroyed or outlawed. Tibet in particular was subject to planned acts of destruction and little in the way of distinctive cultural practices sur-vived this period. There were Tibetan as well as Chinese Red Guard factions, and those for and against the ruling Communist authorities. Some of the worst violence appears to have been the result of a 'Rebel' (*Gyenlo*) faction mobilising widespread discontent with collectivisation against the controlling 'Supporters' (*Nyamdre*) faction.[55] Xinjiang was similarly riven by violent clashes between rival 'Red Guard' groups and factions within the military, but this was generally the preserve of Chinese taking up Mao's call to 'rebel'. Turkic Muslims were nonetheless in the firing line as 'nationalities' issues were subordinated to the assimilationist 'class struggle'. Destruction and desecration of mosques, madra-sas and cemeteries occurred, while religious leaders and intellectuals were persecuted and humiliated in struggle sessions.[56] This extraordinary period of turmoil throughout China, with its combination of Mao's orchestration against his political enemies and collective violence from the 'bottom' up, marked the low point in the cultural practices of the minority peoples.

The Cultural Revolution swept away the state's attempts to implement forms of government tailored to the special problems of the minority border-lands. As part of their broader 'nationalities' policy for governing non-Han regions, Xinjiang (1955) and Tibet (1965) were declared 'autonomous regions' (*zizhi qu*). This policy adapted practices reaching back to the Qing dynasty, and borrowed from the Soviet Union's nationalities policy. In practice the system was designed to facilitate partial self-rule while discouraging separatism. Critics of China's system of local autonomy see it as a 'throwback' to an archaic impe-rial form of governing non-Han peoples, but the Communist form of autonomy was both more sophisticated and more tightly controlled.[57] The declaration of the Tibetan Autonomous Region (TAR) was complicated by the extensive Tibetan populations within the provinces of Sichuan, Qinghai, Gansu and Yunnan, who were to be administered as sub-provincial autonomous prefec-tures and counties. This consolidated a political division between eastern and western Tibetan populations which only began to emerge in the final years of the Qing dynasty. The legacy of the 1959 rebellion and military occupa-tion made the TAR a closed region under the heavy surveillance of the Tibet

Regional Committee of the CPC and the Tibet PLA. In Xinjiang a divide-and-rule approach to the various nationalities resulted in thirteen different groups being identified, with at least six of these (Kazak, Kyrgyz, Hui, Mongol, Tajik and Sibe) given autonomous status at various levels of local government. Of the twenty-seven autonomous units in Xinjiang, an identified nationality formed the majority in only twelve. Being in the majority, the province as a whole was designated 'Uyghur', but the parcelling out of autonomy to different groups at the local level diluted the potential political weight of this majority. This form of 'autonomy' translated to little more than the appointment of members of the recognised nationalities to local representative bodies and government offices. While the leaders of autonomous areas were drawn from the nationality with a demographic plurality, in a curious echo of Manchu Qing monitoring of Chinese officials, their deputies were generally high-ranking Chinese Party members. All autonomous levels of government were under the rule of central authorities and the Communist Party, whose leaders in Tibet and Xinjiang were almost always Chinese. The regional branch of the Party answered directly to the Central Party in Beijing, and all major economic development and infrastructure projects were determined from Beijing. Political authority was thus more centralised than ever once the conversion to an 'autonomous region' was implemented.[58]

In addition to the convoluted system for dividing the political authority of nationalities at the local level, the CPC leadership revived the Qing dynasty practice of settling Chinese in 'minority' regions. In Xinjiang they combined military state farms with civilian and penal colonies in a system designed to secure and develop border frontiers while reducing population density in eastern China. In the early 1950s the system was reorganised into the Production and Construction Military Corps (*Shengchan Jianshe Bingtuan* or *Bingtuan* for short). This unique hybrid of civilian and paramilitary organisations became the primary vehicle for recruiting hundreds of thousands of Chinese migrants, as well as absorbing large masses displaced by famine or 'rusticated' youth sent down to the countryside, to Xinjiang through to the mid-1970s. It is estimated that the *Bingtuan* managed the resettlement of over five million Chinese during this period. Around 90 per cent of the members of *Bingtuan* are Chinese, and these constitute about one-seventh (2.8 million) of the total population of Xinjiang.[59] The *Bingtuan* are increasingly dedicated to urbanisation and the commercial and industrial development that goes with it, and less focused on agricultural and paramilitary roles, but they continue as the major instrument of state policies for the development and integration of Xinjiang with the greater Chinese economy.[60]

The socio-economic discrimination resulting from either tacit or explicit forced migration in large part follows from the rapid development models of the state, which favoured those with the work and language skills suited to urbanisation.[61] But at heart it is a consequence of the lack of precisely the sort of political autonomy that minority nationalities policy appears to promise. For many Uyghurs, Tibetans and other 'minorities' the system of autonomy itself became the main conduit for repression and regular abuse at the hands of 'outsiders'.[62] This system is not one of monolithic repression or deprivation, but one in which the central authority of the state attempts to control the dimensions of minority identity. Many minorities have taken this politically assigned identity and 'sought to define and exploit it on their own terms'.[63] As in other areas that potentially challenge its authority, the state cultivates and co-opts an acceptable or 'patriotic' face of minority identity. There are thus officially sanctioned standards of political appointment, economic opportunity, religious practice, and cultural, linguistic and educational attainment that are tolerated and promoted. It is the tightly controlled limits of this identity and the denial of genuine self-determination that are the causes of contentious politics and violence. Accordingly, the fortunes and life conditions of Uyghurs, Tibetans and other minority peoples have tended to follow the policy swings emanating from Beijing rather than their assigned 'autonomous region'.

The relatively more liberal reform period of the early 1980s, when there was some support from Beijing for allowing minorities more local autonomy and reducing the role of Han officials, also proved to be a mixed blessing for Tibetans and Xinjiang. Beyond the rapid if unequal economic growth already noted, there was greater local political representation, more scope for religious and cultural expression, and even attempts to cajole the exiled Dalai Lama to visit Tibet. Local autonomy laws were strengthened in 1984 and, within the limits of the Party remaining in control of 'nationalities' policy, minority peoples did become more actively involved in determining their daily lives. The promotion of policies for greater autonomy, like the general direction of liberalising policies at the time, became ensnared in the looming political struggles that culminated in the 1989 Tiananmen massacre. The relatively more tolerant political environment produced a wide range of criticisms of the Party and calls for a more open and responsive political system. This atmosphere stimulated more demanding calls for autonomy in both Tibet and Xinjiang, with more activist groups outbidding their senior, more cautious community leaders. When political pressures on the CPC leadership began to make them nervous about political reforms in particular, from around 1987 the promises of greater autonomy for minorities were again withdrawn. Even the moderate Dalai Lama then decided to pursue his cause internationally, focusing his calls for a demilitarised 'zone of peace' in Tibet on the US. This infuriated the CPC authorities, but the internationalisation of the Tibetan problem sparked protests in Tibet that grew into drawn-out and widespread 'riots' (around two hundred demonstrations occurred over a six-year period). Another violent protest on the fortieth anniversary of the 1959 military occupation brought the imposition of martial law in Tibet. Similarly, in Xinjiang protests, demonstrations and violent clashes with authorities increased, ranging from calls for genuine 'equality between the nationalities' to separatist independence. As the forces against reform in the Party hardened, the rise in anti-government demonstrations and separatist sentiment were blamed on the liberalising policies of the period. The 1989 Tiananmen massacre was only the most dramatic and widely publicised event in the turn to political control and repression.

The subsequent collapse of the Soviet Union and the formation of newly independent states in Central Asia intensified this repression. For over twenty years now the CPC has followed a dual strategy of the 'loosening of economic policy with political tightening'.[64] The state's crackdown on separatism continued through the 1990s and the CPC seized the opportunity of the 9/11 attacks upon the US to exploit the most uncompromising boundary category of 'terrorism' in framing its nationalities problems. Those accused of the so-called 'three evils' of 'terrorism, separatism (or splittism) and religious extremism' experience longer prison terms, a higher rate of death sentences and more frequent violent conflict with state authorities than any other perceived threats to national security.[65] The resort to 'counterinsurgency' tactics in response to separatist threats underscores the gravity of the problem from the state's standpoint, notwithstanding a degree of political opportunism that exaggerates security threats in a post-9/11 context.[66] More importantly, the continued application of the most intensive state violence in dealing with minority populations exposes persistent failures in the PRC's national unification and 'multi-national' state. Serious 'riots' involving Tibetans in 2008 and Uyghurs in 2009, and continuing episodes of violent conflict down to the present, suggest national unification is moving further away from completion.

Discovering terrorism, stoking inter-communal conflict?

China's rapid expression of support for the global 'war on terror' appeared to mark the state's newly discovered frankness about what it described as 'terrorism' within its own territories. Just ten days before 11 September 2001, the Secretary of the Communist Party Committee for Xinjiang, Wang Lequan, declared that 'Xinjiang is not a place of terror'.[67] Such reticence had dissipated by January 2002, with the release of its comprehensive official report on China's brand of terrorism. 'Over a long period of time – especially since the 1990s', the report stated:

> the 'East Turkistan' forces inside and outside Chinese territory have planned and organized a series of violent incidents in the Xinjiang Uyghur Autonomous Region of China and some other countries, including explosions, assassinations, arsons, poisonings, and assaults, with the objective of founding a so-called state of 'East Turkistan'.[68]

The report claimed that from 1990 to 2001 these same unspecified forces were responsible for over two hundred terrorist 'incidents', resulting in the deaths of 162 people (of 'all ethnic groups') and injuries to over 440 people, even though only fifty-seven deaths were specifically enumerated. Perhaps most importantly from the perspective of the 'war on terror', the report also claimed that there were intimate links between East Turkestan terrorists, Osama bin Laden and the Taliban. Both bin Laden and the Taliban allegedly supported, trained and co-ordinated the activities of a group called the East Turkestan Islamic Movement (ETIM, said to be led by Hasan Mahsum), as well as other 'East Turkestan' terrorist groups. Members of these groups, it was said, engaged in terrorist acts not only in Xinjiang, but also in Afghanistan, Chechnya and other parts of Central Asia. The official report did not, however, directly link the ETIM to any 'terrorist' attack inside China.[69]

The state thus seized the opportunity afforded by its 'membership' of the 'global coalition' against terrorism to openly re-define Xinjiang as part of the problem. The most immediate reason for doing so was to proceed with its suppression of separatism in Xinjiang, with less fear of international censure from the international community and the US. Although this response was hardly surprising, it was built upon a misleading representation of Xinjiang. As already noted, the diversity among the people of Xinjiang and the Uyghur population, and the fragmentation of separatist groups, has assisted the state in enforcing control through a divide-and-rule approach. But this diversity and division was entirely absent from China's post-11 September report, which chose to tar all separatism with the same terrorist brush. The tenor of the report betrayed the profound political problems confronting the state in its continuous efforts to counter resistance and separatism in Xinjiang. Their position appeared alarmist and coy at the same time, a feature of official statements since 9/11 noted by several academic observers.[70] Association with the most lethal forms of international terrorism condemned purportedly widespread separatist violence in Xinjiang. Yet the government reassured the populous that its 'crackdown' on such violence 'targets only a few core members and criminals'. 'Toward the majority of the people involved, who have been hoodwinked', the government claimed to adopt an 'attitude of educating and helping them, and welcomes them back to the true path'.[71]

The combination of alarm and reassurance suggests a level of political opportunism and the need to establish the *bona fides* of terrorism to an international audience while playing down its scope to law abiding Uyghurs and potential supporters of Xinjiang's economic development. But in raising Uyghur 'terrorism' to the level of the 'global war on terror' the Chinese state 'securitised' the issue of separatism as both a domestic and international threat. This means it is 'presented as an existential threat, requiring emergency measures and justifying actions outside the normal bounds of political procedure'.[72] While the state may have achieved some short term gains in its ability to prosecute its own 'war on terror', subsequent events, such as the 'riots' in 2008 in Tibet and 2009 in Urumqi, showed that the state's capacity to contain violence was weakened rather than increased.

Prior to the events of 2008 and 2009, there were good reasons to question aspects of the state's accounts of terrorist violence in China. Its own estimates of deaths and injuries over more than a decade appeared relatively low in comparison with the human cost of separatist violence in such areas as Chechnya, Sri Lanka, Mindanao and Aceh. The casualties also appeared to be the consequence of small-scale attacks, with one or two deaths in each incident. Nor was there a clear indication of the criteria on which the violence was judged to be 'terrorist' rather than separatist or even criminal. Careful, scholarly studies of the claims of terrorism have cast doubt on the nature and extent of the violent incidents listed in this official report.[73] The balance of available evidence suggests that while the Chinese government has indeed experienced problems with periodic violent opposition and protest, including some terrorist-style attacks, it faces a more significant political problem in trying to contain and control broader hostility to its rule in its key minority regions. At the same time, there has been a tendency in official reports to trawl for violent incidents and cast them as separatist or terrorist after the event.[74] Leading up to the Beijing Olympics of 2008 there were reports of kidnappings and attempted hijackings by Uyghur 'terrorists', and for the first time official media reports drew a link between Uyghur terrorism and the violent protests in Tibet, pointing the finger at the Tibetan Youth Congress.[75]

The most significant incidents of violent resistance or protest demonstrate the close relationship between the state's policies and the responses of Uyghurs and Tibetans. In Xinjiang there has been a steady (if low-level) series of violent clashes between Uyghurs and local authorities since the late 1980s Among the most serious were the Baren 'incident' of April 1990 and the Ghulja (Yining) 'incident' of February 1997. Official accounts of the most serious events retrospectively portray them as examples of Islamic terrorism carried out by various East Turkestan movements.[76] The state's 'strike hard' (*yanda*) anti-crime campaigns, conducted every year in Xinjiang since 1996, which are designed to prevent or respond to anti-government Uyghur demonstrations or protests, appear to exacerbate tensions and provoke further protest. They are often combined with broad security sweeps to warn against separatist activity or detain people for questioning.[77]

Many violent incidents have been blamed on the East Turkestan terrorist movement linked to the international terrorism and Islamic extremism of Al Qaeda and the Taliban. But the state's 2002 report manages to link only four incidents with particular groups. The organisation accused of direct links with the international terrorism of Al Qaeda and the Taliban was the ETIM. These links were said to include a meeting with Osama bin Laden, funding from Al Qaeda and training in Al Qaeda and Taliban camps. Almost nothing in detail is known about several other groups mentioned in China's 2002 report. In December 2003 China's Ministry of Public Security issued a new list of terrorist organisations linked to Al Qaeda, which mentioned, in addition to the ETIM and East Turkestan Liberation Organisation, the World Uyghur Youth Congress and the East Turkestan Information Centre, based in Munich. The leaders of each group (Dolqun Isa and Abduljelil Qarkash, respectively) were the main targets, standing accused of financing, instructing and participating in terrorist acts associated with Xinjiang separatism. Before these accusations were made, both groups were primarily associated with publicity, the calling of congresses, and political promotion for Uyghur and Xinjiang issues.[78]

The 'strike hard' campaigns have become a fixture of state policy dealing with any form of organised opposition or separatist sentiment. One of the most extensive campaigns against Uyghur separatism was launched early in 2001, and was stepped up after 9/11. According to Amnesty International, this resulted in over 3,000 arrests and twenty executions from 11 September to the end of 2001.[79] Later reports suggested that tens of thousands of people had been detained for investigation, with hundreds being charged and some being executed. The state-run *Xinjiang Daily* reported that in 2005 18,227 individuals were detained for endangering state security.[80] These crackdowns make any form of opposition or separatist sentiment extremely difficult to express. They represent the more aggressive aspects of a broader government strategy to stifle separatism. In more recent years this has included attempts to clamp down on the development of religious, cultural and language practices. The authorities have not been prepared to tolerate unauthorised gatherings for religious purposes, and they have strictly enforced rules prohibiting religious instruction or mosque attendance for children under eighteen. The government has also reduced the amount of class instruction given in 'minority' languages and merged some dedicated Uyghur schools with mainstream Chinese schools. These measures appear to be part of a more intensive policy to 'Sinicise' minority cultures. Since at least 2004 the state has openly promoted a policy of integration through development. In an attempt to delegitimise nationality claims by minorities, official documents in Chinese switched from referring to 'nationalities' (*minzu*) to 'ethnic groups' (*zuqun*).[81]

Perhaps the most devastating blow to China's nationalities policy after 9/11 has been the serious outbreak of violence associated with the 2008 and 2009 riots in Tibet and Xinjiang respectively. In both cases the level of violence had not been seen since the Cultural Revolution or perhaps even since 1959 in Tibet. The March 2008 protests were of such magnitude, extending to all parts of the Tibetan Plateau, including beyond the TAR, that they have been characterised as a 'Tibetan national uprising'.[82] As with past protests, they began with monks demonstrating against the repressive controls on the practice of their religion and culture, taking advantage of the publicity surrounding the Beijing Olympics. When the initial protesters were beaten and arrested and further planned protests were prevented, demonstrations quickly spread throughout the region, culminating in serious Tibetan–Han violence. China's media emphasised this communal violence, ignoring the initially peaceful start to demonstrations. Official statements pointed to the usual suspects for stirring up trouble: the 'Dalai Lama clique' and 'hostile Western forces', as well as the 'terrorist' Tibetan Youth League. To mitigate international criticism, Beijing offered to hold a dialogue with the Dalai Lama, but returned to its hard-line uncompromising position not long after the Olympic Games. A severe crackdown was implemented, with thousands detained and hundreds arrested and tried, while extensive 'patriotic education' campaigns were implemented. State policy became even more intractable and inflexible. The current line is to deny the validity of Tibetan discontent, and this stokes a widespread resentment among the Han population of the 'ungrateful' Tibetans. Smaller scale but significant protests nonetheless continued, and over one hundred self-immolations stoked anxiety among security authorities, extending an intrusive presence across the region down to the present. The most concerning development is the communal violence between Han and Tibetans, with official discourse reinforcing popular prejudices against minority nationalities. This risks driving Han nationalism towards more extreme expressions of ethnic, religious and cultural intolerance.[83]

Although again clouded by a lack of open reporting and independent evidence to match official accounts of what occurred, the July 2009 riots in the Xinjiang provincial capital of Urumqi initially appeared to follow the pattern of previous demonstrations that turned violent. A group of perhaps hundreds of Uyghurs gathered in the northern parts of Urumqi to protest against what they believed to be lenient treatment of Chinese accused of killing at least two Uyghur workers in a factory in the southern province of Guangdong. These workers were reportedly killed, and hundreds injured, after a false rumour spread that the Uyghur men had raped two Chinese woman. News of this incident spread to Xinjiang through the Internet and social media, sparking the 5 July demonstration in Urumqi. When the People's Armed Police and possibly PLA troops attempted to force the demonstrators southward, away from a public square, attacks upon shops and Chinese in the vicinity allegedly broke out. What role the police and paramilitary may have played in the violence remains unclear. The rioting that followed, and the actions of Chinese vigilante groups over subsequent days, reportedly led to the deaths of 197 people and thousands of injuries, the majority of them Chinese according to official reports. Communication networks within Xinjiang were shut down and the events were considered serious enough for then President Hu Jintao to return from a state visit in Italy to take charge. In an unusual measure, the Urumqi Party Secretary, the highest ranking official in the city, was removed from his position. Some official accounts linked the 'riots' to terrorism and the ETIM, and accused Rabiya Kadeer and the World Uyghur Congress of agitating events.

But the Uyghur demonstration appears to have been prompted by perceived injustice towards fellow Uyghurs in the south of China and showed few overt signs of separatist sentiment or even demands for greater autonomy. Once again, the most troubling development was the rapid escalation of communal violence between Uyghurs and Han, and this was further exacerbated by a reported spate of syringe attacks, many of which were based on rumour, that set off further Uyghur–Han violence and large demonstrations of Chinese concerned with their security. This serious breakdown of relations between Uyghurs and Han in Xinjiang, from which Urumqi has not yet fully recovered, is in large part the legacy of the hard-line policies against separatism since 9/11 and the increasing attempts to integrate Uyghurs into a Han-centric vision of national unity. More intense resentment on both sides appears to be the result.[84] Subsequent violent clashes between Uyghurs and local police authorities in and around Kashgar, in southern Xinjiang, have occurred on a regular basis. A prominent Muslim imam from Turpan, Abdurehim Daomalla, was killed in August 2013, allegedly due to his perceived support for the official line that blames violence on terrorists. Although more reluctant to name a particular terrorist group, such as the ETIM, state media continues to blame violent acts on 'separatism, terrorism and religious extremism', while occasionally reporting the discovery of extremist Islamic views, calling for 'jihad', on social media. In mid-2013, President Xi Jinping met with provincial leaders who then issued a report declaring that 'ethnic separatist forces at home and abroad continue to intensify their activities, and deep-seated problems harming social stability in Xinjiang remain fundamentally unsolved'.[85] The apparent explosion of a car that had driven into Tiananmen Square, towards the famous portrait of Mao, killing the occupants and several bystanders, and the serious knife attack on civilians in the southern province of Yunnan, have reinforced reflex official reporting of such violent attacks as Uyghur terrorism.[86]

As with some violent incidents in the 1990s, a level of coordination and the targeting of civilians indicate terror tactics. At the same time, the sporadic and unsophisticated nature of the violence suggests that the organisation and capacity of well-established terrorist groups is lacking in China. Not all incidents, such as the bloody July 2009 'riots', can readily be identified with 'an explosion of separatist sentiment, much less "jihadism" or "Islamic terrorism"'. Sources both hostile and sympathetic to Uyghur separatism have tended to reach the same exaggerated conclusion: 'Xinjiang is in crisis and the Uyghurs [are] poised to erupt in violence'. Like the Tibetans, Uyghurs may well have become more concerned about 'cultural autonomy' than the 'unattainable' goal of an independent state.[87] But this lack of cultural autonomy is symptomatic of the state's failure to 'win recognition as the sole legitimate representative of Uyghur interests and to make Uyghurs think of themselves as Chinese (*jonggoluq*) and citizens of the PRC'.[88] The sense of Uyghurs being 'strangers in their own land' has not been overcome: relations between Uyghurs and Han 'will probably get worse in the near term', while 'significant improvement will take at least a generation, if it happens at all'.[89]

Conclusion

For over two hundred years the Chinese state has experienced violent convulsions from forces within and without. The state today still endorses a national history that reminds its citizens that the greatest threat to China is the combination of 'chaos within, aggression without' (*neiluan, waihuan*).[90] Although a warning of ancient heritage, it resonates because it speaks the language of modern nation-state sovereignty and its vulnerability in a 'globalising' world. The Communist Party has restored the continuity of China's integrity as a civilisation, a people, and a territory. Yet the 'core interests' of the PRC nation-state signal incomplete sovereignty – Taiwan and disputed island territories – and vulnerable regions of 'minority nationalities' – Tibet and Xinjiang. The trace of insecurity and a defensive re-building of the state against internal strife and 'hostile foreign forces' are still visible in the failure to successfully govern or integrate the 'nationalities' of Tibet and Xinjiang. China's claim to these territories is a legacy of its own imperial past. The last dynasty, the Manchu Qing, conquered these hinterland regions to eliminate any potential security threat, secure proto-modern sovereign borders, and implement the eighteenth-century Qing's imperial vision. The Qing expansions were comparable to European states as war machines, but they remained imperial projects towards subordinate 'others' of the hinterland who were only incorporated into the central state administration in the late nineteenth century. By then the Qing were under siege from within and without, and their Manchu origins became an easy target for Han nationalism. State disintegration was fertile ground for horrific competitive violence and foreign wars, but it also cracked open fissures to multiple claims to national statehood among Tibetans and the Turkic Uyghurs, among others. Both the Nationalist Party and the Communists simply denied there were independent nationalities outside the greater Han race. They also denied the need for more than one party monopoly to represent all Chinese. A preparedness to uphold this univocal nation-state came into tragic conflict not just with the multi-ethnic, but also the plural social and political realities of China. Despite the PRC state's concessions to multi-ethnic 'autonomy', persistent resistance among Tibetans and Turkic Muslims were met with tighter political controls at best and brutal military force at worst. Such 'nationalities' were particularly vulnerable to the modernist socialism of the Communist Party and its attempts to subordinate all politics to class struggle.

China's modern state has never been more powerful than at present, and it continues to expand its national wealth and capacity for regional and international influence. Yet the assertion of control over the 'minority nationality' hinterlands has intensified. Continuing resistance to nationalities policy and increasing incidents of state-minority and Han-minority communal violence represent continuing and deep-seated policy failure. In casting separatism as 'terrorism' the state effectively securitised the issue, raising its international profile and intensifying state coercion and national unification policies. The risk is that this will further consolidate divisions between 'minority' and Chinese people, expanding the opportunity for mobilising political violence at a communal level. Tibetans and Uyghurs cannot in sober reality hope for the independence of a separate state, and the majority do now seek 'genuine autonomy' instead. Concessions in this direction would ameliorate conflict, but would also challenge the Communist Party's commitment to a monopoly of power and risk escalating demands towards separatism or secession. This at times tragic dilemma for China's minority nationalities appears only further away from satisfactory resolution.

NOTES

1 Possibly a misattribution, Stalin is quoted as saying in reply to Churchill's warning about the costs of a premature second front in Europe: 'When one man dies it is a tragedy. When thousands die it's statistics'. See D. McCullough, *Truman* (New York: Simon and Schuster, 1992), p. 510.

2 C. Tilly, *Capital, Coercion, and European States, A.D. 990–1990* (Cambridge, MA: Basil Blackwell, 1990).

3 On national unification or nation-building as never finished but always in the making, see R. Brubaker, *Nationalism Reframed: Nationhood and the National Question in the New Europe* (Cambridge: Cambridge University Press, 1996); R. G. Suny, 'Ambiguous categories: States, nations, empires', *Post-Soviet Affairs*, 11:2 (1995), pp. 185–96.

4 C. Tilly, *The Politics of Collective Violence* (Cambridge and New York: Cambridge University Press, 2003), p. 73.

5 M. Rossabi, 'Introduction', in M. Rossabi (ed.), *Governing China's Multiethnic Frontiers* (Seattle: University of Washington Press, 2004), p. 8.

6 Rossabi, 'Introduction', p. 8.

7 On boundary conflict, see Tilly, *The Politics of Collective Violence*, pp. 75–7.

8 M. D. Swaine, 'China's assertive behaviour, part one: On "core interests"', *China Leadership Monitor*, 34 (22 February, 2011), pp. 7–8.

9 A. Carlson, *Unifying China, Integrating with the World: Securing Chinese Sovereignty in the Reform Era* (Stanford: Stanford University Press, 2005), p. 230.

10 X. Jinping, 'On several experiences and understandings in studying the theoretical system of socialism with Chinese characteristics', *Qiushi*, 1 April 2008, cited in T. R. Heath, 'What does China want? Discerning the PRC's national strategy', *Asian Security*, 8:1 (2012), p. 55.

11 V. B. Shue, 'Powers of State, Paradoxes of Dominion: China, 1949–1979', in K. Lieberthal,

J. Kallgren, R. MacFarquhar, and F. Wakeman, Jr. (eds), *Perspectives on Modern China: Four Anniversaries* (Armonk, NY: Sharpe, 1991), p. 218.

12   P. C. Perdue, *China Marches West: The Qing Conquest of Central Eurasia* (Cambridge, MA: Belknap Press, 2005), pp. 506–11.

13   Swaine, 'China's assertive behaviour, part one', pp. 1–25.

14   R. Ma, 'Reflections on the debate on China's ethnic policy: My reform proposals and their critics', *Asian Ethnicity*, 15:2 (2014), p. 237.

15   A. J. Nathan and A. Scobell, *China's Search for Security* (New York: Columbia University Press, 2012), pp. 196, 198.

16   Perdue, *China Marches West*, p. 546.

17   Ma, 'Reflections on the debate on China's ethnic policy', p. 237.

18   J. Waley-Cohen, 'Commemorating war in eighteenth-century China', *Modern Asian Studies*, 30:4 (1996), p. 873.

19   On the Manchu 'final solution' for the Mongol threat, military campaigns in the Turkic Muslim northwest, and incorporation of Tibet see Perdue, *China Marches West*, pp. 4, 227–40, 289–92. On Tibet see D. D. Ho, 'The men who would not be Amban and the one who would: Four frontline officials and Qing Tibet policy, 1905–1911', *Modern China*, 34:2 (2008), pp. 215–16.

20   F. Wakeman, Jr., *The Fall of Imperial China* (New York: Simon and Schuster, 1977), p. 92.

21   J. A. Millward, *Beyond the Pass: Economy, Ethnicity, and Empire in Qing Central Asia, 1759–1864* (Stanford: Stanford University Press, 1998), pp. 50–2.

22   M. C. Goldstein, *A History of Modern Tibet, 1913–1951: The Demise of the Lamaist State* (Berkeley, CA: University of California Press, 1991), p. 815.

23   J. A. Millward, *Eurasian Crossroads: A History of Xinjiang* (New York: Columbia University Press, 2007), pp. 201–10, 226; G. Bovingdon, *The Uyghurs: Strangers in Their Own Land* (New York: Columbia University Press, 2010), pp. 51–60; A. D. W. Forbes, *Warlords and Muslims in Chinese Central Asia: A Political History of Republican Sinkiang, 1911–1949* (Cambridge: Cambridge University Press), pp. 135–44.

24   On how experience of past independence can be a catalyst for separatism see J. Cuffe and D. S. Siroky, 'Paradise Lost: Autonomy and Separatism in the South Caucasus and Beyond', in J-P. Cabestan and A. Pavkovic (eds), *Secession and Separatism in Europe and Asia: To Have One's Own State* (Abingdon: Routledge, 2013), pp. 37–53.

25   J. Fitzgerald, *Awakening China: Politics, Culture and Class in the Nationalist Revolution* (Stanford: Stanford University Press, 1996), pp. 103–6, 122; C. Kaishek, *China's Destiny* (New York: Macmillan, 1947), p. 13.

26   D. Howard, 'The dialectics of chauvinism: Minority nationalities and territorial sovereignty in Mao Zedong's New Democracy', *Modern China*, 37:2 (2011), pp. 177, 178–9.

27   Fitzgerald, *Awakening China*, pp. 346–8.

28   R. Mitter, *China's War with Japan, 1937–1945: The Struggle for Survival* (Oxford: Oxford University Press, 2013), pp. 34–49, 186–95.

29   Estimates of the total number of deaths in twentieth-century China through wars, famine, mass murder and political persecution vary between thirty million and over one hundred million. See R. R. Rummel, *China's Bloody Century: Genocide and Mass Murder Since 1900* (New Brunswick, NJ: Transaction Publishers, 1991).

30   M. Taylor Fravel, 'Regime insecurity and international cooperation: Explaining China's compromises in territorial disputes', *International Security*, 30:2 (2005), pp. 55–9.

31   A. Heraclides, 'The ending of unending conflicts: Separatist wars', *Millennium: Journal of International Studies*, 26:3 (1997), pp. 704, 707.

32   Tilly, *Politics of Collective Violence*, pp. 50, 51, 53.

33   B. He and B. Sautman, 'The politics of the Dalai Lama's new initiative for autonomy', *Pacific Affairs*, 78:4 (2005/6), pp. 601–29; B. He, 'A deliberative approach to the Tibet autonomy issue: Promoting trust through dialogue', *Asian Survey*, 50:4 (2010), pp. 709–34; M. Ramos-Lynch, 'Sino-Tibetan dialogue: Much misunderstanding, little room for compromise', *China Security: A Journal of China's Strategic Development*, 6:3 (2010), pp. 67–74; T. Shakya, 'Tibetan questions', *New Left Review*, 51 (2008), pp. 5–27; E. Sperling, *The Tibet–China Conflict: History and Polemics* (Washington DC: East-West Center, 2004).

34   C. A. Ford, *The Mind of Empire: China's History and Modern Foreign Relations* (Lexington: University of Kentucky Press, 2010), p. 84.

35   S. van Schaik, *Tibet: A History* (New Haven: Yale University Press, 2011), p. 215.

36   Millward, *Eurasian Crossroads*, p. 237.

37   Millward, *Eurasian Crossroads*, p. 238.

38   van Schaik, *Tibet*, p. 218; D. Gladney, *Muslim Chinese: Ethnic Nationalism in the People's Republic* (Cambridge, MA: Harvard University Press, 1996), p. 88.

39   G. Bovingdon, *The Uyghurs*, p. 5; M. Dillon, *Xinjiang: China's Muslim Far Northwest* (London: Routledge/Curzon, 2004), pp. 52–5; Millward, *Eurasian Crossroads*, p. 238.

40   Bovingdon, *The Uyghurs*, p. 7.

41   C. McGranahan, 'Tibet's Cold War: The CIA and the Chusi Gangdrug Resistance, 1956–1974', *Journal of Cold War Studies*, 8:3 (2006), pp. 102–30.

42   Exact casualties cannot be verified. See Y. Hao, 'Tibetan Population in China: Myths and facts re-examined', *Asian Ethnicity*, 1:1 (2000), p. 20.

43   On the uprising and its aftermath, see van Schaik, *Tibet*, pp. 241, 231–42.

44   T. Shakya, *The Dragon in the Land of Snows: A History of Modern Tibet Since 1947* (London: Penguin Compass, 2000), p. 273.

45   D. M. Crowe, *War Crimes, Genocide, and Justice: A Global History* (New York: Palgrave Macmillan, 2014), p. 291.

46   van Schaik, *Tibet*, p. 241.

47   Mao Zedong, cited in F. Dikotter, *Tragedy of Liberation: A History of the Chinese Revolution 1945–1957* (London: Bloomsbury Press, 2013), p. 84.

48   Dikotter, *Tragedy of Liberation*, p. 83.

49   B. Harff and T. R. Gurr, 'Toward empirical theory of genocides and politicides: Identification and measurement of cases since 1945', *International Studies Quarterly*, 32:3 (1988), pp. 363–4.

50   J. Yang, *Tombstone: The Untold Story of Mao's Great Famine* (London: Allen Lane, 2012), pp. 394–431.

51   R. MacFaquhar and M. Schoenhals, *Mao's Last Revolution* (Cambridge, MA: Belknap, Harvard University Press, 2006), pp. 87–92.

52   Y. Su, *Collective Killings in Rural China During the Cultural Revolution* (Cambridge: Cambridge University Press, 2011), pp. 1–38.

53   Millward, *Eurasian Crossroads*, p. 264; Bovingdon, *The Uyghurs*, p. 60.

54   Millward, *Eurasian Crossroads*, pp. 271–4.

55   M. C. Goldstein, B. Jiao and T. Lhundruup, *On the Cultural Revolution in Tibet: The Nyemo Incident of 1969* (Berkeley: University of California Press, 2009), pp. 6–8.

56   Millward, *Eurasian Crossroads*, pp. 271–6.

57   W. Smith, *China's Policy on Tibetan Autonomy*, East-West Center Working Paper No. 2 (October 2004), pp. 1–2.

58   Smith, *China's Policy on Tibetan Autonomy*, p. 13; B. Hillman, 'China's many Tibets: Diqing as a model for "development with Tibetan characteristics?"', *Asian Ethnicity*, 11:2

(2010), p. 276; Millward, *Eurasian Crossroads*, pp. 242–6.

59   N. Becquelin, 'Xinjiang in the nineties', *China Journal*, 44 (2000), pp. 77–84; D. H. McMillan, *Chinese Communist Power and Policy in Xinjiang, 1949–1977* (Boulder: Westview Press, 1979), pp. 61–6; D. H. McMillan, 'Xinjiang and the Production and Construction Corps: A Han organisation in a non-Han region', *Australian Journal of Chinese Affairs*, 6 (1981), pp. 65–96; Millward, *Eurasian* Crossroads, pp. 251–4; J. D. Seymour, 'Xinjiang's Production and Construction Corps, and the Sinification of Eastern Turkestan', *Inner Asia*, 2:2 (2000), pp. 174–5.

60   T. M. J. Cliff, 'Neo Oasis: The Xinjiang *Bingtuan* in the twenty-first century', *Asian Studies Review*, 33:1 (2009), pp. 84–5.

61   Bovingdon, *The Uyghurs*, pp. 52–4.

62   Millward, *Eurasian Crossroads*, p. 237.

63   D. C. Gladney, *Dislocating China: Muslims, Minorities and Other Subaltern Subjects* (London: Hurst & Co., 2004), p. 225.

64   Bovingdon, *The Uyghurs*, p. 53; M. Goldstein, *The Snow Lion and the Dragon: China, Tibet and the Dalai Lama* (Berkeley: University of California Press, 1997), pp. 67–76; Millward, *Eurasian* Crossroads, pp. 276–84; Smith, *China's Policy on Tibetan Autonomy*, pp. 18–22; van Schaik, *Tibet*, pp. 256–61.

65   Wedeman, 'Strategic Repression and Regime Stability in China's Peaceful Development', in S. Guo (ed.), *China's 'Peaceful Rise' in the 21st Century: Domestic and International Conditions* (Aldershot: Ashgate, 2006) pp. 105–9. On China's development of the 'three evils' and its adoption by the Shanghai Co-operation Organisation in Central Asia see M. Clarke, 'China, Xinjiang and the internationalisation of the Uyghur issue', *Global Change, Peace and Security*, 22:2 (2010), p. 222.

66   L. Odgaard and T. G. Nielsen, 'China's counterinsurgency strategy in Tibet and Xinjiang', *Journal of Contemporary China*, 23:87 (2014), pp. 1–21.

67   Amnesty International, *China's Anti-Terrorism Legislation and Repression in the Xinjiang Uyghur Autonomous Region*, 2002, available at: http://web.amnesty.org/aidoc/aidoc_pdf.nsf/index/ASA170102002ENGLISH/$File/ASA1701002.pdf, p. 7 (accessed 12 April 2014).

68   Information Office of the State Council of the PRC, 'East Turkistan Terrorist Forces Cannot Get Away with Impunity', *People's Daily* (21 January 2002), available at: http://english. people.com.cn/200201/21/eng20020121_89078.shtml (accessed 12 April 2014). In Chinese, 'Guowu Yuan Xinwenju Fawen 'Dongtu Kongbu Shili Nan Zuize', *Renmin Gang* [Union News Net], *Renmin Ribao* [People's Daily] (21 January, 2002) available at: www. peopledaily.com.cn/BIG5/shizheng/20020124/655189.html (accessed 12 April 2014).

69   It is not entirely clear which groups operate outside Xinjiang, but other groups named in this official report include: East Turkestan Liberation Organization, Shock Brigade of the Islamic Reformist Party, East Turkestan Islamic Party, East Turkestan Islamic Party of Allah, East Turkestan International Committee, Uyghur Liberation Organization (Kyrgyzstan), Islamic Holy Warriors (Afghanistan). Those named as 'ringleaders' include: Tursun Turdi, Muhammat Tursan, Yasin Muhammat, Hogaxim Qasim, Muhammatjan Huzir. The report claims the Chinese police have arrested over 100 terrorists who were trained in Afghanistan and 'other countries' and then 'sneaked' back into Xinjiang. On these groups and the official accounts of casualties from 'terrorism' see also J. A. Millward, *Violent Separatism in Xinjiang: A Critical Assessment*, Policy Studies 6 (Washington, DC: East-West Centre, 2004), pp. 12–18; Millward, *Eurasian Crossroads*, p. 340.

70   Bovingdon, *The Uyghurs*, p. 105; M. Clarke, 'China's "War on Terror" in Xinjiang: Human security and the causes of violent Uighur separatism', *Regional Outlook Paper*

No. 11, 2007, pp. 271–301; Y. Shichor, 'Blow up: Internal and external challenges of Uyghur separatism and Islamic radicalism to Chinese rule in Xinjiang', *Asian Affairs: An American Review*, 32:2 (2005), pp. 119–35.

71 Information Office of the State Council of the PRC, 'East Turkistan Terrorist Forces' (accessed 12 April 2014).

72 B. Buzan, O. Weaver and J. de Wilde, *Security: A New Framework for Analysis* (Boulder: Lynne Rienner, 1998), p. 24.

73 Bovingdon, *The Uyghurs*, pp. 113–28, 174–90; Clarke, 'China's "War on Terror" in Xinjiang'; J. A. Millward, 'Violent separatism in Xinjiang: A critical assessment', *Policy Studies*, 6 (2004), pp. 1–41; S. Roberts, *Imaginary Terrorism? The Global War On Terror and the Narrative of the Uyghur Terrorist Threat* (Washington, DC: Ponars Eurasia, 2012).

74 Bovingdon, *The Uyghurs*, pp. 188–90.

75 W. W. Smith, Jr, *Tibet's Last Stand? The Tibetan Uprising of 2008 and China's Response* (Lanham: Rowman and Littlefield, 2010), p. 7; C. Cumming, 'Quiet death in Xinjiang', *Guardian* (5 April, 2008), available at: www.guardian.co.uk/commentisfree/2008/apr/05/china.tibet (accessed 14 April 2014).

76 Millward, *Eurasian Crossroads*, pp. 326–7.

77 Bovingdon, *The Uyghurs*, pp. 131–4; Amnesty International, *People's Republic of China: Gross Violations of Human Rights in the Xinjiang Uyghur Autonomous Region* (New York: Amnesty International, 1999), pp. 18–25.

78 Millward, 'Violent separatism in Xinjiang', pp. 22–8.

79 Amnesty International, *China's Anti-terrorism Legislation and Repression in the Xinjiang Uyghur Autonomous Region* (New York: Amnesty International, 2002), p. 19, available at: http://web.amnesty.org/aidoc/aidoc_pdf.nsf/index/ASA170102002ENGLISH/$File/ASA1701002.pdf (accessed 15 April 2014).

80 Uyghur Human Rights Project, 'Persecution of Uyghurs in the Era of the "War on Terror"' (16 October 2007), available at: http://docs.uyghuramerican.org/Persecution_of_Uyghurs_in_the_Era_of_the_War_on_Terror.pdf (accessed 15 April 2014), p. 4.

81 Ma, 'Reflections on the debate on China's ethnic policy', p. 238.

82 Smith, *Tibet's Last Stand?*, p. 2.

83 A detailed account of the 2008 'riots' can be found in Smith, *Tibet's Last Stand?*, pp. 11–79. On self-immolation in Tibet see Y. Sun, 'Ethnic, sectarian, or localized grievances? On Wang Lixiong's analysis of Tibetan self-immolation', *Asian Ethnicity*, 14:3 (2013), pp. 376–80.

84 On the July 2009 'riots' see J. A. Millward, 'Introduction: Does the 2009 Urumqi violence mark a turning point?', *Central Asian Survey*, 28:4 (2009), pp. 347–60; Amnesty International, *'Justice, Justice': The July 2009 Protests in Xinjiang, China* (New York, Amnesty International, 2010); C. Mackerras, 'Xinjiang in 2013: Problems and prospects', *Asian Ethnicity*, 15:2 (2014), pp. 247–50.

85 Cited in Mackerras, 'Xinjiang in 2013', p. 248.

86 E. Wong, 'Chinese governor signals crackdown on separatists', *New York Times* (6 March 2014), available at: www.nytimes.com/2014/03/07/world/asia/chinese-governor-signals-crackdown-on-separatists.html?_r=0 (accessed 15 April 2014).

87 Millward, 'Does the 2009 Urumqi violence mark a turning point?', pp. 349, 355, 357.

88 G. Bovingdon, 'The not-so silent majority: Uyghur resistance to Han rule in Xinjiang', *Modern China*, 28:1 (2002), p. 44.

89 Bovingdon, *The Uyghurs*; Mackerras, 'Xinjiang in 2013', pp. 249–50.

90 S. Shirk, *China: Fragile Superpower* (Oxford: Oxford University Press, 2007), p. 64.

4

Instruments of state violence in hybridising regimes: the case of post-communist Russia

Matthew Sussex

RANSITIONAL REGIMES FACE specific challenges in their attempts to consolidate power. In many cases transitions occur smoothly, with the polity accepting a new order without the need to resort to violence. However, political violence remains an attractive instrument for leaders of states, as well as old and new elites within them, to achieve their objectives. In this chapter, I examine how violence is utilised in transitions that are derailed away from democratic consolidation towards hybrid forms. Using the case of post-communist Russia I identify three distinct types of violence. Despite some overlap between them, each broadly coincided with a particular phase of the Russian Federation's political trajectory. The first type, which I refer to as *ablation*, took place early after the emergence of the Russian Federation as a proto-democracy. This is rare. In spite of the literature on voting and violence that links problematic transitions to a predisposition to militarism (primarily as a foreign policy strategy by disgruntled former elites),[1] it is unusual for democratising states to turn to violence in order to silence opponents at home or abroad. The second type, which can be termed *scapegoating*, occurred alongside Russia's political reformulation in the late 1990s and early 2000s, and was driven by the more authoritarian vision for Russia articulated by Vladimir Putin. The third and chronologically most recent type is *nullification*. This accompanied the consolidation of the present hybrid semi-authoritarian Russian state. It refers to a targeted attempt to create external conditions favourable for regional hegemony over its neighbours through violent means.

It is important to note that each type of violence identified in this chapter is a mechanism in its own right for encouraging national unification, and each has been employed in a variety of different forms by states for centuries. What is interesting, though, is that each type reflected different tactics, and represented a differing level of severity, linked directly to the severity of internal and existential threats facing the state, as well as the extent to which ruling elites perceived their hold on power to be under serious challenge. As the post-communist Russian case demonstrates, the motivations to engage in violence in states where transitions fail have not altered appreciably. Instead, ideas and identities continue to be manipulated by political elites for pragmatic reasons pertaining to power and influence. In Russia, whether this referred to attempts by Boris Yeltsin to quash anti-democratic forces, two wars in Chechnya, or the identification and neutralisation of alternative centres of political influence by Putin, the reasons for employing violence remained remarkably consistent.

Conceptualising violence: democratisation, transition and security

When conceptualising violence, the literature on democratisation tends to exhibit a preference for explanations that focus on legitimacy, morality and domestic-level variables.[2] This is understandable. Whether the cause of violence is seen as a matter of construction, as witnessed by studies that focus on 'stateness',[3] or alternatively ascribed to strategies of regime unification,[4] it becomes easier for the researcher to explain away triggers of violence without compromising democracy as an ideal. As a result, bad institutions, bad leaders, bad elites or bad sections of society can be blamed for their instigation. This also means that the solutions proposed to counter state violence revolve around ideational and institutional factors. So, for instance, to resolve violence long embedded in a society one might seek to confront such deep causes through truth and reconciliation, and through new discourses of nonviolence. One might also seek to achieve legal and/or institutional change in order to remove triggers for violence, mobilise popular support in order to challenge bad leaders, appeal to external actors such as the UN, or suggest various socio-economic reforms in order to achieve political community.

This is all very well for successful and stable transitions. But what happens when transition goes wrong? In such cases neither diagnoses (because it is hard to tell when transition is failing), nor prescriptions (because by then it is generally too late) are particularly useful. Moreover, transitional states – even those that succeed – generally do not operate with a common understanding of the 'rules of the game' necessary for a pluralist society to function. Without these, it is impossible to determine when violence can be legitimately employed. Transitional regimes also tend to lack the institutional rigour, societal stability or economic dynamism to peacefully manage what may be a whole host of different cleavages within a given polity. And whether one defines democracy in specific Dahlian terms as polyarchy,[5] or more loosely to accommodate liberal, electoral or illiberal democracies,[6] it is still difficult for the researcher to identify exactly when democracy's supposedly peace-promoting characteristics start taking effect. To do so one must either invoke Kant and make a series of increasingly speculative judgement calls, or alternatively adopt methodologically dubious discourses relating to norm diffusion, norm cascades, or norm entrepreneurship.[7]

Hence while scholarship on democratisation is often inherently politicised when looking at questions about violence, much of the contemporary scholarship on international relations exhibits the same tendency. Given its broader epistemological reach, international relations tends to focus on war rather than violence, but it is nonetheless prone to similar errors. In particular the recent enthusiasm for human security locks the analyst into following a predetermined path to resolve violence because it is seen to come from the same broad set of normative causes. Following the literature on 'new war', much of today's violence is regarded as being linked to forces of globalisation.[8] This produces not only new actors but also – in Mary Kaldor's classic formulation – new economics, new modes of violence, and new (or no) rules of the game.[9] Instead of being products of rational calculations of power, violence is the direct result of a new radicalised politics of identity. Efforts to resolve such multifaceted forms of violence typically take the form of calls to make international law much more muscular, to locate, capture and try perpetrators of genocide, and to engage in tolerant cosmopolitan discourses.[10]

In addition to being virtually unworkable in practice, this is akin to treating a disease without first properly understanding its symptoms. In this chapter I do not focus on the desirability of reducing violence, or ascribe blame for it to any particular individual, structure or group of actors. I am also not interested in taking sides in the debate over whether violence is structural (and therefore operates at all levels of society) or more diffuse. Rather, I am more concerned with the types of violence that transitional regimes utilise in order to achieve their ends, without commenting on whether that violence was appropriate. I adopt a minimalist definition of violence: the direct use or threat of physical coercion against an agent or agents deemed for whatever reason to be a threat to the security of the state.

Thus this chapter makes no distinction between force and violence, as some have done, or necessarily between violence and war. By 'state violence' I mean the use of coercion by governments to achieve their ends. This does not presuppose, in Weberian terms, a monopoly on *legitimate* violence, or over the ability of other actors to utilise violence for instrumental purposes. Put simply, states tend to be better equipped to use violence because they tend to control the major apparatuses through which compliance or consent is enforced. Given such a conventional (and some might say old-fashioned) approach, it is reasonable to ask why it might be interesting to focus mainly on the types of violence that transitional states can employ.

Three types of violence: ablation, scapegoating and nullification

Transitional regimes facing significant challenges to their authority can employ violence in a variety of ways. To begin with, it is often the case that old elites are not provided with 'golden parachutes' that soften their fall from power. Faced with the prospect of being relegated to political obscurity (at best), or becoming a target of persecution by a liberated populace (at worst), marginalised groups can agitate for a return to the old order – and in doing so seek to regain their privileged positions. As Michael McFaul once famously pointed out, this can often include the formation of anti-government parties of protest. Ironically, then, former authoritarian elites often still find themselves participating in democratic processes, despite the fact that their public pronouncements and policy platforms seek to overthrow the proto-democratic state.[11]

Such eventualities are generally unproblematic for the democratising state. After all, if radical groups are part of the development of multi-party systems, there can be some confidence that their views will eventually be moderated. This is because they will eventually need to gravitate towards the political centre in order to compete for influence, for votes, and ultimately for power.[12] If they become more worrisome, or if the potential for them to attract a significant following is considered likely, disgruntled elites can be marginalised by simply banning the organisations and political parties that they might seek to form. This takes away not only a potential operational base, but also a hub for ideas, for a unifying narrative, and in some cases opportunities for funding. When memories of an authoritarian past are particularly raw, the new democracy can engage in campaigns of truth and reconciliation, in which old elites are afforded a chance at rehabilitation, and eventual acceptance through reintegration into society.[13] Finally, at the more coercive end of the spectrum, former elites can be exiled or imprisoned for various crimes against the people. The process by which this occurs can be an important component of the state's development in respect to the rule of law.

Although each of these strategies certainly reflects the use of political power to various degrees, none of them crosses the line into actual state violence. They may be just or unjust, or involve intimidation, but they do not employ physical harm (or the threat of it) against certain sections of society. But what happens when an old elite rapidly gains sway over public sympathies, comes to control important agencies and institutions of the state, or even engages in violence itself? Under those conditions, the democratising state sometimes has little recourse except to use violence itself. This is especially so if the institutions for managing law and order are weakly defined, are poorly funded and/or are ill coordinated. It can also be the case that the security services, the military and other agencies with the capacity to use violence become part of the political tug-of-war between the new elite and the old one.

In order to head off clashes, or even outright civil war, between these groups, the proto-democratic state can turn to a strategy of what I call *ablation*. This refers to the removal of a specific threat, often with surgical precision. While primarily a term that is used in medicine (and sometimes in geology),[14] its definition is especially appropriate to describe the behaviour of proto-democratic states in which the risk of violent conflict is high, or there is good reason to suspect that the democratic project is under significant threat. It is indeed a violent response because it requires direct intervention by the state through forceful means. The goal is not to wage wholesale war on a set of rival ideas, but to eliminate those individuals primarily responsible for the threat, taking care to ensure that violence does not spread. It is therefore used against a specific set of regime opponents, with the aim of removing them from the political spectrum, and is limited to violence on the domestic level rather than inter-state conflict. Once ablated, regime opponents have little opportunity to return to power in the short term, and the proto-democracy can return to the business of state-building. But this is also potentially an important marker of problematic transition, since new democracies are often highly averse to the use of violence against their own people.[15]

Violence can occur when a state is under threat from a specific group, whether defined along ethnic, religious, geographical or socio-economic lines. Such groups may seek to secede, or demand that the political centre should devolve political power to it. When faced with such claims for autonomy or self-determination, state elites must calculate carefully the relative worth of acquiescing against the costs involved in doing so. It may be, for instance, that a particularly rebellious province contains large material resources, delivers significant industrial capacity, or occupies an important trade route or other strategically vital position.[16] The state's determination of implications and consequences will ultimately shape its decision to capitulate, negotiate, coerce or use violence.

Yet states also have another option that has less to do with risks and how to manage them, and more to do with national unification projects. Here a state can engage not only in violence, but a particular type of violence designed to unite and mobilise the majority of the population at the expense of the alien 'other'. In this chapter I refer to such a form of violence as *scapegoating*. In this case, the state not only securitises the threat from would-be secessionists, but also inflates it as one upon which future national survival and/or prosperity depends.[17] It can range in severity from small-scale violence to keep restive populations in check, to broader campaigns of elimination. It can encompass media campaigns of demonisation, use law enforcement agencies to segregate and demoralise the target group, and can wage military operations against it.[18] This has the twin effect of removing a challenge to the existing order, as well as sending a powerful deterrent message to others who might harbour similar aspirations.

This is a well-documented phenomenon, and is not limited to transitional states. It is practised by authoritarian governments, but also by democratic ones. The Israeli–Palestinian conflict is potentially a good example of scapegoating. In this context, the Palestine Liberation Army (PLA) and other militant Palestinian groups have been held responsible for a broader cross-section of the ills facing Israeli society, arguably to a greater degree than the actual threat represents, and the state's response often involves disproportionate force. The People's Republic of China (PRC) practises scapegoating against the Uyghur population in Xianxiang Province,[19] and until the end of World War II Japan had a long history of playing on domestic fears of a geographic 'dagger' pointed at its heart, in the form of the Korean peninsula.[20] Hence while ablation refers specifically to internal threats, scapegoating is a type of state violence that sits at the nexus of the domestic and the external – and also potentially the transnational, in the case of terrorist and insurgent campaigns that cross state borders.

The third type of violence identified in this chapter is *nullification*. This refers to the use of violence as part of a more overarching strategy to create an external environment favourable to regional primacy. It is tied centrally to material power, and assumes that the state exercising such a form of violence has the capacity to shape regional order in line with its interests. Here the literature on regionalism offers two different conclusions in relation to whether such an order will be stable. On the one hand, balance-of-power theorists would argue that prospects for conflict are lower when material capabilities are more or less balanced between major actors, regardless of whether there are two, three or more vying for hegemony.[21] On the other hand, hierarchal theorists expect stability to be enhanced when there is an acknowledged central focal point of power. Regional Security Community theorists sometimes refer to this as a 'centred' community,[22] whereas realists tend to focus on a specific dominant actor, with a clear acknowledgment by second-tier actors that the hegemon has the right to manage regional order. Most states within the second tier choose to bandwagon with the dominant power, and derive material benefits from doing so.[23] But those who seek to defect, or to challenge the existing order, can often be the targets of violence by the dominant state, which takes action to preserve its privileged position, as well as to deter similar behaviour by others. This may or may not be enduring: as John Mearsheimer has noted, one of the tragedies of great powers is that the concentration of power in one state tends to attract power to counterbalance it.[24]

While this can help to explain whether regional orders will be stable or unstable, it says little about the types of strategies – especially those utilising violence – that can help to shore up regional dominance, and have the added domestic benefit of shoring up a regime's legitimacy internally. Much of the scholarship on security 'architecture' is focused on a similar objective, although it stresses the need for overlapping institutions to ensure that aspirant hegemons have a stake in continued stability.[25] And the writing on rising great powers is also relatively vague on the topic, noting mainly that as states enhance their power they will also look to construct and preserve institutional, legal and other mechanisms of dominance.

Sometimes, though, violence is deemed by the state to be necessary in order to accomplish its objectives. Hence a nullification strategy can be employed if institutions and threats fail to achieve the desired outcome. It can be a pursued by a strong state, or one seeking to manage its retrenchment by shoring up a stable geopolitical buffer zone around it. This can be targeted, in short, sharp bursts (and limited in the form of police actions); it can seek to destabilise or Balkanise a recalcitrant state; or it may take the form of a broader strategy of conquest. The Mexican–American war, as well as Nazi Germany's *Anschluss* with Austria and its campaign in the Sudetenland can all be seen in terms of the use of violence to facilitate a more compliant and stable regional environment. Of equal importance to the goal of regional stability, though, was that they were also important components of national unification and regime consolidation.

Each of these types of violence operates at a different level of analysis. Ablation is an internal strategy only. Scapegoating can be either domestic or international, depending on the type of threat faced by the state. And nullification is solely focused on the external environment. But as noted above, the three strategies of ablation, scapegoating and nullification are by no means limited to transitional regimes. Each strategy can be (and has been) practised in some form or another by any state. Various US interventions in Latin America during the Cold War could be seen as nullification, and they occurred when the US was near the height of its powers. So too could the Soviet invasion of Afghanistan, at a time when its power was beginning to wane.

How, then, are these types of violence useful as analytical categories, specifically in relation to transitional or hybrid states? The answer lies in the potential correlation between each strategy being employed and a specific moment at which democracy is failing (as opposed to when it is succeeding). The point is not that any of these types of violence is especially unique to transitional nations. Rather, it is the time and context in which they may occur. This is also not to imply a direct line of causation between democratic derailment and the use of state violence. Other factors, such as national power for instance, are vital considerations here. It is unrealistic to expect a new democracy, often very much weakened by the circumstances that led to it to alter its regime-type, to immediately embark on violence as nullification against its neighbours. But by the same token, it is equally unrealistic to expect a developed and mature democracy to need to resort to violence against its own people through a strategy of ablation. Domestic politics, not to mention the external and internal threat environment is also important: it is necessary to assume that at least some neighbours will be hostile to claims by a state to regional hegemony; that internal-transnational challengers will seek to exploit state weakness; and that domestic elites will seek to derail the process of democratisation.

It makes sense, then, to see the use of each type of violence as a means for a transitional state to accomplish political objectives as the domestic institutional obstacles to that violence are removed and alternative voices are silenced. A working multi-party system, for example, is a natural check against the routinised use of military power for gain. So too is a free and independent media. And so are other institutions such as courts, parliaments and the pluralism of elites that can be found in developed civil societies. As democracy fails, political power is centralised. In the process of 'strengthening the vertical',[26] various types of violence – internal, local and international – are progressively enabled for use by a regime as it moves away from democracy and towards authoritarianism.

To demonstrate this, I turn to the case of the Russian Federation's experience with democracy following the collapse of the USSR in 1991. The rest of the chapter examines the Russian government's use of ablation, scapegoating and nullification during three specific periods. First I examine ablation in respect to the constitutional crisis of 1992 that led to former President Boris Yeltsin using force against his own parliament. This created a power vacuum that was subsequently used by Yeltsin to push through a controversial 'super-presidential' constitution. Second, the chapter argues that President Vladimir Putin's use of disproportionate force to resolve the conflict in Chechnya was an excellent example of scapegoating that consolidated his power and helped to unify the nation against an internal-external 'other'. Finally, the chapter demonstrates that Russia's war with Georgia in 2008 over South Ossetia, as well as its incursion into Crimea in 2014, are reflective of state violence as nullification – part of Putin's desire to create a stable regional environment by punishing potential defectors.

Violence as ablation: the 1993 crisis and constitutional reform

The ideological and ideational landscape of Russia in 1992, just one year after the dissolution of the USSR, reflected a plethora of competing visions for statehood. In addition to liberals in the Congress of People's Deputies (including technocrats who had risen in the ranks of the Communist Party under Mikhail Gorbachev), Stalinist hardliners and other former Communist Party of the Soviet Union apparatchiks were also represented. There were also more strident elements emerging on the domestic political scene. Nationalists like Vladimir Zhirinovsky – the 'clown prince' of Russian politics – urged the recreation of an anti-Western and pan-Slavic empire that sought the immediate return to Russia of former Soviet republics. These nationalist rumblings were recognised by then-Foreign Minister Andrei Kozyrev, who wrote of 'fledgling red-and-brown fuehrers' promising to 'shower the prodigal sons of the [Soviet] empire with radioactive waste'.[27] And while kotowing to the US for aid was initially tolerated, this changed markedly when Russia voted in favour of a UN resolution instituting an economic sanctions regime against Serbia and Montenegro. Patriotic parliamentarians interpreted this as a betrayal of brother Slavs. At the same time, the plight of ethnic Russians in the 'near abroad', especially in Moldova and Estonia, was seen as a form of 'ethnic apartheid'.[28]

Eventually the tensions between the legislature and the executive, which had solidified during disagreements over the management of the economy and the new Russian Constitution, spilled over into outright hostility. Yeltsin was faced with a parliament that vetoed virtually his entire agenda, but rebel leaders such as Vice President Alexandr Rutskoi were unable to win the support of the major power ministries in their attempts to seize control. For a while Russia seemed to have two governments, with both passing legislation to marginalise the other. Matters came to a head when Yeltsin decided to bypass the parliament altogether, introducing 'special presidential rule'.[29] The parliament responded by readopting the old Brezhnev-era Soviet constitution and declaring the Presidency defunct.[30] In September 1993 Yeltsin dissolved the Congress of People's Deputies and the Supreme Soviet (the upper house) of the Russian Federation and called for new elections for the Federal Assembly. But since the army wavered on which side to support, with Defence Minister Pavel Grachev attempting initially to stay out of the imbroglio, the parliament continued to meet. It also armed itself, and on 3 October 1993 its forces attacked the main Moscow TV station and the Moscow mayor's office in a bid to seize power. Yeltsin eventually won the backing of the military and laid siege to the White House where parliament sat. Eventually the decision was taken to storm it, and tanks fired on the parliament until an assault captured the parliamentarians, leading the main organisers to Lefortovo prison. The official death toll was 187 killed, with 437 wounded.[31]

Following his successful victory over the legislature, Yeltsin held a referendum that linked support for fresh elections to a new parliament with alterations to the Russian Constitution. The Constitution was quickly branded 'super-presidential' in nature, given that it provided Yeltsin with the power to rule by decree. Faced with a series of fractious parliaments in the mid-1990s, Yeltsin did so on numerous occasions. But his new powers went further, instituting a strong line of authority leading directly from the office of the President. Under the terms of the Constitution, any legislation rejected by the Duma (parliament) on three occasions did not lead to the President being forced to withdraw it. Instead, it stipulated that the *parliament* would be dissolved, and fresh elections would take place. Moreover, any challenge pertaining to the legality of Presidential behaviour would go before the Constitutional Court, which Yeltsin himself appointed. Hence the Russian president was able to hold the threat of new elections constantly hanging over the legislature if they did not back his agenda. In turn the Duma would routinely exercise the only avenue of dissent that was open to it: rejecting legislation twice, and then passing it on the third submission.

With the new Duma virtually emasculated, and the Prime Minister appointed by the President rather than by election from the leading political party, the executive branch had virtually no check upon its power. It is unsurprising, then, that elections in 1993 saw significant gains to far-right parties such as the misnamed Liberal Democratic Party of Russia. Subsequent elections in 1995 resulted in a so-called 'red-brown alliance', with the Communist Party of the Russian Federation holding the largest number of seats, supported by various nationalist groups. But this was little more than a protest vote by the populace. When it came time to choose between Yeltsin and the Communist candidate Gennady Zyuganov in the 1996 Presidential elections, Russians chose overwhelmingly to stick with Yeltsin, even though his health was failing (he underwent a quintuple heart bypass just before the election campaign) and had behaved increasingly erratically in the lead-up to the poll. Hence while much Western scholarship has laid the blame for the abandonment of Russia's democratic transition at the feet of Vladimir Putin,[32] this is not completely accurate. Indeed, better-informed analyses acknowledge that it was Yeltsin – the notional democrat – who took the legal steps of strengthening the executive branch to such an extent that other organs of government were little more than a rubber stamp.

What is more interesting, though, is that Yeltsin's moves against the rebel parliament represented an excellent example of a strategy of ablating opponents. The physical violence unleashed in the 1993 siege of the White House, from which Yeltsin emerged the victor, was the perfect pretext to ensure that political opponents could not challenge his authority. In this context the use of violence by the state was difficult to avoid under the circumstances, but it was certainly not randomised. Instead it was a focused use of force against a clear and present threat to Yeltsin's power. It is also instructive to note that the rebellious deputies were swiftly rehabilitated. Along with the other 'coup plotters', former Vice President Rutskoi was granted amnesty in February 1994, and went on to be elected governor of Kursk oblast. Ruslan Khasbulatov, the Speaker of the old Congress of People's Deputies, ran unsuccessfully as a moderate candidate for the office of President of Chechnya against Jokhar Dudayev, and then became a prominent political commentator at the Plekhanov Institute.[33]

This did not mean that all opposition to Yeltsin ceased after the violence of 1993, and nor did it mean that Russia's transition to democracy had been completely abandoned. If anything, Yeltsin was forced to move to the new (moderately nationalistic) centre on issues such as foreign policy. Already tenuous, Russia's initial 'friends with everyone' approach to diplomatic relations with the international community was fairly quickly replaced by a more muted strategy of multipolarism. The new doctrine explicitly sought to engender the end of US unipolarity, and increased Russian cooperation with non-democratic states such as China, Iran and North Korea. Nonetheless, it is hardly coincidental that the use of armed force by the Russian government was the precursor to wide-ranging political reforms that marginalised opponents from the central decision-making process, and formalised a system of political rule that was effectively by the executive, from the executive (and increasingly for the executive). This was paradoxically assisted by crippling economic weakness, rampant organised crime, social stagnation and the rise to prominence of a new financial elite that backed Yeltsin to the hilt. In many ways, then, Russia's clan-based oligarchic politics of the mid-1990s was as least in part a product of the decision not to engage in bargaining and compromise to unite different warring factions, and to use violence instead.

Violence as scapegoating: Russia's (second) war in Chechnya

Russia's frequent past persecutions of Chechens have been well documented. Events in the twentieth century – especially Stalin's deportation of the Chechens as part of his ethnic divide-and-rule campaign – were merely a more recent manifestation of long-running mistrust that commonly saw Chechens routinely branded as thieves, liars and murderers by ethnic Russians. Before the disintegration of the USSR, Chechnya was one of the poorest Soviet republics. It had the lowest number of doctors per capita in the USSR, and poor education levels. Over 58 per cent of the population had not completed secondary schooling and only 4 per cent went on to higher education. In addition, Chechnya had the highest proportion of the population among Soviet republics classified as rural (73 per cent), coupled to high birth rates (16.1 per 100,0000 people as compared to the national average of 2.2 per 100,000).[34] And whereas Russia's first war in Chechnya from 1994–96 was essentially a short but bloody war of self-determination at a time of weakness in the political centre, the second war of 1999, triggered after a series of apartment bombings in Moscow and Volgograd, came at a time of increased state consolidation and capacity.

In the first Chechen conflict a variety of essentially secular nationalist groups employed a national identity dynamic as a force for liberation, and to garner support in local presidential elections. However, nationalism quickly grew into a negative mixture of ethnic hegemony and anti-pluralism. The Yeltsin administration eventually negotiated a compromise agreement via the 1996 Khasavyurt Accord between General Alexander Lebed and the rebel leader Aslan Maskhadov. While it sought to demilitarise the capital of Grozny, the agreement essentially postponed any final decision over the status of the proposed autonomous Chechen Republic of Ichkeria until 2001.

Given the 'frozen' nature of the conflict with Chechnya, with a political decision on future autonomy left awaiting resolution, it was not surprising that the conflict erupted again just three years later. A weak and under-resourced Russian policing capacity was unable to prevent the region from turning into a hub for banditry and lawlessness. Organised crime, kidnapping and extortion were endemic, as Chechen leaders played out long-held personal animosities between themselves at the local and clan level. It is also unsurprising that the second conflict, unlike the largely secular struggle characteristic of the first one, was perceived as a heavily radicalised variant of transnational terrorism. Certainly individuals like the Saudi-born Ibn-al Khattab, with direct links to Al Qaeda, played a role in running weapons and funds to support the separatists. Chechen pro-independence propaganda also became heavily influenced by Wahhabi dogma. It is also often forgotten that a substantial part of Russia's population is Muslim. It comprises approximately twenty million people out of a total of some 144 million. The fastest growing religion in Russia is Islam, and many Muslims are found on Russia's south-western flank.[35] As the precursor to the Russian Federation, the Soviet Union had the world's fifth-largest Muslim population after India, Indonesia, Pakistan and Bangladesh; and a Muslim population greater than either Egypt or Turkey.[36]

The perception that state violence against the Chechens was necessary due to a civilisational war against radical Islam was assisted by a series of high-profile atrocities. This included the 1995 attack by the infamous Shamil Basayev, field commander of the Sabotage Battalion of Chechen Martyrs, who took patients and staff in a Budyonnovsk hospital hostage. The operation to remove Basayev's forces resulted in 129 deaths, most of whom were civilians. It also included the Moscow Nord–Ost crisis of 2002, in which Chechen fighters took 850 theatregoers hostage. Some 130 died from suffocation, blast and gunshot wounds after Russian Alpha teams pumped a tranquilising gas into the building, and then stormed it. And it included the 2004 siege at Beslan, where 334 people (including 156 children) died in an attempt to liberate a school that Basayev's forces had seized in order to demand independence for Chechnya and Putin's resignation.[37]

Yet despite branding the struggle against the Chechens as a war against transnational terrorism Islam – which became especially useful after the 9/11 attacks and the onset of the US 'war on terror', it was a much more complex phenomenon prompted by both domestic and external considerations. To begin with, Moscow exaggerated the impact of external Wahhabi fighters in the conflict. Even Putin's press secretary put the number of jihadists in Chechnya at not more than two hundred.[38] Indeed, for Putin the war was less about Islamic insurgency per se and much more about security on three levels: personal, domestic and international. In this way it matched almost exactly the expectations about scapegoating articulated earlier in this chapter.

Using violence in Chechnya was the ideal opportunity for Putin to make a successful transition from Prime Minister to President in a fragmented domestic political landscape. The war had started in September 1999, and Yeltsin stepped down on 31 December the same year. The popularity of the war amongst parliamentarians and the public alike allowed Putin to make further alterations to Russian political institutions without fear of attracting too much criticism. And the pacification of Chechnya was crucial given that its territory represented a vital corridor for the transit of energy supplies to Europe, which by the mid-2000s had become the cornerstone of Russia's economic revival.

Hence a radicalised politics of identity that treated the Chechens as scapegoats operated as a powerful unifying force for the conflict, offering a means to securitise the threat of Chechen terrorism for ordinary Russians. Soon after the war began, Moscow's mayor Yuri Luzhkov made it mandatory for all Chechens to register with local authorities. Individuals who were Chechen, part-Chechen or even simply looked swarthy were subjected to random searches and temporary detention without standard requirements for reasonable suspicion of having committed a crime.[39]

Under Putin, Russia's conduct of the second war – in contrast to the first – was epitomised by brutal violence. The military was allowed to interpret its rules of engagement more liberally, and hence did not need to establish the difference between civilians and enemy combatants. Frequent stories of Russian forces using tube artillery to level villages before advancing into the ruins began to appear, as did reports of broader scorched-earth policies. These took the form of *zachistki* (literally 'a little clean-up') operations that often involved follow-on forces engaging in door-to-door searches for teenagers deemed to be of fighting age. They were frequently arrested, many of them disappeared, and others were simply executed. Families of any individual captured on suspicion of aiding the separatists were subjected to intimidation and the loss of personal property, and their homes were burnt to the ground. Estimates of total casualties vary significantly, but a 2007 Amnesty International report suggested that at least 25,000 civilians had died since 1999. Other estimates put the number at 40,000, with at least 200,000 displaced.[40] This amounted to about a fifth of the pre-war population.

The popularity of the second war, as opposed to the first, is instructive. Yeltsin was almost impeached in May 1999 on charges of conducting an illegal and genocidal war in Chechnya from 1994–96 (with the Duma vote in favour at 283, just seventeen short of passing).[41] An *Interfax* poll taken in 1995, at the height of the first conflict, put disapproval with Yeltsin's performance at 75 per cent.[42] In contrast, according to VTsIOM polling, Putin's popularity rose from 3 per cent upon taking office as Prime Minister to over 60 per cent by January 2000.[43] During this period he had made no policy announcements of any substance with the exception of taking charge of the war.[44] Over the course of the conflict Putin referred to Chechens with colloquial language, which was also well received by the public. This ranged from calling Chechen separatists 'bastards' and 'bandits', to promises to 'wipe them out in the shithouse'.[45]

Putin's popularity also came at a time of heavily reduced information about the conflict. The Kremlin took advantage of the opportunity to make governmental sources the primary conduit of information, tightening media laws to restrict reporting on the conflict. In January 2000, Andrei Babitsky, a prominent Radio Liberty reporter often seen as pro-Chechen, was kidnapped by the Russian military. An agreement to release Babitsky only came after direct intervention by US Secretary of State Madeline Albright, and he was eventually handed over to Chechen warlords in exchange for three captive Russian soldiers.[46] By 2005, the Duma had passed a law requiring journalists to source information about terrorist attacks only from official channels. One year later, the Law on Fighting Extremist Activity meant that any journalist critical of public officials could be found guilty of spreading extremism, and sentenced to up to three years' imprisonment.[47]

Putin also exploited the national unification benefits of violence through scapegoating the Chechens by making further enhancements to executive power. In 2000, in a move taken partly to better respond to national emergencies, he created seven new federal districts, each with a Presidential appointee as a representative. He weakened the Federation Council (comprised of regional governors) by removing its oversight over legislation or budgetary processes, and created the State Council with an agenda set by the Presidential administration.[48] Following the Beslan siege he announced a major new reform to 'strengthen the unity of the country'. On 13 September 2004 he proposed a change to replace all eighty-nine elected leaders of Russia's regions with Presidential appointees.[49] While these appointments would be subject to approval by local legislatures, two consecutive rejections of his nominations would result in those legislatures being dissolved. The parliament, by then dominated by Putin supporters, passed the proposal by 356 votes to 64. Even regional governors and presidents – whose positions were under threat – came out in support of the idea.[50]

The conduct of the war had further importance for Russians still struggling to adapt to a post-Cold War era in which Moscow's influence had waned. Losses in prestige and territory after the collapse of the USSR were exacerbated by the economic and social policy failings of the Yeltsin administration. For this reason, any policies that threatened to weaken Russia further were perceived negatively. Putin tapped into popular frustration at Russia's diminishing power as a potent vehicle during his initial election campaign. This went a long way towards shoring up his position as a strong leader with broad-based support, and gave him an increasingly potent domestic rationale for escalating the Chechen conflict. In this way, Russia's main international objectives were geopolitical and geoeconomic, but also a matter of preserving Russian territorial integrity. In particular they were necessary to prevent spillover.[51] The risks involved in granting independence to Chechnya would have been to see Dagestan and Ingushetia quickly follow suit. This would have had disastrous domestic consequences, and denied Russia access to the strategically significant Caspian Sea.

Russia's second war with Chechnya therefore neatly highlights the inside–outside nature of scapegoating as a mechanism of state violence. Both external considerations and domestic ones were significant enablers of subsequent changes to Russia's fortunes. This was true in respect to its future regional ambitions, its further movement away from democratic governance, and Putin's own political longevity. The threat from Chechen separatists was heavily securitised as a fundamental challenge to Russian territorial integrity. The Kremlin played on public fears of a domino effect that could lead to the breakup of Russia itself, and thus presented the Chechen war as a potent national survival narrative. Internally this had the effect of allowing for further tightening of executive power, the restriction of free and independent sources of information, and the silencing of political dissent. On the external level it ensured that Russian control over energy supply lines would allow it to exert political leverage over its near neighbours, and create vulnerable over-dependencies in a broader European context.

Violence as nullification: war with Georgia and the annexation of Crimea

The final type of state violence assessed in this chapter concerns nullification as an instrument for cementing local hegemony. While many actors have followed such a strategy in the past, the Russian experience in both Georgia and Crimea – in 2008 and 2014 respectively – is especially instructive in relation to the theme of transition from proto-democracy to authoritarianism. Both the Crimean peninsula and the South Caucasus (Armenia, Azerbaijan, and Georgia) occupy a crucial geo-strategic position at the intersection of East–West trade routes, as a theatre for great power rivalry, and the source of regional and local instability and conflict. The South Caucasus in particular became even more important after the collapse of the USSR and then the onset of the 'war on terror'. At least seven external actors (eight including China) have interests there. The US has encouraged 'multi-vector' foreign policies from states in Russia's 'near abroad', especially over trade in resources. Turkey and Iran both have economic and security interests in the South Caucasus, while EU expansion has seen it moving nearer the area, and putting forward its own good offices to try and settle local disputes. The Commonwealth of Independent States (CIS) and NATO have also played a role: the former attempting to prevent extra-regional influences from the West, and the latter trying to encourage them. But due to extensive ethnocultural links, a large diaspora population, and the danger of conflict spillover, Russia is the state that has most to risk from losing control over this part of the former Soviet space.[52]

A further problem for Russia was that Abkhazia and South Ossetia had different reasons for wanting to secede from Georgia. Many Abkhaz wanted full independence, and saw their relationship with Russia as a pragmatic one, since it was most likely to assist them. South Ossetians, meanwhile, were split between pro-independence forces and those ethnic Russians who wanted to be re-incorporated into the Russian Federation.[53] Since Abkhazia and South Ossetia had been virtually independent for almost twenty years, Russia's options were: to fully recognise their autonomy; to assimilate them into Russia; or encourage them to re-integrate with Georgia. But only one of these options was realistic. The first risked all-out conflict with Tbilisi, while the third was unthinkable after the conflict between Georgia and South Ossetian and Abkhazian forces in the 1990s. As Richard Sakwa correctly put it:

> Had the war not occurred, it is likely that Russia would have continued a policy of 'Russification' in Abkhazia and South Ossetia that would have fallen short of out-right independence. While this option also would have guaranteed the continuation of the 'frozen conflicts', the outcome of 2008 put the situation in Georgia on ice, given the unwillingness of either side to compromise or concede defeat.[54]

The actual conflict over South Ossetia in 2008 was a short one, lasting only five days. It came about after Georgian forces invaded Tskhinvali, the South Ossetian capital, on 7 August. Russia responded quickly and with massive force: within forty-eight hours it had pushed Georgian forces back deep inside their own territory, while Russia's Crimean Black Sea Fleet blockaded the Georgian coastline and then landed 4,000 marines at the port of Poti.[55] Speculation at the time that Russia was prepared to take Tbilisi proved unfounded, yet the success of the Russian *blitzkrieg* operation certainly demonstrated that it had the capacity to do so. As one report put it, Georgia lost its entire air defence network, its air force and its navy – effectively its entire war-fighting capabilities.[56] By the end of hostilities Russian losses amounted to sixty-four soldiers dead, and South Ossetian/Abkhazian civilian casualties stood at 133.[57]

Nearly four years later, following another 'colour' revolution in Ukraine that removed the pro-Moscow Viktor Yanukovych from power, Russia quietly took over the Crimean Peninsula. But in Crimea, Russian strategy had shown considerable evolution from its raw application of overwhelming force in 2008. Large numbers of well-armed 'friendly green men' without identifying insignia quickly gained control over Sevastopol and Simferopol.[58] They deliberately avoided direct provocation of Ukrainian forces, and only a few shots were fired in anger. As an exercise in *maskirovka* (disguised warfare), it reflected an approach that may have stretched plausible deniability, but achieved Russian objectives swiftly, and with minimum violence.

Russia's decision to use violence in South Ossetia and in Crimea was an excellent example of nullification: in this case, to help embed Russian influence in the post-Soviet space; to shut out external influences; and to serve as a warning to others. Indeed, it was part of a broader strategy to preserve sub-regional primacy, and it was intended for both international and domestic audiences. The fear from the Kremlin is for a future order in which Russia's overall power continues on a downward trajectory while China's rise continues. Under those conditions Russia would be left as little more than a resource appendage to either the PRC or the EU. The main aspect of its strategy has been institutional: to construct political, economic and security architecture in and around the former USSR. It includes the Collective Security Treaty Organisation, which Russia has dubiously touted as a military-security counterweight to NATO. It also incorporates the CIS, Putin's Eurasian Union, various energy trading clubs, and the Shanghai Cooperation Organisation.[59] While comparatively little has come yet from them, Putin's intention has been for a number of institutional carrots and sticks binding neighbouring states closely to Russia.

An equally important aspect of Russian strategy has been to use the West's own logic against it. This makes it look hypocritical and ineffectual, and highlights how malleable 'global' international legal and human rights rhetoric can be. Putin's justification for intervening in South Ossetia in 2008 was the 'Responsibility to Protect' (R2P).[60] Similarly in Crimea – and then in Eastern Ukraine – Putin pushed the line that he was protecting ethnic Russians from right-wing nationalists. His message was simple: if the West can back a coup against a democratically elected government, Russia can as well. Crimea, and potentially Eastern Ukraine (as an energy transit corridor and with a large manufacturing base), is an important part of that vision. By intervening in Crimea, Putin's calculation was that it would show any vacillators how far he was prepared to go to secure Russian interests.

By August 2008, when Russia went to war with Georgia over South Ossetia, Putin's consolidation of his domestic power base had long been completed. While he had shifted from the Presidency to the office of Prime Minister for one term, giving way to the notionally more liberal Dmitry Medvedev, he remained at the political power centre due to his role as Russia's kingmaker. The same constitutional powers, in which the media and rival parties had been significantly emasculated, also gave him a direct path back to the presidency at the election in 2012, two years before Russia's intervention in Crimea. Thus the type of state violence practised by Russia in 2008 and 2014 had much more to do with projecting Russian power than any lingering notions of a relaxation of executive power, and a potential return to liberal democratic transition.

Yet this was also an indication of the enabling effect of previous episodes of state violence on the Kremlin's ability to act with domestic impunity. Exemplifying the notion of nullification described earlier in this chapter, the use of violence by Russian leaders in South Ossetia/Abkhazia and then Crimea was targeted, limited and circumspect. The idea of any large-scale Russian military intervention in the 'near abroad' during the 1990s, for instance, would have been unthinkable. It was not just because Russia was relatively weaker, but also because domestic institutional checks upon executive power – although weak – would have been a potent barrier to violence. Yeltsin had discovered this himself during the first Chechen war. But by the end of the first decade of the twenty-first century, the Putin–Medvedev alliance was domestically strong enough to justify an attempt to impose a Russian-dominated regional order. And following the turnaround in Russia's economic fortunes it had not only the will, but also the wherewithal, to do so.

Conclusions: state violence as markers of problematic transitions

How can these three types of state violence – ablation, scapegoating and nullification – be understood in terms of flawed democratic transitions more generally? To begin with, it is certainly not the case that each episode of violence automatically predisposed the Russian state to lurch further away from democracy. After 1993, for instance, there was still an opportunity for political liberalisation, and commentators even speculated that Dmitry Medvedev would restart the process when he took over the Presidency in 2008. Second, the reasons that the state employed violence were on each occasion different, even though all of them were important in relation to domestic identity and national unification. The 1993 crisis was specifically undertaken as a targeted and very brief campaign against counter-elites who had become a rival centre of power. The war in Chechnya was justified as necessary for national survival, even though it had domestic benefits for Putin, as well as safeguarding external Russian interests over the transit of energy resources. And the 2008 and 2012 interventions in South Ossetia/Abkhazia and Crimea were articulated according to domestic rationales (to assist ethnic Russians abroad), but in reality had their origins in geopolitics and Moscow's efforts to maintain regional primacy.

However, each of these instruments of violence occurred in linear sequence for a reason. It would not have been possible for a Russian leader to embark on a campaign of national unification without having first silenced domestic challengers and marginalised institutional sites of opposition to presidential decision-making. Moreover, Russia could not have used violence in an attempt to consolidate its grip on the former Soviet space if it was simultaneously confronting internal separatist movements, and if domestic sentiment had not been previously consolidated behind Putin. In this way the gradual derailment of Russian democracy was an enabler for a new type of violence. This is not to say that each type might not have been employed had Russia emerged from its transition a stable and prosperous pluralist state. Yet it is nonetheless instructive that each form of violence occurred during Russia's shift from a proto-democracy to an illiberal democracy, and finally to a neo-authoritarian state. And while one case by no means proves a rule, it opens up the potential to examine the correlation between types of violence as markers for democratic derailment elsewhere.

NOTES

1   On this, see J. Gowa, *Bullets and Ballots: The Elusive Democratic Peace* (Princeton: Princeton University Press, 2000); E. Mansfield and J. Snyder, 'Democratisation and war', *Foreign Affairs*, 74 (1995), pp. 79–97; E. Mansfield and J. Snyder, 'Democratisation and the danger of war', *International Security*, 20:1 (1995), pp. 5–38; J. Snyder, *From Voting to Violence: Democratisation and Nationalist Conflict* (New York: Norton, 2000).

2   See for instance T. Clifton Morgan, 'Domestic structure, decisional constraints and war: So why Kant democracies fight?', *Journal of Conflict Resolution*, 35:2 (1991), pp. 187–211; C. Laynce, 'Kant or can't: The myth of the democratic peace', *International Security*, 19:2 (1994), pp. 5–49; R. Cohen, 'Pacific unions: A reappraisal of the theory that democracies do not go to war with one another', *Review of International Studies*, 20:3 (1994), pp. 207–23.

3   T. Kuzio, 'Transition in post-communist states: Triple or quadruple?', *Politics*, 21:3 (2001), pp. 168–77.

4   See for example A. Dukalskis, 'Stateness problems or regime unification? Explaining obstacles to democratization in Burma/Myanmar', *Democratization*, 16:5 (2009), pp. 945–68.

5   R. A. Dahl, *Polyarchy: Participation and Opposition* (New Haven: Yale University Press, 1972).

6   For instance, F. Zakaria, 'The rise of illiberal democracies', *Foreign Affairs*, 76:6 (1997), pp. 22–43; J. Herbst, 'Political liberalisation in Africa after 10 years', *Comparative Politics*, 33:3 (2001), pp. 357–75; L. Diamond, 'Thinking about hybrid regimes', *Journal of Democracy*, 13:2 (2002), pp. 21–35; S. Levitsky and L. Way, 'The rise of competitive authoritarianism', *Journal of Democracy*, 13:2 (2002), pp. 51–64; A. Schedler, 'The menu of manipulation', *Journal of Democracy*, 13:2 (2002), pp. 36–51; P. H. Smith and M. R. Zeigler, 'Liberal and illiberal democracy in Latin America', *Latin American Politics and Society*, 50:1 (2008), pp. 31–57.

7   On norm cascades see M. Finnemore and K. Sikkink's seminal 'International norm dynamics and political change', *International Organisation*, 52:4 (1998), pp. 887–917. For norm diffusion see A. Acharya, 'How ideas spread: Whose norms matter? Norm localisation and institutional change in Asian regionalism', *International Organisation*, 58:2 (2004), pp. 239–57; J. Prantl and R. Nakano, 'Global norm diffusion in East Asia: How China and Japan implement the Responsibility to Protect', *International Relations*, 25:2 (2011), pp. 243–58. For simple (and simplistic) definitions, see F. Gilardi, 'Transnational Diffusion: Norms, Ideas and Policies' in W. Carlsnaes, T. Risse and B. Simmonds (eds), *Handbook of International Relations* (Thousand Oaks: Sage, 2012), pp. 453–77.

8   M. Kaldor, *New and Old Wars: Organised Violence in a Global Era* (Cambridge: Polity, 2nd edn, 2006). See also M. Shaw, *War and Genocide: Organised Killing in Modern Society* (Cambridge: Polity, 2003); M. Shaw, 'War and Globality: The Role and Character of War in the Global Transition', in H-W. Yeong (ed.), *The New Agenda for Peace Research* (Aldershot: Ashgate, 1999).

9   Kaldor, *New and Old Wars*, 2006, p. 37.

10 See D. Held, 'Democracy: From city-states to a cosmopolitan order', *Political Studies*, 40 (1992), pp. 10–39; M. Kaldor, *Human Security: Reflections on Globalisation and Intervention* (Cambridge: Polity, 2007).

11 M. McFaul, 'Russia's "Privatized" State as an impediment to democratic consolidation: Part I', *Security Dialogue*, 29:2 (1998), pp. 25–33.

12 S. White, R. Rose and I. McAllister, *How Russia Votes* (Chatham: Chatham House Publishers, 1996). See especially p. 183 on the formation and abandonment of parties.

13 The evidence in favour of such commissions is mixed. See M. Ben-Josef Hirsch and M. Mackenzie, 'Measuring the impacts of truth and reconciliation commissions: Placing the global "success" of TRCS in local perspective', *Cooperation and Conflict*, 47:3 (2012), pp. 386–403.

14 A medical definition of the term: http://medical-dictionary.thefreedictionary.com/ (accessed 12 April 2014).

15 J. Linz and A. Stepan, *Problems of Democratic Transition and Consolidation: Southern Europe, South America and Post-Communist Europe* (Baltimore: Johns Hopkins University Press, 1996). See especially p. 6 which refers to a democratic regime being consolidated when 'no significant national, economic, social, political or institutional actors spend significant resources attempting to achieve their objectives by [turning] to violence'.

16 Such was the case, for instance, during the breakup of Yugoslavia in the 1990s, and also in relation to the industrialised heartland of eastern Ukraine during the crisis with Russia in 2014.

17 See for instance M. C. Williams, 'Words, images, enemies: Securitization and international politics', *International Studies Quarterly*, 47:3 (2004), pp. 511–31.

18 B. Coppieters, 'The politicisation and securitisation of ethnicity: The case of the southern Caucasus', *Civil Wars*, 4:4 (2001), pp. 73–94.

19 See B. Kernen and M. Sussex, 'The Russo-Georgian War: Identity, intervention and norm adaptation', in M. Sussex (ed.), *Conflict in the Former USSR* (Cambridge: Cambridge University Press, 2012), p. 82.

20 The use of the term is commonplace. For context, see the address by Tommy Koh, then Singapore's Ambassador to the US, at a series of lectures at Stanford University in 1995. Available at: http://news.stanford.edu/pr/95/950417Arc5282.html (accessed 20 April 2014).

21 See C. Layne, 'The War on Terrorism and the Balance of Power: The Paradoxes of American Hegemony', in T. V. Paul, J. Wirtz and M. Fortmann (eds), *Balance of Power: Theory and Practice in the Twenty-first Century* (Stanford: Stanford University Press, 2004), pp. 103–27. See also D. Kang, 'Why China's rise will be peaceful: Hierarchy and stability in the East Asian region', *Perspectives on Politics*, 3:5 (2005), pp. 551–4; and R. Powell, 'The inefficient use of power: Costly conflict with complete information', *American Political Science Review*, 98:5 (2004), pp. 633–48.

22 On the Regional Security Community, see its primary tomes by B. Buzan and O. Waever, *Regions and Powers: The Structure of International Security* (Cambridge: Cambridge University Press, 2003); B. Buzan, O. Waever and J. de Wilde, *Security: A New Framework for Analysis* (Boulder: Lynne Reinner, 1997).

23 Paul *et al.*, *Balance of Power*, p. 113.

24 J. Mearsheimer, *The Tragedy of Great Power Politics* (New York: W. W. Norton, 2001).

25 See, for example, J. McMillan, R. Sokolsky and A. C. Winner, 'Toward a new regional security architecture', *Washington Quarterly*, 23:2 (2004), pp. 161–75.

26 R. Sakwa, *Putin Redux: Power and Contradiction in Contemporary Russia* (New York: Routledge, 2013). See especially his chapter on 'Putin's Constitutional Coup' of 2004, and pp. 112–14.

27 *Izvestiya* (2 January 1992), p. 3.

28 See the article by S. Stankevich in *Rossiskaya Gazeta* (23 June 1992), p. 1.

29 For a good summary of events, see R. Sharlet, 'Russian constitutional crisis: Law and politics under Yeltsin', *Post-Soviet Affairs*, 9:4 (1993), pp. 314–36.

30 Sharlet, 'Russian constitutional crisis', pp. 314–36.

31 S. White, 'Russia: Presidential Leadership under Yeltsin', in R. Taras (ed.), *Postcommunist Presidents* (Cambridge: Cambridge University Press, 1997), pp. 57–61.

32 See for instance the special event held by the National Endowment for Democracy on the theme 'Putin versus civil society'. Available at: www.ned.org/events/putin-vs-civil-society (accessed 10 April 2014). See also L. Aron, 'Putin versus civil society: The long struggle for freedom', *Journal of Democracy*, 24:3 (2013), pp. 62–74.

33 For some of Khasbulatov's thoughts on the violence, see T. De Waal, 'Khasbulatov's Mixed Omens', *Moscow Times* (10 January 1994), available at: www.themoscowtimes.com/news/article/khasbulatovs-mixed-omens/211888.html (accessed 15 April 2014).

34 See P. Shearman and M. Sussex, 'Globalisation, "New Wars" and the War in Chechnya', in R. Sakwa (ed.), *Chechnya: From Past to Future* (London: Anthem, 2005), pp. 199–221.

35 T. Heleniak, 'Regional distribution of the Muslim population of Russia', *Eurasian Geography and Economics*, 47:4 (2006), pp. 426–8.

36 For details, see P. Shearman and M. Sussex, 'The roots of Russian conduct', *Small Wars and Insurgencies*, 20:2 (2009), pp. 251–75 (especially pp. 255–7).

37 A. Higgins, G. Chazan and G. White, 'How Russia's Chechen quagmire became a front for radical Islam', *Wall Street Journal* (16 September 2004), available at http://www.wsj.com/articles/SB109528796620919041 (accessed 18 January 2015).

38 M. Sussex, 'Beslan's lessons: Is pre-emption better than cure?', *Australian Journal of International Affairs*, 58:3 (2004), pp. 414–18.

39 S. Karush, 'Local Chechens fear being scapegoats, again', *Moscow Times* (10 August 2000), p. 12.

40 Amnesty International, 'What Justice for Chechnya's Disappeared?' (23 May 2007), available at: http://web.amnesty.org/library/print/ENGEUR460152007 (accessed 15 April 2014). See also the report in the *Jamestown Foundation Chechnya Weekly*, 8:21 (2007). On displacement figures see M. Holland, 'Chechnya's internally displaced and the role of Russian non-governmental organisations', *Journal of Refugee Studies*, 17:3 (2004), pp. 334–46.

41 *New York Times*, 'Drive to impeach Russian president dies in parliament' (16 May 1999), available at: www.nytimes.com/1999/05/16/world/drive-to-impeach-russian-president-dies-in-parliament.html (accessed 10 April 2014).

42 See the report in the *Independent*, 'Chechnya rocks Yeltsin's rule in peril', *Independent* (1 January 1995), available at: www.independent.co.uk/news/world/chechnya-rocks-yeltsins-rule-in-peril-1566236.html (accessed 28 March 2014).

43 All-Russia Centre for Public Opinion (VTsIOM), 1993–2000, available at: www.wciom.com/index.php?id=58 (accessed 30 March 2014).

44 BBC News, 'Putin takes over as Yeltsin resigns' (31 December 1999), available at: http://news.bbc.co.uk/onthisday/hi/dates/stories/december/31/newsid_4102000/4102107.stm (accessed 15 April 2014).

45 J. Strauss, 'Putin's language is becoming the talk of the vulgar', *Telegraph* (8 November 2003), available at: www.telegraph.co.uk/news/uknews/1446241/Putins-language-is-becoming-the-talk-of-the-vulgar.html (accessed 15 April 2014).

46 The Babitsky case was raised in the US Senate on 4 May 2000, with a subsequent referral to the Committee on Foreign Affairs. The text of the resolution is available at: www.gpo.gov/fdsys/pkg/BILLS-106sres303is/html/BILLS-106sres303is.htm (accessed 10 April 2014).

47 Human Rights Watch, 'Extremist legislation in Russia', 18 August 2006.

48 See J. Koehn, 'Putin's reforms and Russia's governors', *Kennan Institute, Woodrow Wilson Centre*, 16 October 2001, available at: www.wilsoncenter.org/publication/putins-reforms-and-russias-governors (accessed 28 March 2014).

49 For a much more comprehensive evaluation, see M. Evangelista, 'Ingushetia as a microcosm of Putin's reforms', *Program on New Approaches to Russian Security (PONARS)*, Policy memo 346, November 2004.

50 Evangelista, 'Ingushetia as a microcosm of Putin's reforms'.

51 See Z. Brzezinski, 'An agenda for NATO', *Foreign Affairs* 88 (2009), pp. 2–20; B. Nygren, *The Rebuilding of Greater Russia: Putin's Foreign Policy Toward the CIS Countries* (London: Routledge, 2007), p. 131. For a full analysis see M. Sussex, 'The Shape of the Security Order in the Former USSR', in M. Sussex (ed.), *Conflict in the Former USSR* (Cambridge: Cambridge University Press, 2012), pp. 29–45.

52 See C. Ziegler, 'The Russian diaspora in Central Asia: Russian compatriots and Russian foreign policy', *Demokratizatsia*, 14:1 (2007), pp. 103–26.

53 R. Sakwa, 'Great Powers and Small Wars in the Caucasus' in Sussex (ed.), *Conflict in the former USSR*, p. 49.

54 Sakwa, 'Great Powers and Small Wars in the Caucasus', p. 49.

55 For details see M. Barabanov, 'The August War between Russia and Georgia', *Moscow Defense Briefs*, 1:16 (2009).

56 C. Sweeney, 'Georgian rebel confidence grows after fighting', *Reuters* (13 August 2008).

57 BBC News, 'Russia scales down Georgia toll' (20 August 2008), available at: http://news.bbc.co.uk/2/hi/europe/7572635.stm (accessed 30 March 2014).

58 R. McDermott, 'Black cats in a dark room: Moscow's denials of military involvement in Eastern Ukraine', *Jamestown Foundation Eurasia Daily Monitor*, 11:75 (2014), available at www.jamestown.org/single/?tx_ttnews%5Bswords%5D=8fd5893941d69d-0be3f378576261ae3e&tx_ttnews%5Bany_of_the_words%5D=torture&tx_ttnews%5Bpointer%5D=3&tx_ttnews%5Btt_news%5D=42255&tx_ttnews%5Bbac kPid%5D=7&cHash=f83cd2487c1692e169c74c5426e8244f#.VAWbtksqYds (accessed 14 April 2014).

59 A. Cohen, 'Russia's Eurasian Union could endanger the neighborhood and U.S. Interests', *The Heritage Foundation*, available at: www.heritage.org/research/reports/2013/06/russias-eurasian-union-could-endanger-the-neighborhood-and-us-interests (accessed 14 April 2014).

60 For the BBC interview with Sergei Lavrov, in which he made this claim, see the Russian Federation Ministry of Foreign Affairs website, which also includes a transcript. Available at: www.mid.ru/brp_4.nsf/0/F87A3FB7A7F669EBC32574A100262597 (accessed 10 April 2014).

5

Crimea as a Eurasian pivot in 'Arc of Conflict': managing the great power relations trilemma

Graeme P. Herd

As THE international strategic landscape evolves, with power shifting ever more rapidly from the US and Western Europe to East Asia, the continued viability of existing cooperative security governance frameworks is being brought into question. As the Permanent Secretary of Singapore's Ministry of Foreign Affairs put it, 'A global transition of power and ideas is under way. Transition to what, no one can yet say. We have no maps and will have to improvise our way forward the best we can'.[1] Charles Kupchan notes that an unstable multipolar order has emerged after US withdrawal from a bipolar and then unipolar order, and argues that transitional multipolar orders especially, are volatile. As Kupchan recently commented, the end of the US era was not only the end of US primacy, nor a return to multiple power centres. It was also 'the end of the era that America has played such a large role in shaping – the era of industrial capitalism, republican democracy, and the nation-state'.[2] The accelerated power shift to East Asia, as well as regime instability in Tunisia, Egypt, Libya, Syria and the other implications of the Arab Spring all provide an immediate strategic context within which states will need to adapt or fail. Gideon Rachman of the *Financial Times* concludes: 'If neither the United States nor some form of world government can provide the leadership to tackle the world's common political problems, then a third alternative will emerge, with China and Russia spearheading an "axis of authoritarianism"'.[3]

There is some credence, then, in the claim that disorder is the new order. This has the potential to produce a 'G-Zero world' in which no global leadership is in evidence. Since no single country or bloc possesses either the political or economic leverage that can produce a global agenda, uncertainty and conflict is the norm. This applies to international economic coordination as well as trade policy, and even issues such as climate change. There is also no global consensus on strategy. A Bretton Woods II agreement – with a reformed International Monetary Fund, World Bank, and UN Security Council – has not been agreed upon. This global power vacuum is the product of a lack of self-confidence amongst European states, as well as a lack of strategic clarity in the US. The sprawling size of the G-20 underscores both the loss of European power (the G-8 consists of five European states while the G-20 includes six European countries and the European Commission) but also accounts for the consequent lack of shared values of its members. China, India and Brazil are unwilling to bear the financial and political costs of growing international responsibilities. The resultant power vacuum, as Ian Bremmer convincingly argues, will benefit some governments, institutions and companies that can adapt in a leaderless world. Turkey and Brazil, for example, are best placed to pivot to new markets, allies and partners as necessity demands.[4]

This chapter investigates the potential for the new disorder in the context of a specific geographical locus: Crimea. It is in this historical pivot-point that relations between great powers will be most significantly tested, and here that one finds political, economic and security quandaries that are best conceptualised in terms of a 'trilemma'.[5] This occurs in terms of competing themes of democracy, self-determination and economic globalisation. My contention is that managing each of these three themes will be a difficult task in general, and virtually impossible where the major power centres of the post-unipolar world ultimately meet. Accordingly I examine the preconditions for Russian involvement in Crimea, the instruments it employed, its normative justifications for doing so, and the domestic and foreign policy gains it sought to engender. I then turn to an analysis of Security Sector Reform (SSR) and Security Sector Governance in the broader Central Asian space in order to demonstrate that the trilemma between the US and Russia will continue to deepen.

Understanding trilemmas in contemporary world politics

A trilemma occurs when policy-makers are faced with three desirable objectives but find that only two of the three can be combined. In other words, one objective has to give. In financial terms, for example, a monetary policy trilemma suggests a stark trade-off among exchange stability, monetary independence, and capital market openness. Rodrik Dani, author of *The Globalization Paradox*, identifies a 'fundamental political trilemma' of the global economy that shapes contemporary security and stability, namely the notion that although democracy, self-determination and globalisation are key contemporary dynamics, only two can exist in conjunction and harmony. If democratic governance is the goal then either a state can embrace national sovereignty or democracy, but not both. In this example, fuller globalisation demands sacrificing the democratic political process of the state.[6]

Contemporary modernisation projects/pathways have certain recurrent core characteristics that engender legitimacy and so lead to sustainability. These include democracy (with attributes such as self-determination, transparency, human rights, freedom); stability (understood in terms of security, safety or peace); and prosperity (through economic growth and markets). Yet some states in this arc of instability support stability and prosperity but are not democratic. This raises the question: will democratic processes and practices gradually grow within a garden of stability and prosperity? At the same time, other states exhibit stability and democracy, but not prosperity. Hence the question becomes how long might they remain stable and/or democratic without prosperity? Others still enjoy prosperity and democracy but not stability. This gives rise to the question of how much instability is needed to derail attempts to consolidate democratic transitions? On current indications, debtor democracies may become more dependent on creditor autocracies, such as China. Hence one must also consider whether democracies are dysfunctional relative to state capitalist and other authoritarian political systems.

Turning to warfare, Lorenzo Zambernardi has identified the trilemma of counter-insurgency, in which it is impossible to simultaneously protect one's own forces, distinguish between combatants and non-combatants, and eliminate insurgents.[7] In his 2012 Annual Report, NATO's Secretary General Anders Fogh Rasmussen wrote of an 'arc of instability' stretching from the Sahel to Central Asia. Since then, following civil war in Iraq with the Islamic State of Iraq and Syria's (ISIS) attempted creation of an Islamic caliphate,[8] instability has proliferated. The worsening of civil war in Syria, Israeli-Hamas rocket launches and growing fears of spill-overs following the International Security Assistance Force's withdrawal from Afghanistan have all combined to reinforce the notion of a strategic agenda characterised by armed conflict involving new types of violence.

Such violence is connected to regional crises, fragile states, political extremism, terrorism and proliferation and looks set to shape the global conflict strategic agenda for the next twenty to thirty years. New tactics to counter such instabilities involve cyber warfare, drones, special forces and proxy forces on the ground that would maintain lethality while generating a 'light footprint doctrine'. These are encapsulated by the notions of 'leading from behind' and 'leading from the air'.[9] If successful, such a doctrine would be enabled by new types of cooperative partnerships, with new divisions of labour, ownership compacts and burden sharing.

Yet a trilemma is embedded in this paradigm, especially with respect to recent US–Russian rivalry. On the one hand, the US and Russia seek to maintain the great power truce and avoid a great power conflict. But at the same time, Russia seeks to undermine US hegemony and consolidate itself as an independent pole in a multipolar world. And a third complicating factor is that Russia's strategy of *maskirovka* or 'disguised warfare' is increasingly unsustainable in a globalised and technologically advanced world. Events in Crimea and eastern Ukraine highlight the nature of this trilemma.

An autopsy of Russia's annexation of the region should ideally identify the major factors that are relevant to understanding its significance. In this chapter I examine five of these key themes. First, what were the necessary preconditions for Russian action in Crimea during 2014? Second, what tools or capabilities did Russia employ in order to act? Third, what norms, values and beliefs did Russia invoke to legitimate its position? Fourth, what were the domestic gains? Fifth, what were the foreign policy benefits? The answers to these questions can help answer whether these factors are unique to Crimea and eastern Ukraine or whether they resonate elsewhere in former Soviet space. If the latter, the prospects for a deepened trilemma with the US are enhanced.

Russia's *maskirovka* model: an autopsy of the annexation of Crimea

The dominant Western narrative about Russia's annexation of Crimea in 2014 is centred on a number of questionable assumptions. To begin with, it assumes the revolution that toppled the corrupt (and yet nonetheless democratically elected) Viktor Yanukovych from power in 2013 was inherently good since it was an expression of democracy. Second, it assumes that Vladimir Putin was the puppet master pulling the Ukrainian President's strings, and that hence Russian motivations for annexing Crimea were opportunistic, aimed at recreating a 'greater Russia'. Third, it assumes that the West was merely trying to assist Ukraine to make a peaceful transition towards greater association with the EU. However, each of these is regarded as deeply flawed by Russian observers. To begin with, there was a strong Ukrainian ultranationalist presence in the events of Maidan Square in Kiev, as well as indications that Ukraine's Right Forces bloc had some involvement with the use of force against protesters, in order to trigger a crisis. Faced with a situation in which the Far Right would swiftly move towards the EU, crossing one of Russia's 'red-lines' regarding Western encroachment in its sphere of influence, Moscow had little option but to act in Crimea. This was especially since the symbolic but nonetheless important Russian Black Sea Fleet at Sevastopol would have been an inevitable casualty of the Ukrainian transition, not to mention potentially the many ethnic Russians living in Crimea and the eastern industrialised Donbas region. And finally, Russian commentators have pointed out that the EU was in fact forcing Ukraine to choose between an Association Agreement and Putin's proposed framework for regional integration, rather than permitting it to be a part of both. While the truth with respect to these competing narratives is probably somewhere in the middle, it is certainly the case that Russian accounts of the lead-up to a move into Crimea are difficult to reject out of hand.

Moreover, Russian moves in Crimea were heavily influenced by years of disenchantment with Western security policies, which Moscow feels – rightly or wrongly – to be deliberately exclusionary, and following old power structures rather than adapting to post-Cold War realities. From Moscow's perspective, the European security system is characterised by NATO-centric dominance and balance-of-power Cold War 'bloc mentalities' which the West has yet to over-come. Russia had been excluded from strategic decision-making in Europe and felt that unless it acted with force to uphold its legitimate state interests it would simply be ignored. These interests were partly institutional, currently being pursued through Putin's Eurasian Union. They were also related to identity, as Russia's conservative modernisation within a Greater Russian space takes shape. Finally, they were shaped by domestic and elite preferences for a strong executive authority within a 'sovereign democracy'. But even though bipolarity has ended, Russia's relations with NATO have been marred by a continued Cold War paradigm. According to this perspective this accounted for the survival of Cold War alliance structures such as NATO, the mentalities of its members and provided reflexive Soviet benchmarks through which actions of the Russian Federation would be viewed. As a result, Russia views NATO as a threat, par-ticularly with regards to missile defence and the perception of its ability to com-promise its own strategic second strike capability.

According to NATO it was Russia itself, as the legal successor state to the Soviet Union, that continued to perceive of NATO as an 'aggressive bloc', while NATO member states attempted to reformulate the alliance as an engine of democratic security building in central and eastern Europe. Following this annexation of Crimea, Russia–NATO relations have reached a nadir. As NATO's Deputy Secretary General stated: 'Clearly the Russians have declared NATO as an adversary, so we have to begin to view Russia no longer as a partner but as more of an adversary than a partner'.[10] As Rasmussen put it:

> We have seen Russia rip up the international rulebook. President Putin and his government have tried to change borders at the barrel of a gun. They have actively subverted the government of a neighbouring state. And they have proclaimed a right to limit the sovereignty of territories which have at some point in history been part of Russia, or where large Russian-speaking communities live. All these actions call into question fundamental principles that Russia subscribed to, and they put at risk the post-Cold War order that we have built with such effort together with Russia, not against it.[11]

Such a view runs directly counter to Russia's own self-image. Russia represents a state that has significant influence as a European player but remains margin-alised and perceives itself to be unfairly victimised by the West, which is unwill-ing to take Russia's legitimate interests into account. Moscow neither trusts the West nor believes Russia has received (or currently receives) the respect it deserves. It is a key European actor of three hundred years standing, since the Treaty of Nystadt (1721), which saw the defeat of Sweden in the Great Northern War. The lack of trust can be attributed to perceived double standards

and hypocrisy regarding Western interventions or approaches to possible interventions in Kosovo, Iraq, Libya and Syria.

The preconditions for Russian action

Putin's strategy in Crimea was one of increasingly (im)plausible deniability, with
a highly coordinated 'citizen's militia' that lacked any unit markings, but had all
the bearing of professional Russian combat forces. The thinking in Moscow was
that as long as it could create sufficient doubt about its role, an occupation could
be swiftly accomplished and then presented as a *fait accompli*. But this was not a
knee-jerk response. Indeed, broader social and political preconditions needed to
be met in order for such a policy line to be pursued. The key lesson here is that
history mattered in Russia's decision to annex Crimea. Ancestral memories of
1812, 1919 and 1941 still influence the Russian collective psyche, as do enduring myths in Russian political discourse centred on NATO's broken promises.
So too does the fact that Russia has only been a nation-state – as opposed to the
centre of an empire – since 1991.

Central to President Putin's foreign policy philosophy is the notion of Russia
as a resurgent great power, with the country rescued under his leadership from
the dustbin of history. Power-shifts and the rise of non-Western centres of global
authority and influence promote the emergence of a multipolar world with
Russia as one of the independent poles and thus a key actor in global decision-
making. Given the relative decline of the US, Russia sees itself as a power that is
now firmly on the 'right side of history'. Whereas the Five Day War with Georgia
in 2008 over South Ossetia and Abkhazia served as a Kremlin 'red-line' warning
to NATO concerning its eastward expansion, the recent conflict in Ukraine is
directly attributable to this new-found sense of Russian confidence. And despite
Western misinterpretations of his domestic standing as based on radicalised
nationalism, Putin is seen at home as a moderate. He is also genuinely popular,
regarded as having restored a Russian sense of *Derzhavnost* (thinking and acting
like a great power). In relation to the industrialised Donbass region Putin in
2014 made several references to *novorossiya*: the term used in the 1700s and
1800s to refer to the area of the Black Sea north of Crimea which is currently
part of Ukraine. The increasingly transparent employment of Russian military
power throughout 2014, especially the use of T-72B1 tanks – which are not
part of the Ukrainian armed forces – was also indicative of a shift away from
plausible deniability and towards more overt intervention.

Russia's confidence in its power is broadly based and rests on its economic
strength. It is one of the top ten global economies (eighth in the world), with the
third largest sovereign wealth fund.[12] With the waning of the West, market-
democratic universalism loses its appeal and the political and economic model
of a 'sovereign democracy' rises.[13] This alternative and, in Russia's view an

increasingly attractive model, is one in which human rights, democracy and humanitarian interventions are subordinated to the stability of government and societies. It is a vision that Moscow has attempted to use as a model for other post-Soviet states in Central Asia to follow, and has also been promoted via soft power and transformational aspects of diplomacy to parts of Southeast Asia, especially Singapore. Underpinning the alternative Russian narrative for political order are its armed forces, which have become increasingly sophisticated since capability gaps were identified during the 2008 conflict with Georgia. The hardware beginning to enter operational service for Russian front-line forces increases the flexibility of its overall posture, permitting doctrinal shifts to take advantage of new capacities. In turn, overlaying its conventional forces, Russia's nuclear triad secures strategic autonomy and stability, and is therefore prized as a core political value.

Understanding this self-image is critical to assessing Russia's actions in Crimea and eastern Ukraine. Three main necessary preconditions for Russian action were present in the case of Crimea. First was the assertion that a collapse of 'legitimate executive authority' had taken place (with President Yanukovich fleeing the country) to be replaced by a far right, neo-Nazi 'junta', as interim authorities in Kiev were characterised in the Russian media and by leading political figures in Russia.[14] Second, Crimea boasted a majority 'ethnic Russian' population, a common language, heritage, and identity, with supportive local elites making up the majority of society with deep local knowledge. Last, Russia had prepositioned military bases and proximate military forces based on Russian territory itself. In relation to its less rapid approach to the separatist movements in Luhansk and Donetsk, a similar justification was used, with the exception that threats to ethnic Russians were securitised even more visibly. Russian assistance was provided to rebels unofficially through access to surface-to-air missile systems, small arms and training, as well as logistical support and training. Later the ranks of Ukrainian separatists were bolstered by Russian troops 'on leave' from their regular assignments. The provision of armour and artillery support also augmented the capabilities of separatist forces, permitting them to undertake more coordinated offensive manoeuvres instead of the hit-and-run tactics characteristic of operations conducted by militia and guerrilla units.

Tools and capabilities

The tools and capabilities Russia needed to act can also be understood as threefold. First, Russian media propaganda provided a one-sided but compelling narrative of Western hypocrisy, double standards, and interference in the domestic affairs of Ukraine, resulting in chaos and the potential for spillover into Russia.[15] Second, Putin had the 'political will' to act and was supported by compliant state institutions such as the Duma and Constitutional Court. Third, strategic directives from the Kremlin were translated into action by Russian military intelligence exercising operational control through local paramilitaries (*Samoobrona*), who were members of the separatist 'Self-Defence Force' on the ground. They were supported by Russian Special Forces, who were euphemistically referred to as 'little men in green'.

The role of such forces is highly contested. Is the conflict in eastern Ukraine *maskirovka*, in which so-called instruments of humanitarian and social war technology are utilised? Does such new-generation warfare use psychological warfare, intimidation, bribery and propaganda to undermine resistance to the point that firepower is not needed? Do 'polite, little green men', Special Forces, paramilitaries and local elites act in a coordinated manner in opposition to the centre? Edward Lucas argues that a new generation warfare is moving away from the scripted rhetoric-kinetic sequence characterised by 'ultimatums, declarations of war, invasions, counterattacks, second and third fronts, and finally a negotiated surrender, payment of reparations and a new territorial settlement'.[16] The new trend, he argues, is invasion by stealth. The point here is to use psychological warfare, intimidation, bribery, and propaganda to undermine resistance to the point that firepower is not needed:

> First is to prepare the ground – or rather, to tilt the playing field – by a mixture of economic, political, diplomatic and psychological pressure. Next come operations to confuse the already weakened political and military leadership of the targeted country, with leaks and disinformation to degrade their decision-making abilities ... Third comes intimidation and bribery so that state officials do not carry out their orders and duties ... Fourth is destabilising tactics aimed at the population, using propaganda to whip up discontent among the population, and groups of trained provocateurs (who may be intelligence officers, private contractors, or political activists). Fifth come blockades, perhaps in the form of no-fly zones, or on the ground with the siege and occupation ... of military bases and government buildings. Sixth are cyber-attacks, covert deployment of special forces, industrial sabotage, intense diplomatic pressure and propaganda aimed at the outside world. Only then does something close to old-style warfare break out, with (seventh) the use of precision munitions, but also those based on electro-magnetic radiation and non-lethal biological weapons. The eighth phase is to eliminate remaining points of resistance – identified by special forces and then attacked with advanced weapons and if necessary airborne assault.[17]

John R. Schindler, a former National Security Agency counterintelligence officer who currently teaches at the Naval War College, characterises such actions as 'special war'. In such circumstances, strategy is 'an amalgam of espionage, subversion, even forms of terrorism to attain political ends without actually going to war in any conventional sense'.[18] Jacob W. Kipp, an expert on the Russian military and the former deputy director of the US Army's School of Advanced Military Studies at Fort Leavenworth, suggested that the Russian military assumed that civilians were part and parcel of the modern battlefield, rather than a hindrance to operations, and were trained to operate in such tactical environments.[19] By the same token, the US State Department has argued that Russia has been actively seeking to destabilise eastern Ukraine, noting that Russia's actions did not match its rhetoric. The State Department's official assessment was that Russia has provided separatists in the region with heavy weapons, other military equipment and financing, and was an active conduit for militants to freely travel between Russia and Ukraine. It acknowledged that Russia denies this, but noted with some irony that this was exactly what Russia had done during its operations in Crimea – until after the fact. As General Philip M. Breedlove, NATO's top military commander, reported on NATO's website:

> It's hard to fathom that groups of armed men in masks suddenly sprang forward from the population in eastern Ukraine and systematically began to occupy government facilities. It's hard to fathom because it's simply not true. What is happening in eastern Ukraine is a military operation that is well planned and organised, and we assess that it is being carried out at the direction of Russia.[20]

A Russian analysis provides an alternative assessment. For Moscow, so-called 'colour revolutions' themselves are in fact 'camouflaged aggression', a new type of warfare in which the actions of an armed opposition are coordinated by foreign states' military staffs rather than manifestations of inhabitants protesting against authoritarian rule. The actions of separatists in southeast Ukraine can be seen as a kind of 'colour counterrevolution'. The use of covert means, including non-governmental organisations (NGOs), as a feature of contemporary warfare, has been highlighted by Chief of the General Staff of the Russian Armed Forces, Valeriy Gerasimov, who regarded the activities of Greenpeace activists in the Arctic, events in Ukraine as well as in Syria as symptomatic of this tendency. Gerasimov went on to note that 'The reaction time for the transition from political-diplomatic measures to the use of military forces has been maximally reduced. Decisions on the creation, use and support of line-unit groupings are being made in a real-time scale'.[21] Andrey Novikov, the head of the Commonwealth of Independent States' (CIS) Anti-Terrorism Center, also emphasised that some NGOs were using mercenaries in internal social conflicts such as Kyrgyzstan in 2010 and Ukraine in 2014. In addition, NGOs were taking part in training mercenaries as well as financing them, especially with respect to carrying out psychological operations in the field. For Novikov, such NGOs often became more active during the 'ripening' of social conflicts. At the same time, he argued 'the NGOs are often informational cover for the mercenaries' activities. Here we can see a new and very dangerous symbiosis'.[22] Building on this view, Aleksandr Golts, a Moscow-based defence correspondent and participant in a Russian Ministry of Defence 2014 international conference on security issues has noted that:

It transpired that 'colour revolutions' are no more and no less than a new type of warfare. Colour revolutions are increasingly acquiring the form of an armed struggle and are devised in accordance with the rules of warfare, and all available instruments are set in motion in the process ... This rich idea was developed by Valeriy Gerasimov, chief of the General Staff, and Vladimir Zarudnitskiy, chief of the Main Operations Directorate. [It] described a scary scheme for the new type of warfare: To begin with the military potential ... of countries organizing the ousting of an undesirable government is utilized to exert overt pressure on it. The aim of this pressure is to prevent the utilization of security structures to restore law and order. Then, when the opposition initiates military actions against government troops, foreign states provide military and economic aid to the rebels. Thereafter a coalition of countries ... may carry out a military operation with a view to routing government troops and providing assistance to armed opposition forces in seizing power.[23]

Norms and beliefs

In terms of norms, values and beliefs, Russia invoked moral and legal imperatives such as the restoration of stability through support for 'legitimate executive order'[24] in the face of illegitimate Western-backed fascists determined to instigate a pogrom, bloodbath and even genocide. President Putin and Foreign Minister Sergey Lavrov with respect to Crimea and eastern Ukraine expressed a determination to protect co-ethnics and Russophone compatriots from danger.[25] In addition, the notion of righting perceived historical injustice and reuniting historically Russian lands was used to justify intervention.

Not only does political, social, economic and even cultural estrangement from the West provide ideal incubation conditions to nurture this conception, but to repudiate Crimea's annexation would be to undermine Russia's foundational narrative and special mission, its very identity. If the West has been training mercenaries and snipers, and supporting neo-Nazi, anti-Semitic and pogromist far-right fascists in Ukraine (which prominent Duma deputies and serious analysts are at least publically contending), why should Russia be concerned with criticism from such quarters? Rather the opposite, criticism is an indicator of good practice. Lev Gudkov, head of the Levada Centre, has highlighted a two-week-long propaganda and disinformation campaign, unprecedented in post-Soviet times, aimed at manipulating public opinion. It is built on several simple ideas and techniques. These include the identification of the infringement of rights of Russian and Russian-speaking populations, a threat to their wellbeing and lives. It also discredited the supporters of Euro-Maidan, labelling them bandits, Nazis and Banderites. This has ensured a negative mobilisation of a greater part of the Russian society, reviving its dormant imperial complexes.[26]

More generally, Russia has often utilised legalistic arguments in favour of its campaign to return what it sees as its former territory to the new Russian sphere. It did so in 2008 during the conflict with Georgia over South Ossetia, when Lavrov stated without noticeable irony that Russia was invoking the 'Responsibility to Protect' doctrine to defend ethnic Russians. Using the West's norms against it, in a way that China has also done with respect to the Uighurs in Xinjiang province, has provided an alternative narrative to that proffered by the 'global' human rights regime, dominated as it is by Eurocentric notions of individualism. In addition to this, the notion of 'sovereign democracy' establishes a point of demarcation with both the EU and US, with Moscow articulating a specific ideological vision for a reconstructed post-Soviet identity. This is a project that had been languishing for many years prior to Putin taking office, as the Russian Federation emerged from the collapse of the USSR, and the attendant destruction of a unifying national idea.[27] And as Timothy Snyder argues: 'Eurasia was meant from the beginning as an ideological and political rival to the European Union, not just something that sits next to it and has a similar name. It is based on opposite principles – not the support of liberal principles but opposition to liberal democracy'.[28]

In this way, norms and values expressed by Russia in its campaign to liberate Crimea revolved very much around the twin ideas of perceived historical injustice and the requirement for Russia to be a great power in order to ensure regional peace and stability. Coupled to attendant notions of legal-normative justifications for Russian territorial expansion, as well as accusations of Western hypocrisy in permitting the rise to prominence of a Ukrainian government dominated by the far right, the Russian legitimation effort is statist in character, but notionally humanitarian in aspiration. The aim is to lock the West into an ideational pincer between nationhood and law, where support for Moscow's adversaries is characterised as one-sided and deliberately vexatious. This has flow-on effects on both the domestic level and international level.

Domestic gains

With regards to domestic gains for Russia, the benefits of annexing Crimea are numerous. First, Putin has carefully calibrated Russian action that can demonstrate military and national power in order to mobilise and consolidate his oligarchic and *siloviki* support base, as well as harness a real conservative rebound in society in support of the regime, and so maintain and enhance his legitimacy and the legitimacy of the system.[29] Domestic political 'consolidation' – a further tightening of the screws – can now be justified as a necessary response to Western sanctions and in opposition to Western values, norms and beliefs, propagated in Russia by an unpatriotic '5th column' and 'national traitors'.[30] One examination of intra-elite politics in Russia notes: 'Like a 17th-century tsar, Mr Putin needs to maintain a rough balance among various business clans, preventing them from fighting each other and posing a threat to his own ultimate authority'.[31] Putin's regime, theoretically in power until 2024, can become 'anti-fragile' and resilient. Continuous short, victorious virtual or actual wars/ crises with consequent external reactions maintain regime legitimacy as domestic economic performance stalls due to a falling industrial and economic base on the cusp of authoritarian stagnation. Such a foreign policy further squeezes a minority entrepreneurial and creative class unable to function at home in the face of a state-sponsored 'sovereign democracy' ideology morphed into triumphalist conservative nationalism, in the context of an ongoing chronic state of emergency.

Second, Russia has instrumentalised the Ukrainian crisis to consolidate its wider conception of an alternative conservative national patriotic domestic order. Russia has framed Ukraine's crisis in terms of a contest between rival civilisational models that rest on different norms, values and beliefs – Russia invests itself as a bearer of alternative values it is prepared to defend, with force if necessary: 'The country's conservative rebound is real. The question is the degree to which he [Putin] can manipulate social change'.[32] Under those conditions, 'Orthodoxy, Autocracy, Nationality' becomes the neo-traditional state dogma – fuelled by paranoia and populism. Russia understands itself as leading an ideological alliance of states that privilege ultra-conservative traditional family values and respect for authority above the relativist liberal values of a morally bankrupt West.[33]

Russia has therefore moved from a soft vision of Europe (via the failed 'Medvedev Initiative' – a legally binding collective security treaty)[34] to hard division via the use of undeclared military force with impunity in response to what Russians see as the West's *de facto* and *de jure* refusal to end the Cold War. The EU is viewed through a zero-sum prism, with the EU's Association Agreement declared incompatible with Russia's Eurasian Union. Increased antagonism towards NATO as a strategic adversary helps reinforce a besieged fortress mentality and justify a US$770 billion, ten year rearmament and modernisation programme,[35] while virtual/cyber and proxy normative battles with NATO can increase as Russia pressures CIS states to limit Partnerships for Peace military exercises.

At worst Putin calculates that the West will be alienated in the short term, at best that Russian action can divide and highlight splits between states that view Russia as a strategic partner and those that see it as an adversary.[36] This thinking would be informed by Western historical practice, not least the experience of a divided and half-hearted EU and NATO reaction to the Georgia crisis in 2008. Following the global financial crisis, solidarity and shared responsibility are less in evidence since Western states prefer to act according to their own immediate interests and priorities, privileging these above the longer term interest of the preservation of peace in the system. Economic interests and interdependence, whether it be Russian gas (Germany), arms sales (France) or investments (UK), also moderate Western responses. Washington's perceived need to use Moscow's leverage in global strategic hotspots, to act with it in concert to contain the fallout in Syria, and to manage the Iran nuclear dossier or Democratic People's Republic of Korea six-party talks, constrains the backlash. The ability of Russia's public intellectuals to articulate a compelling narrative of moral equivalence shapes an internal perception that Russia is now a free actor in the international system.[37] And though annexation by force on protection of minorities is anathema to China,[38] Russia could still maintain an equality of relations with that state. Indeed, a display of calibrated power would enhance Russia in the eyes of its Asian strategic partner.

Foreign policy benefits

There are two main foreign policy gains from Russia's annexation of Crimea. First, regarding Ukraine, Russia is presented with a geopolitical victory in its ability to 'divide and destabilise' or 'partition and destroy' Ukraine. Nana Gegelashvili, Director of the Centre for Regional Problems at the Russian Academy of Sciences, argues Russia's role as a power broker in the CIS has been reinforced, since;

> Russia, as the successor of the USSR, is still capable of regulating and determining their territorial integrity – the key problem of practically each post-Soviet country. This has a demonstration effect, binding the wider CIS periphery to a dependency relationship with the Russian Federation. It reinforces the notion that it is 'order-producing' and playing a managerial role in the region as a centre of global power.[39]

And it has broader implications in terms of Western norms regarding humanitarian intervention:

> The principle of responsibility to protect is perceived in Russia as nothing more than the efforts by the society of democratic states to reap the benefits of democratic peace theory by means of military intervention. Russia is worried that the West has a pre-established consensus about which side to support in internal conflicts (rebels over non-democratic governments) and that its frequent commitment to regime change leads not to settlement but to the further escalation of conflicts.[40]

Second, Russia can challenge 'North Atlantic interests' and the US's credibility as guarantor of order and NATO as legitimising framework of the US as a European power. The Atlantic order is challenged by Russia's ability to question the territorial status quo that has remained sacrosanct for twenty five years. In doing so it has activated a new confidence in the Russo-phone population. Russian passports provide a security blanket to a potential 100 million ethnic Russians in the CIS.[41] Faced with the example of the Maidan, the Russian Federation now offers a new alternative to local nationalism: majorities in localities can threaten state stability by the renewal of street protests leading to the overthrow of elected presidents.

Russia's actions in Ukraine have also questioned US credibility as a post-Cold War world order guarantor. For example, the US is a signatory to the 1994 Quadrilateral Budapest Memorandum that provides statehood guarantees to Ukraine in return for denuclearisation. The result of the Ukrainian imbroglio is that the Nuclear Non-proliferation Treaty regime is further undermined. Under what circumstances, one might ask, would the Democratic People's Republic of Korea and Iran ever give up a nuclear capability as Ukraine once did? For Russia, weak Western responses are symptomatic of the end of Western-centric structure and order.

In sum the message from Moscow is that the hegemonic status of the West is over. It is no longer the unquestioned bearer of geopolitical order, economic power and military supremacy. From a Russian perspective the unipolar system is harmful – 'the system of distain for the law by the US has exceeded all bounds'.[42] The US imposes its own model of globalisation, economy, policy and culture, and the role of other countries is secondary. But Russia is able to pivot to Asia and so avoid diplomatic isolation and demonstrate that an Asian future is a real alternative to a European past. Finally, as relations with the West deteriorate Russia increasingly will view itself as a free actor in the liberal international system. In other words, it is able to challenge not just the cornerstone of that system – the Atlantic order – but, with support from other states, challenge the wider norms and rules that underpin that system itself.

From Crimea to Central Asian trilemmas and security sector governance: strategic divorce?

What lessons might be drawn from Russia's annexation of Crimea with respect to the nature of contemporary conflict in general, and the specific idea of 'trilemmas' identified earlier in the chapter? There are limits to the Russian challenge to the US and the West, based as it is on a new type of warfare. To begin with, the West has numerous financial, institutional and reputational levers to punish Russian intransigence. So-called 'market deterrence' can close international credit markets forcing Russia to rely on its own state banks. Economic growth will be affected not so much by sanctions but by anti-Western rhetoric. This damages entrepreneurship and encourages capital flight – and hence stagnation and corruption. The narrow legal positivist view Russia took on interventions in Yugoslavia, Iraq, Libya and Syria now looks tactical rather than principled, and Russia has lost the political and moral advantage in doing so. Moreover, the Russian Federation has no grand vision of an alternative to the liberal, capitalist and democratic order led by a US network of alliances, institutions, geopolitical bargains, client states and democratic partnerships. It is also clear that Ukraine constitutes a regional squabble that does not define world politics. The emerging powers are not lined up with the East or West, as in 1956 or 1968, but rather they tend to follow their own interests and priorities.

In the introduction to this chapter it was suggested that a trilemma was at play in this arc of instability that characterised security politics in this region, in which three preferences are identified but only two are possible to achieve at any one time. An examination of contemporary Security Sector Reform (SSR) and Security Sector Governance efforts in Central Asia, coupled to the roles of the UN and the Organization for Security and Cooperation in Europe (OSCE) in driving this agenda highlight the difficulties of navigating this trilemma. As Heiner Hanggi and Fred Tanner put it, security sector governance means simply that 'if we accept the perspective that every issue-area, including military and non-military security, is subject to certain systems of governance on the substate, state or international level, then we arrive at the concept of security governance'.[43] Central to this is that parties in dispute about the threat environment can nonetheless devise ways to manage them cooperatively under a common governance umbrella. But the strategic divorce between Russia and the West (where parties can neither agree the nature of certain strategic threats nor how to address them in a cooperative or at least compatible manner) suggests that the SSR/G agenda will be further politicised. International organisations will be less able to agree common action to best effect, and the power of host states to instrumentalise the engagement of such international organisations will become all the greater.

Obstacles to change continue to matter more than technical modalities or conceptual compatibilities around the delivery of assistance. If host states are unable or unwilling to learn lessons identified, change is circumscribed. This is particularly the case following the crisis in Crimea, where Central Asian states are likely to learn what the West considers to be precisely the wrong lessons. There is a direct relationship between the OSCE and the UN's promotion of SSR/G in Central Asia and political will and enthusiasm of host states to receive and implement it. If the overriding priority of all regimes in Central Asia is political survival – an existential issue – then the interest will be to 'train and equip'. This means the reform and modernisation of the security sector in order to better defend the regime against potential internal civil society protest, rather than in ensuring accountability, transparency and oversight of the security sector to buttress market-democratic consolidation. The start point for all elite-driven national discourses – Kyrgyzstan aside – is that consolidated authoritarian states provide stability and progress while democratisation is associated with chaos and dysfunctionality.[44] As a result, order is privileged over justice and SSR will remain focused on hardware and infrastructure provision. Indeed, although there is no example of successful SSR/G implementation kick-starting systematic political change (which in a neo-patrimonial Central Asia context would entail regime change), there is a perceived danger that effective SSR/G would lead to regime change, and this may also inhibit moving beyond paying lip-service to the concept.

The rhetoric of mutually shared transnational threats like organised crime, religious and political extremism, terrorism, and trafficking is part of the discourse of all states in the region. It is also used by the UN and OSCE to legitimise their engagement in SSR/G, using the logic that shared threats create a cooperative imperative. This discourse heightened by the fear of transnational threat spillovers from a post-International Stabilization Force Afghanistan into Central Asia prevails. Moreover, though Central Asian states may identify the same threats, they do so for different reasons; have different understandings of the nature of the threat and of the desired consequences of action. Significant differences in regime types as well as foreign policy antagonisms (e.g. a Tajik-Uzbek 'Cold War' in which borders are mined and foreign ministers do not meet) undercuts this potential for joint-confidence building action and cooperation.

A transactional analysis (costs + benefits = +/–?) of SSR/G assistance focused on, for example, border assistance programmes would be difficult to determine. At the same time as external assistance (time and money) spent on counter-narcotics trafficking in Central Asia has increased, drug-related violence and seizures have decreased. However, the volume of drugs trafficked has increased. This suggests criminal clans linked to state security sector apparatus have a monopoly or near monopoly on drugs trafficking in Central Asia and that border management assistance programmes are structurally incapable of succeeding. One could conclude that if the OSCE and UN continue to engage in such assistance then corrupted and repressive authoritarian regimes and systems are further criminalised and this process is legitimised by external assistance. Alternatively, the OSCE and UN may find their assistance used to stamp out corruption that is selectively targeted. Lacking sufficient local knowledge, one criminal-state network instrumentalised donor assistance to exert dominance over another. Lastly, were the OSCE and UN to withdraw assistance, this may weaken existing dominant criminal-security sector networks, encourage competition, increase violence and so destabilise societies and states. The OSCE and UN face counter-intuitive credibility traps and have to manage a difficult balance between staying meaningfully engaged without delegitimising themselves through engagement.

Conclusions

Whichever perspective we adopt with regards to the nature of conflict in eastern Ukraine, it is clear that the role of NGOs and civil society – whose participation is vital to meaningful SSR – is central to both understandings. The net effect is to politicise the independence and integrity of such actors, raising suspicion that they may act as proxies for external agents or harbour internal 'national traitors' and '5th columnists'. In Central Asia, where civil society is relatively less developed as a whole relative to other sub-regions in the OSCE space, such thinking and discourse makes even their limited involvement in SSR oversight harder to sustain.

Looking to the future, a 'Eurasian paradox' may provide some room for meaningful engagement. The 'Asia paradox', as defined by South Korea's president, is that as China is the chief trading partner of all Asia-Pacific states, they naturally look to the US as the chief security provider, and in this way create balanced relationships.[45] In Central Asia China now has that dominant trading partner role, the US is withdrawing security provision from the region, and Russia would appear to have its historical role as security provider reinforced. However, a 'champagne effect' following events in Crimea and Ukraine may see Central Asian states move from 'band-wagoning' with Russia to 'balancing' against Russia. This may occur as the norms Russia now evokes to justify intervention engender a nervousness in a region in where succession plans are not elaborated (like Kazakhstan and Uzbekistan) and co-ethnic Russian populations are numerous (Kazakhstan) or super-nationalism remains an ever ready source of legitimation (Uzbekistan). In addition, foreign policy philosophies in all Central Asian states embrace the notion of having a 'multi-vector' foreign policy.

In such circumstances it is possible to imagine that states balance Russia through encouraging deeper engagement with the OSCE and UN, while at the same time aping Russia's determination to crack down on 'national traitors' and '5th columnists'. In this way they would effectively be using Russia's own discourse to contain its soft-power influence in the region. A new paradox for the OSCE and UN emerges: the political will to engage with the West increases, just as the space for such engagement decreases. Under those circumstances all the trilemmas around engagement, legitimacy and power that the conflict in Ukraine made starkly clear would simply resurface in a new guise.

NOTES

1   B. Kausikan, 'The curse of the highly successful', *Straits Times* (28 July 2012).
2   C. A. Kupchan, *The End of the American Era: U.S. Foreign Policy and the Geopolitics of the Twenty-First Century* (New York: Knopf, 2002), p. 303; C. A. Kupchan, 'The democratic malaise: Globalization and the threat to the West', *Foreign Affairs* (1 January 2012), available online at: www.foreignaffairs.com/articles/136783/charles-a-kupchan/the-democratic-malaise (accessed 4 June 2012).
3   G. Rachman, *Zero-Sum Future: American Power in an Age of Anxiety* (New York: Simon and Schuster, 2011), p. 175. See also Kupchan, 'The democratic malaise'.
4   I. Bremmer, 'Every nation for itself: Winners and losers in a G-Zero world', *South China Morning Post* (25 March 2012), p. 15; I. Bremmer, 'The power of the pivot', *International*

Herald Tribune (15 May 2012), p. 6; I. Bremmer and D. Gordon, 'Rise of the different', *International Herald Tribune* (19 June 2012), p. 8.

5   While primarily a term used in economics, the notion of a trilemma has begun to make its way into assessments of security dynamics, especially at multiple levels of analysis. See for instance F. Kuhn, 'Securing Uncertainty: sub-state security dilemma and the risk of intervention', *International Relations*, 25:3 (2011), pp. 363–80. In its classic economic formulation, see also J. Aizenman, 'The impossible trinity: From the policy trilemma to the policy quadrilemma', *Global Journal of Economics*, 2:1 (2013), pp. 1–17.

6   R. Dani, *The Globalization Paradox: Democracy and the Future of the World Economy* (New York: W. W Norton, 2011), pp. xviii–xix.

7   L. Zambernardi, 'Counterinsurgency's impossible trilemma', *The Washington Quarterly*, 3:3 (2010), pp. 21–34.

8   M. Boot, 'The Iraq takeaway', *Los Angeles Times* (1 May 2014), p. 15.

9   J. Diehl, 'US Model – light footprint doctrine: Foreign policy red flags', *Washington Post* (12 November 2012), p. A19; H. LaFranchi, 'Commando raids: Africa's "arc of instability" reorienting US terror map', *Christian Science Monitor* (7 October 2013); J. Stavridis, 'Spectre of religious war looms over Arab world', *Sunday Independent* (22 June 2014), p. 19; M. Ali, 'Inevitable arc of instability', *Arab News* (26 December 2009).

10   D. Boyer, 'NATO allies criticize U.S. for being caught off guard by Russia's military buildup', *Washington Times* (19 March 2014).

11   A. Vershbow, 'Looking towards the Wales Summit', speech to the NATO Defense College, 13 June 2014, available at: www.nato.int/cps/en/natolive/opinions_111056.htm (accessed 16 June 2014).

12   For economic data see the World Bank, 'Russia Overview', available at: www.worldbank. org/en/country/russia/overview (accessed 8 April 2014). Comparable data is also available in *The Economist*, 'Tipping the scales: Russia's economy and the crisis in Ukraine' (3 May 2014), available at: www.economist.com/news/finance-and-economics /21601536-crisis-ukraine-hurting-already-weakening-economy-tipping-scales? (accessed 2 May 2014).

13   On sovereign democracy see R. Sontag, 'The end of sovereign democracy in Russia: What was it, why did it fail, and what should the United States think about this?', Centre on Global Interests, 3 July 2013. See also the views of the editor of the Carnegie Centre's journal: M. Lipman, 'Putin's "sovereign democracy"', *Washington Post* (15 July 2006), available at: www.washingtonpost.com/wp-dyn/content/article/2006/07/14/ AR2006071401534.html (accessed 8 April 2014).

14   For instance *Russia Today*, 'Western media doing Kiev's job in hiding its fascist allegiances' (19 June 2014), available at: http://rt.com/op-edge/166928-western-media-ukraine-fascist/ (accessed 8 April 2014).

15   See also: U. Clauss, 'Putin's trolls go into the propaganda war', *Die Welt* (13 June 2014), p. 7; U. Clauss, J. Eigendorf and G. Gnauck, 'The anatomy of Russian information warfare', *Die Welt* (2 June 2014), p. 8; K. Mashovets, 'To invent in order to win', *Narodna Armiya* (26 April 2014), p. 6; P. Garkauskas, 'Russian propaganda surprised even experienced experts', *Delfi* (31 March 2014).

16   E. Lucas, 'Is NATO ready for Russia's new-generation warfare?', *Lithuanian Tribune* (4 May 2014), available at: www.lithuaniatribune.com/67571/e-lucas-is-nato-ready-for-russias-new-generation-warfare-201467571/ (accessed 8 April 2014).

17   E. Lucas, 'The Russian way of war', *European Voice* (1 May 2014). 'These changes are particularly important from the standpoint of the tactics known as "myatezhnye" [Russian] (mutinous) wars, which Russia is using in eastern Ukraine. There, regular armed forces

have been at a loss to deal with "little green men" – special forces soldiers concealing their identity, appearing as representatives of the local population.' P. Wronski, 'Reserves just in case', *Gazeta Wyborcza* (12 May 2014).

18 J. Schindler, 'How to win Cold War 2.0', *Politico Magazine* (25 March 2014), available at: www.politico.com/magazine/story/2014/03/new-cold-war-russia-104954.html#.VAk_5OsqYds (accessed 8 April 2014).

19 A. Higgins, M. R. Gordon and A. E. Kramer, 'Photos link masked men in Ukraine to Moscow', *International New York Times* (22 April 2014), p. 1. See also R. Kuzniar, 'Putin has grown fond of warfare', *Rzeczpospolita* (8 April 2014), p. A11.

20 US State Department, 'Russia's continuing support for armed separatists in Ukraine and Ukraine's efforts toward peace, unity, and stability', Office of the Spokesperson, 14 July 2014.

21 V. Gerasimov, 'The general staff plans integrated measures for strategic deterrence for the prevention of military conflicts', *Interfax-AVN Military News Agency* (27 January 2014).

22 Interfax News Agency, 'CIS antiterrorism chief says some NGOs training "mercenaries"' (12 April 2014).

23 A. Golts, 'Defence Ministry breathes life into Putin's phantoms', *Yezhednevnyy Zhurnal* (26 May 2014); 'Russian deputy defence minister Anatoliy Antonov attacks NATO in conference speech', *Interfax-AVN Military News Agency* (9 April 2014).

24 'Having fled from Kyiv on 21 February, Viktor Yanukovych headed to Kharkiv for the Party of Regions Congress. There Mr Yanukovych was supposed to say that power in Kyiv had been seized by fascists funded by the West, to proclaim a Donetsk Republic, and to request Russia to send in troops to provide protection against the Western fascists. But the organizers of the putsch chickened out, the congress was a fiasco, and Yanukovych got drunk and flew off to Donetsk in a helicopter.' Y. Latynina, 'The People and Violence', *Yezhednevnyy Zhurnal* (14 April 2014).

25 See for instance J. Solomon and C. Lee, 'How Putin parried Obama's overtures on Crimea', *Wall Street Journal* (19 March 2014), available at: http://online.wsj.com/news/articles/SB10001424052702303563304579447300718769492 (accessed 8 April 2014); K. DeYoung and A. Gearan, 'Putin rebuffs Obama on Ukraine, says Russia cannot ignore calls for help', *Washington Post* (7 March 2014), available at: www.washingtonpost.com/world/national-security/vladimir-putin-rebuffs-obama-on-ukraine-says-russia-cannot-ignore-calls-for-help/2014/03/07/d322cac0-a60c-11e3-84d4-e59b1709222c_story.html (accessed 8 April 2014).

26 The text of this report, in Russian, is available at www.levada.ru/13-03-2014/situatsiya-v-ukraine-i-v-krymu (accessed 10 April 2014); Moscow News, 'Kremlin to tighten screws in wake of Kiev unrest' (24 February 2014).

27 On the lack of a unifying national idea see P. Shearman and M. Sussex, 'The Roots of Russian Conduct', in P. Rich (ed.), *Crisis in the Caucasus: Russia, Georgia and the West* (New York: Routledge, 2013), pp. 1–25.

28 J. Grimston, 'Moscow meddling in Bosnia, says Ashdown', *Australian* (17 March 2014), p. 9.

29 A. Samarina, 'Vladimir Putin's New Majority', *Nezavisimaya Gazeta* (9 October 2012); L. Shevtsova, 'Death throes', *Yezhednevnyy Zhurnal* (5 February 2013); A. Samarina, 'Kremlin's Theory of Strength of Materials', *Nezavisimaya Gazeta* (24 August 2012).

30 A. Kolesnikov, 'A Game of "Zarnitsa"', *Novaya Gazeta* (24 October 2012). Headline alludes to the Soviet-era wargames known as *Zarnitsa*. See also: B. Taylor, 'Putin's Crackdown: Sources, Instruments, and Challenges', Policy Memo 277, 2013, available at: www.

ponarseurasia.org/memo/putin%E2%80%99s-crackdown-sources-instruments-and-challenges (accessed 12 April 2014).

31 C. Belton and C. Clover, 'Putin's people', *Financial Times* (31 May 2012), p. 11.

32 M. Trudolyubov, 'Russia's culture wars', *International New York Times* (8 February 2014), p. 9. See also L. Biryukova *et al.*, 'Spiritual ties to be exported', *Vedomosti* (13 January 2014).

33 T. Snyder, 'Fascism, Russia, and Ukraine', *New York Review of Books* (20 March 2014), available at: www.nybooks.com/articles/archives/2014/mar/20/fascism-russia-and-ukraine/?pagination=false (accessed 28 February 2014).

34 See for instance M. Galeotti, 'A true Medvedev doctrine', *Moscow News* (26 September 2011), available at: http://themoscownews.com/siloviks_scoundrels/20110926/189070681.html (accessed 28 February 2014).

35 W. Pincus, 'Russia's military is the largest in the region, but it isn't the same force as in Soviet times', *Washington Post* (10 March 2014), available at www.washingtonpost.com/world/national-security/russias-military-is-the-largest-in-the-region-but-it-isnt-the-same-force-as-in-soviet-times/2014/03/10/b3b955b8-a48c-11e3-a5fa-55f0c77bf39c_story.html (accessed 8 April 2014).

36 T. Bielecki, 'Force Putin', *Gazeta Wyborcza* (8 March 2014); L. Hadar, 'Will America re-pivot to Europe?', *Business Times Singapore* (12 March 2014).

37 Aleksey Pushkov, chairman of the State Duma's International Affairs Committee, has stated: 'If the West has recognized the Kiev Maydan as "the speaker of the Ukrainian people's will", then it should recognize that the people of Crimea also have the right to express their will.' See https://twitter.com/Alexey_Pushkov/status/438604919395078144 (accessed 26 February 2014); V. Chepurko *et al.*, 'Fedor Lukyanov, political analyst: is February 2014 in Kiev a copy of October 1993 in Russia?', *Komsomolskaya Pravda* (20 February 2014); S. Karaganov, 'Russia needs to defend its interests with an iron fist', *Financial Times* (6 March 2014), p. 13.

38 With regards to Syria, Russia had embraced international legal positivism meaning that only unilateral or collective self-defence (UN Charter Chapter VII) exceptions to the use of force can be countenanced. There is no link between regime legitimacy and external enforcement action; Russia stresses the centrality of the UNSC as rule maker and final arbiter of standards of appropriate behaviour; and sovereignty and territorial integrity are sacrosanct – to be considered absolute rather than qualified – and stability understood to be of necessity a public good. This is still China's discourse, if not Russia's. See R. Allison, 'Russia and Syria: explaining alignment with a regime in crisis?', *International Affairs*, 89:4 (2013), pp. 795–823.

39 N. Gegelashvili, 'Effects of Ukrainian crisis: Georgian dimension', *Politkom.ru* (11 April 2014).

40 Y. Nikitina, 'Russia's Policy on International Interventions: Principle or Realpolitik?', Policy Memo 312, 2014, available at: www.ponarseurasia.org/memo/russia%E2%80%99s-policy-international-interventions-principle-or-realpolitik (accessed 10 April 2014).

41 On passports see B. Kernen and M. Sussex, 'The Russo-Georgian War: Identity, Intervention and Norm Adaptation', in M. Sussex (ed.) *Conflict in the Former USSR* (Cambridge: Cambridge University Press, 2012), pp. 71–93.

42 See Putin's (in)famous Munich Speech of 2007. R. Watson, 'Putin's Munich speech: Back to Cold War?', BBC News (10 February 2007), available at http://news.bbc.co.uk/2/hi/europe/6350847.stm (accessed 28 February 2014).

43 See Heinner Hanggi and Fred Tanner, 'Promoting Security Sector Governance in the EU's Neighbourhood', *Chaillot Papers*, no. 80, Paris, Institute for Security Studies, 2005, p. 12.

On the concepts more broadly see Elke Krahman, 'Conceptualising Security Governance', *Cooperation and Conflict*, 38:1 (2004), pp. 5–26.

44 For a similar argument see N. Robinson, 'Why not more conflict in the former USSR? Russia and Central Asia as a zone of relative peace', in Sussex, *Conflict in the Former USSR*, pp. 114–42.

45 For President Park Guen-Hye's use of the term, see Washington Post, 'South Korea's President presses Japan during US visit' (9 May 2013), available at http://online.wsj.com/news/articles/SB10001424127887324744104578472530440590490 (accessed 10 April 2014).

6

Violence and the contestation of the state after civil wars[1]

Jasmine-Kim Westendorf

HISTORY IS REPLETE with examples of state violence, state-sanctioned violence and violence aimed at the overthrow or defeat of the state. However, the proliferation of civil wars since the end of the Cold War, and the rise of peace settlements as the preferred way of ending them, has given rise to a new phenomenon in nascent post-civil war states, namely pervasive, low-level violence perpetrated by non-state actors that ranges from criminality and lawlessness, to communal violence and electoral violence, and in some cases results in fatality rates similar to during the war.

This chapter examines the function and purpose of such violence in the aftermath of civil wars, with a particular focus on Liberia, South Sudan and Cambodia. These three countries experienced very different civil wars, and their paths to peace were diverse. Yet all have been faced with high rates of violence during the peacebuilding and state-building processes that followed peace settlements. An analysis of the ways violence was used, and the purposes and interests it served in each of these cases, reveals some clear commonalities across them which reflect broader challenges regarding the processes of re-establishing and consolidating state structures and the state's monopoly on the use of force in the aftermath of civil war.

In all three cases, the violence that was utilised by non-state actors did not directly threaten the existence of the state, but challenged its consolidation, and the newly established sources of power and authority. Peace- and state-building processes rested on the assumption that elites would work within the new frameworks, without recognising the strength of the existing constellations of power to continue to mobilise violence to challenge them. They also underestimated the difficulties involved in shifting the negotiation of power and authority away from the use of violence in the context of political cultures in which it had become deeply embedded. As a result, power-holders, or elites, who could not pursue and secure their interests within the new structures and processes of governance, moved outside of them and used violence to achieve their goals, and reassert that their autonomy and authority existed beyond, and despite, official positions and processes of power. In addition, the peace processes examined suggest that the failure to satisfy the needs and expectations of ex-combatants, particularly in terms of post-war livelihood opportunities, also contributed to violence and instability, as both a backlash to the new system, which they did not benefit from, and a continuation of war-time social and political interaction, which was made possible by the culture of violence that often persists after protracted civil wars. These challenges were particularly stark where post-war state infrastructure, particularly the security sector, was weak. However, the more deeply powerful elites became embedded in state structures, and as those structures were consolidated, the less viable it was for non-state actors to violently oppose them, as the Cambodian case illustrates.

Ultimately, the cases investigated suggest that post-war violence is shaped by conventional political ends, and that the extension of the liberal democratic state-model to newly post-conflict states creates a set of incentives for violence that does not contest the basic existence of the state, but rather its interaction with other forms of political power and authority. Violence continues to disrupt, and at times overwhelm the re-establishment and consolidation of states after civil wars because peace processes do not reflect the constellations of authority within the society, nor acknowledge the importance of satisfying the needs and expectations of elites and power-holders to keep them working within new structures, processes and rules of governance and social interaction.

Civil wars and the challenge of neither war nor peace situations

The post-Cold War era has been characterised by increasing international involvement in the internal conflicts of states, which has been made possible by the growing normative regimes around human rights and the Responsibility to Protect (R2P). This post-Cold War internationalism has meant that the international community, primarily through the UN, but also through other institutions, has become heavily involved in resolving, and building peace after, civil wars. From Latin America and the Caribbean to the Balkans, from the Asia Pacific to Africa, peace processes have attempted to move societies out of often protracted civil warfare, and towards a peaceful system of governance and social relations. Yet, intra-state wars involve complex webs of motives, actors and funding sources, and are notoriously difficult to resolve. The World Bank's *World Development Report 2011* found that repeated cycles of violence and recurrent civil wars are the dominant form of armed conflict, with all civil wars that started after 2003 occurring in countries that have a history of civil war.[2]

What is perhaps most striking in many so-called post-war societies are the high levels of violence and widespread insecurity that continue to characterise them in the aftermath of peace settlements, even where outright civil war does not re-erupt. High criminality rates plague many post-war states, and threaten to destabilise them even decades after the end of violent conflict.[3] Criminal violence in El Salvador increased threefold in the immediate aftermath of the 1993 peace settlement, and the number of killings in Guatemala was far higher in the decade after the peace settlement than at any time during the war.[4] In addition, elections in many post-war states are characterised by violence. And in most post-war states, war-like social and economic conditions continue to characterise everyday life, with high rates of sexual and gender-based violence, severe under-development and lack of access to the basic necessities of life persisting for many years after a peace settlement has been reached. The result is that the consolidation of peace is undermined, as is the establishment of stable, post-war state structures and processes.

Why does this sort of low-level violence persist in the aftermath of civil wars? Much of the violence, though certainly not all, is perpetrated by non-state actors. But the role and purpose of violence is often unclear, especially when one considers that it occurs in societies that have nominally moved towards a set of political and social arrangements based on the non-violent contestation of power and authority. Many scholars have explained this violence as the result of a culture of violence that is established during protracted civil wars, or in other words, 'the system of norms, values or attitudes which allow, make possible or even stimulate the use of violence to resolve any conflict or relation with another person'.[5] Others, including Chrissie Steenkamp, have suggested that by becoming embedded in the culture, or the shared norms and values of a community, violence 'loses its political meaning and becomes a way of dealing with everyday issues: it becomes "trivialized" or "everyday", and becomes a socially acceptable mechanism to achieve power and status in society'.[6] While this explanation sheds light on the context of permissible conditions in which post-war violence is carried out, it leaves open questions about why individuals choose to use violence in certain situations, and not in others, or in other words, what the function of such violence is in the political economy of a post-war society. Examining the post-war experiences of Liberia, South Sudan and Cambodia, this chapter will explore the purposes and functions of the violence that occurred in each country after a peace settlement, and consider the reasons for similar types of violence occurring in each case.

Liberia

The Liberian civil war began in December 1989 when former government official Charles Taylor and his National Patriotic Front of Liberia invaded Liberia in response to the increasingly authoritarian rule of President Samuel Doe. The National Patriotic Front of Liberia overthrew the government in late 1990, but by then the country had descended into civil war with fighting within and between different rebel groups, as well as with the Liberian army and West African peacekeepers. The first civil war came to an end in 1995 with the signing of the Abuja Accords. The Accords brought all rebel factions together under a transitional government ahead of the 1997 elections that saw Charles Taylor's ascension to the presidency. However, anti-government fighting broke out again in 1999 and continued until 2003 when Taylor's troops faced imminent military defeat and he bowed to international pressure to stand down, going into exile in Nigeria.[7] Eight days after Taylor announced his resignation, a Comprehensive Peace Agreement (CPA) was reached in Accra between the Government of Liberia, the Liberians United for Reconciliation and Democracy and the Movement for Democracy in Liberia. The long and brutal civil war destroyed much of Liberia's infrastructure, and left in its wake state structures that were riddled with corruption and had been manipulated to represent only Taylor's interests, and required sweeping reforms to make them relevant and legitimate in the newly post-war society.

The disarmament, demobilisation and reintegration of ex-combatants and the reform of the security sector were central aspects of the peace process, with the international community funding the complete reform of military and police forces, as well as the reconstitution of governance structures in the spirit of liberal democracy as set out in the CPA.[8]

However, despite the broad efforts to demilitarise Liberian society, law enforcement and politics, violence has continued to characterise social and political dynamics. One of the major impacts of the disarmament, demobilisation and reintegration (DDR) programme was rapid urbanisation, which occurred when 45 per cent of ex-combatants chose to be resettled in the greater Monrovia area, rather than their actual areas of origin, probably because of a fear of returning home combined with a perception of the greater opportunities afforded by the capital city.[9] The negative effects of rapid urbanisation were compounded by the ongoing lack of employment opportunities, social services and basic infrastructure in the capital. Furthermore, 88 per cent of those demobilised opted to receive vocational training or further education over agricultural training, which far outnumbered the training and education opportunities available to them, with up to 80,000 ex-combatants left outside the rehabilitation process at least in the initial phases.[10] In addition, the labour market and economy in post-war Liberia had a very limited absorption capacity, meaning that the demand for formal jobs (which was exacerbated by the reintegration programme's emphasis on vocational training and education) far exceeded the opportunities available, leaving many ex-combatants unemployed in a rapidly growing city.[11] The issue of job opportunities was complicated by the fact that recruitment into a new army was not used to absorb ex-combatants, as it often is in DDR processes, leaving former troops with few viable and legitimate income sources given the post-war economic climate, which could destabilise the fragile peace, especially given the large numbers of small weapons still available in the country.

Although some ex-combatants earned a small income doing menial jobs, not all were happy to do so. A former Liberian combatant working as mercenary in Côte d'Ivoire argued that he had no choice but to move across the border to work because they were disarmed, but refused entry into the Liberian army and had no other employment opportunities.[12] According to the International Crisis Group (ICG), undetermined numbers of Liberian ex-combatants were selectively recruited for their fighting experience by both former Ivorian President Laurent Gbagbo and new President Alassane Ouattara during the post-election crisis in 2010–11.[13] These mercenaries were implicated in atrocities in the Côte d'Ivoire, bought back weapons and ammunition when they returned to Liberia, and have been implicated in rising crime rates in the areas to which they returned, and potentially also the violence around the 2011 presidential elections, which will be discussed shortly.[14]

The poor capacity of the police force, despite the police reform that occurred as part of the peace process, also contributed to the insecurity in Liberia. The Liberian National Police (LNP) was compromised because Taylor had embedded his own supporters in it, and so it was completely disbanded and reformed in an effort to restore public confidence, although the United Nations Mission in Liberia's (UNMIL) capacity to do this comprehensively was limited by funding constraints.[15] Officers who joined the LNP after Taylor took power were officially barred from applying for re-entry, and recruits were vetted for human rights abuses, with their names and photos published in the press for the public to see, just as with the army.[16] However, there were serious shortcomings in the recruitment, vetting and training of the police force, and UNMIL's own human rights and protection unit labelled the police vetting system a failure as early as 2005.[17] The ICG argued that the LNP is 'widely considered ineffective and corrupt'.[18] In part this is because of poor management, poor community relations and a severe lack of basic equipment (including vehicles, communications equipment, handcuffs and even torches), but it is also linked to the lack of an effective judiciary in Liberia, which is essential to complement and consolidate the work of the police. Funding deficiencies remain a serious problem, and together these factors have contributed to the police's inability to check rising crime rates.[19]

Data has shown that the situation in Liberia in terms of law and order deteriorated from 2009 with 'an increasing incidence of violent crime, including armed robbery and rape; violent protests over layoffs and employment disputes by youths and former combatants; and deadly land disputes'.[20] The LNP was unable to effectively address many of these issues, sparking UNMIL intervention in some cases. There was a subsequent rise in vigilantism in Liberia, with the public taking responsibility for justice and retribution into their own hands, resulting in at least eight deaths in 2009.[21] Further, although the post-war violence in Liberia was not organised along the same lines of the civil war, it did have communal and political dimensions. In mid-2008, the ICG interviewed a security specialist with access to intelligence on the subject, who suggested that

> there were some signs the rash of robberies might be linked to a coordinated attempt to destabilise the government and prompt violent mass reactions. There are some indications that truckloads of young men have been transported between Kakata and central Monrovia to become involved in the crime spree.[22]

This implies that the rise in criminality was linked to politically motivated organised violence. Mob violence prompted by lack of confidence in the police and judicial system also took on increasingly political connotations in the lead-up to the 2011 elections.[23] That criminality rates remain high and the police are largely unable to address them does not bode well for the stability and security of Liberia in the coming years, or the consolidation of the state's monopoly on the legitimate use of force. This highlights the importance of understanding criminality in post-war societies in terms of the broader political context of the war and peace process, rather than as the result of discrete economic interests that encourage criminality.

In the context of the high levels of generalised violence and insecurity in post-war Liberia, it is surprising that political processes in the aftermath of the CPA were largely peaceful. The Liberian transitional political arrangements, albeit inadvertently, helped avoid the type of major electoral-related violence that is often synonymous with post-war elections, as other cases in this chapter will demonstrate.

The CPA provided for a National Transitional Government of Liberia (NTGL) to be established for a two-year period, to oversee the implementation of the CPA and lead the country to elections. Members of the NTGL were appointed by the parties to the peace talks, and the warring parties were allowed to dominate key ministries and positions, which led to widespread corruption.[24] The CPA precluded any senior NTGL appointees standing for elections in 2005, which meant that there was no incumbent party with an unfair advantage in those elections. David Harris argues that this approach effectively 'bought off' rebel leaders, by not threatening them with war crimes tribunals and 'rightly or wrongly, [presenting] them with opportunities to join the elite and take a slice of the pie without even the need for political participation in the election'.[25] He further argues that 'perhaps because of the realpolitik nature of the CPA and the barely disguised gross corruption of members of the coalition government, the protagonists in the second Liberian civil war (2000–3) complied with the agreement and the peace process held'.[26] Consequently, the 2005 elections were very different from many other post-conflict elections, such as those in Cambodia and South Sudan, in that rebel forces were virtually absent from the political process, opening up space for other participants and for the election to be contested on the basis of policy platforms, rather than party, regional, or ethnic affiliations. Further, violence was largely absent from the electoral campaign and process, which Harris attributes to the dismantling of armed forces, the presence of 15,000 peacekeepers, and the unusual level of cordiality between competing parties.[27]

This demonstrates the benefits of a longer time-frame between signing a peace agreement and holding elections – especially in this case, where the DDR programme took much longer than expected, and where holding elections while the warring groups were still armed could have resulted in a fast return to civil war.[28] It also highlights that political realities and power dynamics shift as actors' interests change. In this case, the interim government provided key elites with an opportunity to satisfy their interests before elections introduced open political competition. This diminished the push factors for violent competition in the immediate aftermath of the peace settlement, and allowed time to consolidate the newly reconstituted state structures. Although this is not something that is easily fabricated, partly because of the problematic ethics of 'buying off' potential spoilers by granting them interim power, it does show that when elites are given the opportunity to work within new state structures and processes to pursue their interests, they may be more likely to help consolidate those processes rather than actively and violently contest them as occurred in South Sudan and Cambodia.

It was predicted that the resulting lack of major parties representing large clan, ethnic or tribal groups in the elections would most likely directly lead to violence; however this was not the case.[29] Nonetheless, politically motivated violence had already begun to rise, with violent uprisings in 2003, 2004 and 2005 due to widespread anger amongst former combatants and members of the armed forces about the non-payment of demobilisation allowances and, in some cases, pensions.[30] Further, government corruption was widespread, despite efforts by President Ellen Johnson Sirleaf to combat it.[31] High levels of government corruption contributed to community dissatisfaction with Liberia's peace, particularly amongst former fighters who received little support and enjoyed few opportunities in the new post-war Liberia. This manifested during the 2011 election in growing opposition to Sirleaf, and support for the opposition who lost, and vowed not to cooperate with her government.

By the second round of post-war presidential elections in October–November 2011 it had become clear that some of the issues around party proliferation and violent competition had become more prominent challenges to the stability and effectiveness of Liberia's government. Although Sirleaf won a second term in government, the elections were marred by violence and an opposition boycott of run-off elections based on claims of electoral fraud. Her main challenger, Winston Tubman, rejected Sirleaf's victory, arguing that the elections were rigged in her favour, calling for a boycott of the run-off elections, and pledging not to cooperate with her government in the legislature.[32] Tubman's claims seem unsubstantiated – the Carter Center's electoral observers monitored 'the tally and the tabulation of final results in Liberia [and reported] a largely transparent process with no evidence of systematic fraud or manipulation of results'.[33] Nevertheless, Tubman's boycott was enacted, and although Sirleaf won 90.6 per cent in the ballot, voter turnout was only 38.6 per cent in contrast with the 71.6 per cent turnout in the first round of voting.[34]

The boycott's success was especially concerning because many of Tubman's supporters who followed his boycott call were unemployed former combatants, who had the means and capacity to regroup into active militias.[35] As a result of these electoral results, Sirleaf faced challenges not only from the opposition within the legislature, as a result of Tubman's pledge not to cooperate with her, but from her constituency, with many disenfranchised by the run-off elections, and a large portion disenchanted with her achievements from her first term in power, particularly her weak or failed anti-corruption efforts, decentralisation and national reconciliation campaigns.[36] Although the transitional arrangements were successful and common vulnerability has characterised governance process and thereby prevented any single party from monopolising power and necessitated cooperative relationships, the combativeness demonstrated in response to electoral results suggests that some actors may not be as committed to due political process as they seemed. Thus, it is clear that the authority of the central governance mechanisms and processes remain contested, informed by a sustained political culture of mistrust, antagonism and corruption which could conceivably lead to further politically motivated violence in the future.

A common problem in post-war states is the weak capacity of governance infrastructure for basic service provision, which can compound people's dissatisfaction with the benefits of the peace established, and lead to conflict between formerly warring groups or amongst the general population over scarce resources, thereby contributing to destabilisation. Poor service provision is not unique to post-war states, but rather a challenge facing many low-income developing countries, as are the interlinked challenges of criminality, poverty, violence, resource competition and instability. But institutional weakness and accountability deficits in post-war states are linked to the way peace processes play out in the governance sphere. Such weaknesses often highlight broader problems with approaches to post-war governance-building, which focus predominantly on establishing the technocratic institutions of government at the expense of engaging with the politics of moving a post-war society towards non-violent modes of social and political interaction.[37]

The Liberian experience of building post-war institutional capacity showcases a range of these issues, particularly around the difficulty of developing institutions nearly from scratch, building community confidence in the government's legitimacy, and addressing corruption. In Liberia, while a great deal of attention has been given to the establishment of the system and structures of electoral politics and to economic recovery, the capital, Monrovia, still has an extremely limited electricity service, a very limited piped water system, no landline telephone service and poor roads. The situation in the rest of the country is similar.[38] Given that post-war Liberia had very little infrastructure left, it is unsurprising that public infrastructure and services remain in this state nearly a decade after peace was established, and that the government's focus has been on rebuilding the economy, which will give it an increased capacity to improve facilities and services. The government's legitimacy in the eyes of many citizens has decreased as service provision has not improved, and economic recovery has been challenged by endemic corruption, which has itself undermined the government's capacity to address poverty, economic development, and provide basic education and healthcare services. Given the context described above, it is not beyond the realm of the possible that this contributes to more violence in Liberia, especially around elections.

The Liberian experience of violence and insecurity in the aftermath of civil war suggests a number of things about why actors chose to use violence when ostensibly living in a newly peaceful state. On the one hand, the transitional political arrangements reflected the political realities of power and economic interests, and moved political competition, at least in the short term, away from war-time politics and divisions by satisfying the self-interest of key actors in the interim period. Essentially, they incentivised against elites using violence to pursue their interests. However, this did not reflect a general commitment to be bound by the new structures of governance, and the 2011 elections and their lead-up demonstrated that when powerful actors could not achieve their ends within the new processes, they moved outside them to mobilise insecurity and violence to contest the state structures and authority. This was facilitated by the disenfranchisement of ex-combatants, and the availability of small arms, which made for easily mobilised opposition to the state. Compounding this insecurity, the high levels of criminality and lawlessness were in part a reaction to the failure of the peace process to generate viable alternative livelihood options for ex-combatants, and partly a backlash to the weak capacity and perceived partisan and self-interested nature of the police force.

South Sudan

The post-war experiences in South Sudan have demonstrated similar challenges to those in Liberia, in terms of the ongoing prevalence of violence and insecurity in both social and political spheres, and the inability of state structures to contain them, culminating in a resurgence of violence in December 2013 that led to renewed civil war. South Sudan's peace process also highlights the complexities of reforming and consolidating governance structures and processes when different groups remain locked in a web of overlapping conflict relationships and power struggles.

The North–South war in Sudan, which began in 1955, had a brief hiatus after the Addis Ababa Agreement of 1972, but resumed again in 1983. The war was just one of a much broader web of conflicts in the Sudan, which were based on 'competing claims by various, shifting groups, to land, water, natural resources, political power or cultural identity'.[39] The discovery of oil in South Sudan in 1978 by Chevron complicated these existing conflicts by adding a further economic dimension to the question of territorial control.

The 1972 Addis Ababa Agreement ended seventeen years of war between the North and the South by granting the South a level of autonomy over its own affairs. However, problems around the integration of guerrilla forces into the national army, support for the South's economic development and the maintenance of the political balance between the central government and the semi-autonomous South were not effectively addressed, which led to high levels of mistrust and tension between the two parties, and eventually to the resumption of full scale civil war.[40] The second civil war was characterised by internal feuding within the Sudan People's Liberation Army (SPLA) – later also known as the Sudan People's Liberation Movement (SPLM) – over the control, direction and goals of the liberation movement. This meant that a great deal of violent conflict occurred not only between the government forces and the SPLA, but between different tribal factions within the SPLA, although the northern government was implicated in funding and arming particular groups in order to undermine the overarching liberation struggle.[41] The government was successful in doing this, at one point entering into a peace agreement with the Nuer southern faction led by Riek Machar which bought him into the central government while leaving John Garang's Dinka faction of the SPLA out. This alliance soon collapsed because the National Congress Party – Omar al-Bashir's dominant northern party – failed to follow through on many promises and agreements, and Machar soon re-joined Garang for the peace talks that eventually led to the 2005 Comprehensive Peace Agreement (CPA). However, the deep divisions between the various Southern groups that fought each other during the second Sudanese war have continued to characterise post-war and post-independence social and political interactions, and much of the violence has occurred along communal lines.

The militarisation of the civilian population was a significant source of insecurity in post-war South Sudan, given the long history of inter-group and tribal violence which was exacerbated by the ethnic dimensions of the civil war. As a result, civilian disarmament was considered a key part of the DDR programme; however it was largely conducted by the SPLM, rather than international actors, as it is in many peace processes. The Government of South Sudan (GOSS) began a forcible civilian disarmament programme in early 2006, with a failed operation in northern Jonglei state, conducted by the SPLA, that collected 3,000 weapons but was ethnically focused and politically motivated, highlighting the ongoing communal dimensions of the insecurity in the South and the way the SPLA was using its newfound authority over state structures to continue its conflict with other groups. This sparked a massive backlash which resulted in 1,600 deaths and did nothing to improve the area's security.[42] This was followed by a second attempt at complete civilian disarmament in 2008, which gave the ten state governors responsibility for its rollout, and included incentives for civilians to surrender their weapons, and also allowed for the use of force to disarm them if they did not do so. The Small Arms Survey found that this programme was largely ineffective due to poor planning and haphazard implementation, and as such had a minimal impact on security, collecting only a small fraction of the total holdings of small arms in Southern communities.[43] These campaigns also deepened communities' mistrust of the SPLM/GOSS because they too seemed to be politically motivated with the aim of neutralising the military capacity of certain tribes, and concerns remain that if disarmament upsets the balance of power between tribes or clans in any given area, it will be strongly resisted.[44] In late 2009, the ICG investigated the imminent civilian disarmament campaign in South Sudan, which was driven by pressure on the GOSS to address the high incidence of intergroup violence. This investigation showed a disturbing acceptance by prominent government and army officials that the campaign might again result in many deaths, with officials arguing that these deaths would be justified by the longer term security gains.[45]

A major challenge to civilian disarmament is the fact that bearing arms is associated with economic, social and political prestige in many communities, and also that in some areas the GOSS has actually encouraged civilians to own guns as a means of protection against armed groups including the Lord's Resistance Army.[46] This issue of violence becoming normalised, through civil war, as a part of political culture and social organisation is a relatively common phenomenon in post-war societies that is often not accorded adequate attention by international actors in their efforts to consolidate post-war security. This is complicated by the estimated two million small arms which are in the possession of civilians in South Sudan. Many civilians see these weapons as integral to their security, which is in part a legacy of the history of inter-group violence and the culture of weapons-bearing, but also a reaction to the new government's inability or unwillingness to ensure security and protect civilians from certain groups from such violence. These factors have contributed to the ongoing insecurity in the region and the armed conflict between Southern groups, particularly since independence in 2011.

The way post-war state structures have been constituted and occupied has contributed significantly to this push factor of the ongoing militarisation and insecurity in South Sudan. The GOSS has been dominated by the two major ethnic groups, the Nuer and Dinka, who controlled the SPLM, dominated the South's engagement in the peace process, and had the capacity and finances to formalise their involvement in the new political structures. While this is unsurprising, it has meant that there is no real opposition in the new state, despite the many smaller ethnic groups not represented by the GOSS. As a result, the new structures, even after elections, have not accurately reflected the constellations and dynamics of political and social authority in the new state, with many power-holders, particularly from minority groups, excluded from formal political processes. In turn, this has contributed to the rise of inter-clan violence to dangerously destabilising levels since independence. For instance, long-standing tensions between Nuer and Murle clans in the Pibor region, which were largely put aside after the CPA for the sake of achieving independence, re-arose and descended to a cycle of violent revenge attacks. These attacks left thousands dead or displaced, hundreds of children abducted and thousands of cattle stolen. While on the surface they appeared to be cattle raids, their deeper causes include poverty, competition for scarce resources, a security vacuum, the availability of small arms left over from the war, and the marginalisation of ethnic minorities in the new South Sudanese political system.[47] In this violence, heavily armed and large militias, including the reconstituted Nuer White Army, have become locked into a cycle of revenge attacks. In 2012, Lou Nuer militias attacked Murle villages, with a Seattle-based fundraising arm issuing a public statement that 'We have decided to invade Murleland and wipe out the entire Murle tribe on the face of the earth'.[48]

The GOSS has not intervened to protect the Murle, because the Nuer-dominated government could not marshal its forces against Nuer militias without sparking even more severe internal conflict.[49] That the levels of inter-tribal conflict escalated to this degree suggests that the system of governance established in South Sudan was not based on a common acceptance of its authority or a will to work together within the new independent state framework. It also reflects the problem that the SPLM's assumption of a large amount of authority through the new government infrastructure leaves little space for a political opposition to occupy, and minority groups feel that their interests are not adequately represented in the new frameworks, and can only be secured through violence. This has enabled a culture of violent competition for power and resources, high numbers of small weapons in civilian hands, and the inability of the new state security forces to constrain such non-state violence.

The widespread violence has been compounded by the poor absorption capacity of the post-independence economy, which, as in Liberia, has meant that many former combatants are unable to establish legitimate livelihoods.[50] In 2010, Julie Brethfeld suggested that ex-combatants had high expectations for their opportunities in peacetime, and that widespread dissatisfaction with the realities of reintegration and income-generation options could push them either into criminality or political violence, which could further destabilise the situation in South Sudan.[51] The recent crisis in South Sudan seems to confirm some of these fears.

South Sudan's fragile post-independence peace crumbled in December 2013 when political disputes at the highest levels of government and a series of attempts to monopolise political control by various power-holders manifested in open violence between the supporters of President Salva Kiir, and his former deputy, Riek Machar. The ethnic divisions that animated the second Sudanese war were re-mobilised by politicians who had spent the post-independence years sharing power under the SPLM, which controlled the state structures. Violence was quick to erupt, old communal rifts re-opened and formerly warring groups re-armed and remobilised. Within a month, an estimated 10,000 people were killed, 200,000 were displaced within South Sudan, 30,000 displaced to neighbouring countries, and thousands more injured.[52] Although the peace process had invested heavily in building the infrastructure for peace through governance and security programmes, the conflict simmered just below the surface.

The widespread violence that has plagued South Sudan in the aftermath of the civil war and its subsequent independence from the North demonstrates the danger of post-war state structures and processes failing to reflect or respond to the realities of political dynamics and competition between different groups. This was in part due to the technical focus of the post-war state-building processes, which focused on the reconstitution of institutions and formal reform processes, at the expense of the informal structures of power, dynamics of conflict and the underlying political culture in the new state.

Ultimately, the violence had clear political dimensions, and was often mobilised in direct contestation of the authority and legitimacy of the new structures, processes and official sources of authority, which had crystallised around two dominant ethnic groups, who also remained in contest with one another. Although it was enabled by the culture of violence that was both a legacy of the war and result of traditional practices, the violence functioned as both a contestation of the new state and an assertion of the autonomy and political will of excluded groups.

South Sudan's experience highlights some further complexities around the political dimensions of post-war security. The civil war not only entrenched the absence of formal law and order in the region (although it must be recognised that law and order does not really exist in much of North Sudan either), but also destroyed traditional forces and sources of law and order, such as paramount chiefs, who were elected by village chiefs to be the highest-level political leader in their region and played central roles in the resolution of conflicts between groups in the region. The SPLA assumed authority over local administrative institutions in areas under its control, removing the power of traditional authorities and replacing it with young, gun-toting men, thereby destroying traditional methods of dealing with inter-personal or inter-group conflict, which are not easily rebuilt.[53] Complicating this reality is the fact that bearing arms is associated with economic, social and political prestige in many Southern communities, which, along with a long history of violent inter-tribal conflict, adds another layer to the incentives for violence in the post-war state, and the resistance to the centralised state establishing a monopoly on the legitimate use of force.[54]

Cambodia

The experiences of violence in post-war Cambodia mirror some of those in Liberia and South Sudan, in terms of the violent contestation of power and authority in reaction to official processes and structures that do not reflect existing power constellations. However, the trajectory of violence was entirely different, with powerful actors eventually capturing the state structures and consolidating them to the point that opposition, including violent opposition, has been all but quashed. This suggests that the extent to which elites are embedded in state structures, and those structures are consolidated, influences the prevalence of the violent contestation of post-war politics.

In 1970, the Cambodian military ousted ruling Prince Sihanouk in a coup, and in 1975 as the Vietnam war ended, the Khmer Rouge, Cambodian communist guerrillas, took control of the capital Phnom Penh, implementing a regime that over the following four years caused the deaths of more than a million Cambodians through forced labour, torture, execution, malnutrition or disease.[55] Their reign was bought to an end in December 1978 with the invasion of Vietnamese troops which pushed the Khmer Rouge into the jungles bordering on Thailand, from where they launched a guerrilla war against the new Vietnamese-backed government. The Khmer Rouge, funded by China, was joined in their anti-government struggle by Sihanouk's National United Front for an Independent, Neutral, Peaceful and Cooperative Cambodia (FUNCINPEC) and the Khmer People's National Liberation Front (KPNLF), led by former Prime Minister Son Sann. FUNCINPEC and KPNLF received support from Thailand and Western states including the US and UK.

The civil war raged through the 1980s, although the roots of the peace process lie in Gorbachev's indications in 1985 that the USSR would soon withdraw material support for Vietnam because of cuts to international spending, which in turn led Vietnam to announce that it 'might be willing to withdraw its troops from Cambodia'.[56] Other factors such as internal political pressure and the 'no win' situation likely in Cambodia were also likely contributors to the Vietnamese policy shift.[57] This led to a series of meetings between and amongst regional and international interest groups, such as the Association of Southeast Asian Nations (ASEAN), and eventually to peace negotiations between the government and the Khmer Rouge, FUNCINPEC, and KPNLF, which culminated in the settlement of the conflict in the Paris Peace Agreement (PPA) of October 1991.[58] The peace agreement set out a detailed plan for Cambodia's transformation into a peaceful and pluralistic liberal democratic state, including provisions for the future government system, DDR, return of refugees, the release of political prisoners and more.

The PPA provided for a democratic election to be held at the end of the transitional period, which was to be organised, conducted and supervised by the UN Transitional Administration in Cambodia (UNTAC). While the agreement outlined principles for a new constitution which included the strengthening of democracy and human rights, it did not outline the process for the transition to democracy in the longer term.[59] Essentially, it did not address the question of how a new state structure would be formed after the elections were held, nor institutionalise the concept of political opposition in the post-war system.[60] It also failed to anticipate the challenges inherent in attempting to move an authoritarian socialist state towards a model of liberal democratic pluralism. These weaknesses were exploited by powerful actors as they sought to embed themselves in positions of authority in the new post-war state structures.

In the years following the signing of the peace agreement, the process of peace consolidation was stymied by ongoing violent conflict between the different groups. Although the PPA established an immediate ceasefire, conflict ceased only briefly, with violence coordinated primarily by the Khmer Rouge's Party of Democratic Kampuchea (PDK) and the Vietnamese backed incumbent Cambodian People's Party (CPP), led by Hun Sen. Between 1992 and 1993, the CPP systematically organised violence against opposition parties, killing around 100 members of FUNCINPEC and the KPLNF successor Buddhist Liberal Democratic Party.[61] Between 1992 and 1998, when the Khmer Rouge collapsed, there were an estimated 3,000 casualties as a result of ongoing conflict between the CPP-dominated government and the PDK, with an additional estimated 700 civilian casualties directly caused by the PDK.[62] Additionally, at least 90,000 people were displaced by fighting between the Khmer Rouge and the government forces in late 1994.[63]

There was widespread political violence in the lead-up to the 1993 elections, carried out largely by the incumbent regime of Hun Sen against FUNCINPEC and KPNLF supporters, and also by the Khmer Rouge against ethnic Vietnamese civilians and UNTAC officials. However, the Khmer Rouge did not ultimately launch the large-scale military offensive it threatened when polling opened, and the elections happened peacefully and on-schedule.[64] This may have been due in part to UNTAC's surprise inspections of certain provinces, deployment of civilian police to deter attacks on vulnerable party offices, and issuance of a directive that prohibited the unauthorised possession of arms which was enforced at checkpoints.

During the elections, more than 90 per cent of registered voters cast ballots, delivering FUNCINPEC victory with more than 45 per cent of the votes, led by Sihanouk's son Ranariddh, while Hun Sen's CPP won around 38 per cent of votes, and the KPLNF won 3.8 per cent.[65] The CPP refused to accept its loss of power, with hardliners led by Sihanouk's son Chakrapong declaring the secession of a number of eastern provinces under its control, and violently attacking UNTAC and FUNCINPEC offices.[66] The interim governing authority also appealed to Prince Sihanouk in the aftermath of the elections and amidst their allegations of electoral fraud (dismissed by UNTAC as insignificant or unfounded), hinting of a return to civil war if their concerns were not addressed.[67] This forced Ranariddh to concede to a power-sharing arrangement, whereby he and Hun Sen would be co-Premiers, and all ministerial posts would be split evenly between FUNCINPEC and the CPP.

General John Sanderson, who was in charge of the military element of UNTAC, and Senior Deputy Chief Electoral Officer Michael Maley argue that the CPP's refusal to accept the results of the elections, and by association, the 'new ground rules' established in the peace agreement, sent a 'powerful and unambiguous signal that, from [the CPP's] viewpoint, the ground rules would not be changing: while use might be made of parliamentary manoeuvres, power would still come, ultimately, from the barrel of a gun'.[68]

Despite a period of relative peace after the 1993 elections, the fragile power-sharing agreement and UNTAC's quick withdrawal after the elections left a fundamentally unstable situation.[69] The unusual power-sharing arrangement entailed a complete duplication of authority in all state systems and structures. Both parties maintained their own armies, police, media and bureaucrats, and maintained dual command structures in all state bodies, which suggested a deep mistrust of plural state structures. Ostensibly, this was designed to ensure that all decisions would be made by consensus; however, the CPP manipulated itself into the dominant position within this coalition government, as it monopolised power at the regional civil administration level, including the courts, and headed the police, gendarmerie and army, undercutting FUNCINPEC's capacity to exercise political authority.[70] There is also evidence that the CPP forcefully intimidated political opponents to ensure its dominance.[71] This caused significant tension between the two parties, leading them to compete for the support of other actors in the system, as discussed above, and resulting in even greater fighting in the lead-up to the 1998 elections.[72]

Political violence peaked in 1997, starting with a grenade attack against a FUNCINPEC break-away demonstration outside the parliament, which resulted in at least sixteen deaths and was organised with the complicity of Hun Sen's bodyguard, according to a UN investigation.[73] Then, in July 1997, Hun Sen coordinated action to undermine FUNCINPEC in the parliament, by fostering a revolt of FUNCINPEC members against Ranariddh, which failed, and then took control militarily. From 2 July 1997, CPP troops disarmed FUNCINPEC-aligned troops first around, and then within, Phnom Penh itself. The fighting in the capital, over the weekend of 5–6 July, left an estimated 100 civilians dead, and spread to Cambodia's western provinces within a few days.[74] While the stated aim of the coup was to arrest Ranariddh on the false pretext that he had brought thousands of PDK soldiers back into Phnom Penh to re-establish the Khmer Rouge regime, it appears that Hun Sen's objective was to dismantle FUNCINPEC's parallel authority structures and consolidate his power within parliament and over the judiciary by establishing a CPP majority in both the Supreme Council of the Magistracy and the Constitutional Council.[75]

After the coup, the CPP reinforced its stranglehold on power by undermining the possibility of democratic opposition through the threat and use of violence against opponents.[76] Nate Thayer, a journalist in Cambodia at the time, told Paris: 'The only reason that there was a coup [in 1997] was that Hun Sen saw himself as being politically outflanked and realized that he would have lost the election [if he had not taken action]'.[77] This reinforces the suggestion that Hun Sen was not committed to the principles of democratisation embedded in the peace agreement. Thus, violence not only signalled the sources of power to opponents to the CPP, but also to those within the CPP who were inclined to uphold the principles and spirit of the Paris Accords.[78]

After the 1997 coup, the UN suspended Cambodia, ASEAN postponed its accession to the regional body, and many donor-states and institutions including the US, Germany, International Monetary Fund and World Bank suspended aid.[79] In the lead-up to the 1998 elections, Hun Sen responded to this isolation by intensifying relations with China, and establishing the framework for credible elections in 1998, so as to regain the international community's recognition.[80] While the 1998 elections were held and declared free and fair by international observer groups, other observer groups highlighted the complete marginalisation of political opposition as well as the killing and torture of political opponents, the electoral commission's partiality to the CPP, the corruption within the electoral process, and the CPP's monopolisation of media access, which suggests that voters had no real options but to support the CPP in the election.[81] Sanderson and Maley argue that by the time of the 1998 election, many voters perceived the balance of power in Cambodia to be such that if the CPP lost power it would respond with the sort of violence it used in the aftermath of the 1993 elections.[82]

The unusual duplicate system of government that was established after the 1993 elections meant that corruption was rife, the political elite became wealthier and more powerful as a result of becoming more deeply embedded in state structures, and 'instead of much-needed reform, the state continued to grow in size and weaken in effectiveness, despite massive foreign aid'.[83] The long standing and complex patronage networks for personal enrichment exacerbated this process, and while they operated at all levels of society, one of the most concerning was between the CPP and the armed forces, as a result of which Royal Cambodian Armed Forces generals control much of Cambodia's natural resource wealth, and Hun Sen can credibly employ the threat of renewed violence as a political strategy.[84]

There was no room within the post-war political system for debate or dissent, and stability was seen to hinge on the denial or marginalisation of political differences – as seen particularly after the 1997 coup, when the country's relative stability rested on Hun Sen's complete monopolisation of power. The first commune-level elections (local government) happened in 2003, with Cambodia's first senate elected in 2006. Until then all local chiefs had been appointed by the CPP, allowing it to maintain its monopoly on power.[85] The centralisation of power has led to a culture of impunity, where the rich and the powerful remain above the law and can manipulate the judicial institutions to their own ends.[86] One consequence was that the public service did not operate as a neutral actor in the years after the peace agreement, with many staff turning to corruption to supplement their low salaries, which meant that civilians often had to pay bribes for basic services.[87]

Much of this account hints at a fundamental problem within the Cambodian peace process: the international community attempted to install a liberal democratic state in a context in which few of the key actors were committed to such reforms.[88] 'Buy in' was absent not only because of the high numbers of State of Cambodia /CPP officials, police, soldiers and 'party hacks' whose livelihoods depended on patronage networks rooted in their power, and threatened by political pluralism,[89] but also because the Paris Accords fundamentally did not represent a true commitment to and desire for peace on the part of the four warring groups. Instead, they represented a rather intense pressure from the groups' international supporters to bring the conflict to an end.[90] As such, consent to the ongoing peace process and democratisation of the state was largely illusory, and powerful elites continued to use violence and to consolidate their existing authority through capturing the new state structures.

Essentially, the international community was working on the unrealistic assumption that political pluralism could be established in Cambodia within eighteen months, largely through electoral processes. Yet while such pluralism was welcomed by large parts of the civilian population, it was not by the State of Cambodia/CPP, and the push towards pluralism led to an upsurge in political violence and a backlash that ultimately resulted in the 1997 coup.[91] According to Caroline Hughes, this has been exacerbated by the fact that since 1991, international engagement has focused on 'eliciting forms of political participation that are atomizing and heavily policed, rather than spontaneous and mass-based, and ... the promotion of stability rather than empowered representation of the collective interests of the poor, has been the overriding concern'.[92]

A central problem of the approach to governance reforms in Cambodia, as well as in Liberia and South Sudan, is that the process has failed to change the underlying sources or modes of political and violent conflict. Violent political culture is a central part of this: Sorpong Peou shows that state leadership in Cambodia has always been most 'interested in preserving or enhancing its hegemonic status quo',[93] and David Roberts emphasises that 'No Khmer leader since independence, whether regal, communist, republican or former peasant, has accepted without resistance a challenge to the absolutism of their authority'.[94] The reality of this political culture and the local power dynamics were ignored by the international community involved in establishing the new post-war state structures. It seems to have assumed, as it also did in South Sudan and Liberia, that the establishment of liberal democratic state structures, as set out in the peace agreement, would ensure pluralism, respect for human rights, and a commitment to the non-violent resolution of political conflict, despite the fact that Cambodia was 'a vulnerable and poor country with primary ideals governed less by specific human rights and more by survival through patronage and loyalty'.[95]

After signing the peace agreement, political actors in Cambodia continued to interact with power and seek its consolidation in the same ways they had in the past. This highlights the need to be aware of existing power structures in peace processes and not 'presume that conflict only happens between the "bad guys" and the "good guys"',[96] but rather is a result of complex power dynamics. In condemning existing power structures and modes of organisation as problems that needed to be solved, the international community implicitly emphasised the 'rightness' of democracy, which meant that it could not respond to the existing power dynamics in Cambodia during the peace process.[97] It was instead stuck peddling a particular set of liberal democratic structures and processes which were understood to be the foundation of a peaceful post-war state, but were at odds with the realities of social, economic and political organisation in Cambodia, and therefore distanced from the realm of realistic outcomes.

Roberts argues that the transition to democracy in Cambodia was undermined by the absence of an alternative to the system of patronage, and by the elite's views of absolutism.[98] He posits that the right societal pillars must be in place to support an overall system, and that the old pillars of society in Cambodia were at odds with the system of democracy that was superimposed onto them.[99] This goes some way to explaining why the new system of plural democratic governance was effectively 'hollow', in that the substance of the system was characterised by a violent political culture, wartime divisions and a rejection of the principles of pluralism and democracy.

The case of the Cambodian governance-building process demonstrates that although there were some technical successes in establishing new systems and structures of governance in the aftermath of the civil war, a violent political culture still characterises the country's politics. This survey of the electoral processes, institutional transformation, institutional capacity, and political culture suggests that the institutions of post-war politics were effectively delinked from the dynamics and structures of power in the post-war state – or in other words, significant political power operated outside of formalised political structures and institutions. This created an incentive for power-holders to mobilise violence to firstly gain entry to those structures and institutions, and then to consolidate their hold over them. As a result, war-time divisions have continued to characterise the country's politics.

Cambodia's post-war competition for power resulted in one set of elites, clustered around Hun Sen, capturing state structures and processes, and consolidating them to the point that opposition groups are too weak to contest them either through formal political channels, or through the mobilisation of violence, as was the case in Liberia and South Sudan. This suggests that elites altered their attitudes to the use of violence depending on the extent to which they were embedded in and benefitted from the new state structures, and the extent to which those structures had the capacity to quash violence mobilised against them.

Ongoing violence and insecurity: negotiating power and authority in post-war societies

This chapter has so far examined the way violence has been used by non-state actors, in the aftermath of civil wars, and asked what the purpose and function of that violence was. The cases analysed have suggested that in many post-war societies, the state structures set up as part of the peace process have been at odds with the existing dynamics and structures of power within their societies. This disjuncture between the official location of authority and the constellations of power within communities gave rise to violence as a contestation of the newly established structures and processes of government. It manifested variously as the establishment of informal systems of authority that challenged formal ones; the refusal to submit political interests to the dictates of due political or electoral processes; the absence of a space for a political opposition to occupy; the dominance of a violent political culture; and widespread criminality and lawlessness.

A number of themes have emerged across the cases examined. On the one hand, it is clear that it is incredibly difficult to shift the role that violence plays in negotiating social and political relations after protracted civil wars. Such wars leave not only weak state infrastructure in their wake, but contribute to the disintegration of social fabric, the destruction of traditional values and authority systems, and leave a legacy of extreme violence.[100] In this context, young people are being raised unaccustomed to the demands of living in peace. This, unsurprisingly, also contributes to the increased rates of violence against women, especially gang rape, which is common in post-war societies.[101] The breakdown of traditional social norms and sanction regimes, according to Michelle Barron, also means that acts of sexual violence that would have previously been punished no longer provoke strong social reactions.[102] In effect, civil wars leave in their wake a set of permissive norms that facilitate the use of violence in social interactions.

However, a culture of violence does not alone explain the purpose to which much of the violence examined in this chapter was mobilised, which is more specifically linked to a violent *political* culture, or the normalisation of the use of violence to contest political power and authority. All of the cases examined demonstrated the ease with which the elites within post-war states slipped back into violence to pursue their interests when they were unable to do so within the newly established state structures and processes. As a result, relationships between different groups continued to be defined by mistrust, and conflictual behaviour dominated post-war political processes and competition. War-time divisions and modes of interaction became embedded in post-war systems. In the cases of Cambodia and South Sudan, this meant that there was no real opportunity for a political opposition to play a role in governance processes, with the ruling elite narrowing the political space to exclude competing groups. In all of the cases examined, it meant that militancy remained a central characteristic of political parties, and that violence continued to be a key characteristic of political culture, with the use or threat of force common in the negotiation of political power or outcomes.

Bad faith and a lack of commitment to peacebuilding and the development of a plural, democratic post-war state lie at the heart of many of these problems, and are often manifested in a weak commitment to the principles and processes of political competition enshrined in peace settlements. This was the case most clearly in Cambodia, where Hun Sen and the CPP manipulated governance reforms to ensure their continued authority went largely unchallenged by democratic process. In Liberia, the weak commitment to agreed-to processes and democratic principles was demonstrated either by elite manipulation of elections to guarantee their victory, or by the refusal of opposition groups to accept the results of largely technically successful elections.

Additionally, a range of other 'push factors', such as the limited opportunities ex-combatants had to develop alternative livelihoods and the suspicion of or resistance to new security structures, contributed to the high rates of violence, particularly criminality and lawlessness. Such violence did not directly contest political power and processes, as the violence associated with electoral processes did, but instead it contested the monopoly official state structures claimed on the legitimate use of violence, and the post-war rules they established around the use of force in social, economic and political interactions. Further, the fact that most post-war states are plagued by weak governance and security institutions meant that they were not only unable to effectively counter criminality and lawlessness, but sometimes provoked it as a backlash against the ineffective institutions. On the other hand, where institutions became strong and power was consolidated within the structures of government, as seen in Cambodia, violence became less common, particularly violence mobilised in contestation of political authority.

This analysis suggests that the political structures and dynamics of post-war societies play defining roles in the success of state-building processes. The cases examined show that despite technical progress in governance reform, the structures of power, dynamics of conflict and underlying political culture in post-war societies continue to define the role violence plays in negotiating power and pursuing interests. If the institutions and processes of governance do not accurately reflect the constellations of power and authority within a post-war society, they are likely to be violently contested by actors who can exercise their power outside of formal channels, for instance through corruption, patronage, or violence. As Roberts argues, in such cases the pillars of society are at odds with the new systems which stand on them, which embeds instability in the system, despite the technical or theoretical 'correctness' of the new systems.[103] Consequently, the state's monopoly on the use of force is not consolidated, and the resolution of political conflict is not moved into the non-violent political arena, but remains determined by violent political cultures characterised by mistrust and conflictual behaviours, and these forces may operate outside of formal channels and systems of governance and act to undermine them.

The cases discussed in this chapter suggest that the conflicts that plague post-war peace consolidation processes are essentially Clausewitzian political conflicts: they are fundamentally contests about power and authority, and not simply a product of a culture of violence which facilitates the use of violence to pursue individuals' interests. Peace processes in civil wars tend to involve the extension of the liberal democratic state-model to new post-conflict states, which creates a set of incentives for violence that does not contest the basic existence of the state, but rather its interaction with other forms of political power and authority. Where elites are excluded from new state structures and processes, but expected to submit to due political process and competition, and where the state is weak, violence is often mobilised to contest the new, official location of authority. In contrast, as Cambodia illustrated, where the use of this violence to contest post-war processes is successful, and leads to the embedding of powerful elites within state structure and the consolidation of those structures, the viability of violence as a mechanism of political competition is significantly reduced.

149

NOTES

1 This chapter draws on material published in J. Westendorf, *Why Peace Processes Fail: Negotiating Insecurity After Civil Wars* (Boulder, Colorado: Lynne Rienner Publishers, 2015).
2 World Bank, *World Development Report 2011: Conflict, Security and Development* (Washington DC: World Bank, 2011), p. 58.
3 For a discussion of the high rates of post-settlement violence and criminality in civil wars, see M. Berdal, *Building Peace After War* (London: International Institute for Strategic Studies, 2009), pp. 49–51.
4 C. Call, 'The Mugging of a Success Story: Justice and Security Sector Reform in El Salvador', in C. Call (ed.), *Constructing Justice and Security After War* (Washington DC: United States Institute of Peace, 2007), p. 39; J. McNeish and O. López Rivera, 'The ugly poetics of violence in post-Accord Guatemala', *Forum for Development Studies*, 36:1 (2009), p. 55.
5 J. Cruz (1998, p. 92) as translated in C. Moser and A. Winton, *Violence in the Central American Region: Towards an Integrated Framework for Violence Reduction*, Overseas Development Institute, 2002, available at: http://kms1.isn.ethz.ch/serviceengine/Files/ISN/104721/ipublicationdocument_singledocument/DDDC09D1-08F6-4C04-AA4A-85E87A6F78B3/en/complete171.pdf (accessed 22 April 2014), p. 11.
6 C. Steenkamp, 'The legacy of war: Conceptualizing a "culture of violence" to explain violence after peace accords', *The Round Table*, 94:379 (2005), p. 254.
7 R. Paris, *At War's End: Building Peace After Civil Conflict* (Cambridge: Cambridge University Press, 2004), p. 95.
8 *Accra Comprehensive Peace Agreement*, 18 August 2003, available at: www.usip.org/sites/default/files/file/resources/collections/peace_agreements/liberia_08182003.pdf (accessed 22 April 2014).
9 W. Paes, 'The challenges of disarmament, demobilization and reintegration in Liberia', *International Peacekeeping*, 12:2 (2005), p. 258.
10 See Paes, 'The challenges of disarmament, demobilization and reintegration in Liberia', p. 258; G. Cleaver and S. Massey, 'Liberia: A Durable Peace at Last?', in O. Furley and R. May (eds) *Ending Africa's Wars: Progressing to Peace* (Hampshire: Ashgate, 2006), p. 192.
11 Paes, 'The challenges of disarmament, demobilization and reintegration in Liberia', p. 260.
12 International Crisis Group, *Liberia: How Sustainable Is the Recovery?* (Dakar/Brussels: International Crisis Group, 2011), p. 15.
13 International Crisis Group, *Liberia: How Sustainable Is the Recovery ?*, p. 15.
14 International Crisis Group, *Liberia: How Sustainable Is the Recovery ?*, p. 15.
15 M. Malan, *Security Sector Reform in Liberia: Mixed Results from Humble Beginnings* (Pennsylvania: Strategic Studies Institute, US Army War College, 2008), p. 43.
16 Cleaver and Massey, 'Liberia: A Durable Peace at Last?', p. 193.
17 International Crisis Group, *Liberia: Uneven Progress in Security Sector Reform* (New York: International Crisis Group, 2009), pp. ii, 17.
18 International Crisis Group, *Liberia: Uneven Progress in Security Sector Reform*, p. 17.
19 International Crisis Group, *Liberia: Uneven Progress in Security Sector Reform*, p. 18.
20 Human Rights Watch, *World Report 2010: Events of 2009* (New York: Human Rights Watch, 2010), p. 136.
21 Human Rights Watch, *World Report 2010*, p. 136.

22   International Crisis Group, *Liberia: Uneven Progress in Security Sector Reform*, p. 7.

23   United Nations Secretary General, *Twenty-First Progress Report of the Secretary-General on the United Nations Mission in Liberia*, United Nations Security Council, 11 August 2010, available at: www.un.org/ga/search/view_doc.asp?symbol=S/2010/429 (accessed 23 April 2014), pp. 3–4.

24   For a discussion of this, see Cleaver and Massey, 'Liberia: A Durable Peace at Last?', pp. 194–5.

25   D. Harris, 'Liberia 2005: An unusual African post-conflict election', *Journal of Modern African Studies*, 44:3 (2006), pp. 393–5.

26   Harris, 'Liberia 2005', p. 375.

27   Harris, 'Liberia 2005', p. 377.

28   For an investigation of this issue, see D. Brancati and J. L. Snyder, 'Rushing to the polls: The causes of premature postconflict elections', *Journal of Conflict Resolution*, 55:3 (2011), pp. 469–92.

29   See Harris, 'Liberia 2005', p. 385. For a full discussion of the electoral results, see Brancati and Snyder, 'Rushing to the polls', pp. 375–95.

30   International Crisis Group, *Liberia: Uneven Progress in Security Sector Reform*, p. 5.

31   United Nations Secretary General, *Twenty-First Progress Report of the Secretary-General on the United Nations Mission in Liberia*, p. 3; Human Rights Watch, *World Report 2010*, p. 138.

32   R. Valdmanis, 'Troubled Liberia poll could slow Sirleaf agenda', *Reuters Africa* (13 November 2011), available at: http://af.reuters.com/article/topNews/idAFJ OE7AC087 20111113?feedType=RSS&feedName=topNews&sp=true (accessed 22 April 2014).

33   Carter Center, *Carter Center Statement on Liberia's Tally Process*, 20 October 2011, available at: www.cartercenter.org/news/pr/liberia-102011.html (accessed 1 May 2014).

34   National Elections Commission, *National Tally Center Tally Report for the Run-off Election of the President and Vice-President on 8 November 2011*, Republic of Liberia, 15 November 2011, available at: http://necliberia.org/admin/pg_img /20111115_NationalProgressiveResultsHandouts%20pdf.pdf (accessed 25 April 2014), p. 3; National Elections Commission, *National Tally Center Tally Report for the Presidential and Legislative Elections on 11 October 2011*, Republic of Liberia, 25 October 2011, available at: www.necliberia.org/admin/pg_img/20111025_ NationalProgressiveResultsHandouts.pdf.PDF (accessed 25 April 2014), p. 3.

35   Valdmanis, 'Troubled Liberia poll could slow Sirleaf agenda'.

36   For a discussion of community dissatisfaction with these campaigns, see International Crisis Group, *Liberia: How Sustainable Is the Recovery?*

37   Westendorf, *Why Peace Processes Fail*.

38   Overseas Security Advisory Council, *Liberia 2009 Crime and Safety Report*, Bureau of Diplomatic Security, US Department of State, 17 January 2009, available at: www. osac.gov/Reports/report.cfm?contentID=116969 (accessed 25 April 2014).

39   M. Simmons and P. Dixon, 'Introduction', in M. Simmons and P. Dixon (eds), *Peace by Piece: Addressing Sudan's Conflicts* (London: Conciliation Resources, 2006), p. 6.

40   For a discussion of this, see T. M. Ali, R. O. Matthews, and I. S. Spears, 'Failures in Peacebuilding: Sudan (1972–1983) and Angola (1991–1998)', in T. M. Ali and R. O. Matthews (eds), *Durable Peace: Challenges for Peacebuilding in Africa* (Toronto: University of Toronto Press, 2004), p. 285.

41   For an account of the dynamics of this internal feuding, see D. Scroggins, *Emma's War: Love, Betrayal and Death in the Sudan* (New York: Pantheon Books, 2002).

42   T. O'Brien, *Shots in the Dark: The 2008 South Sudan Civilian Disarmament Campaign* (Geneva: Small Arms Survey, 2009), p. 10.

43   O'Brien, *Shots in the Dark*, p. 10.

44   See A. Lokuji, *Overview of the Challenges to the Comprehensive Peace Agreement* (Waterloo: Project Ploughshares & Africa Peace Forum, 2006), p. 28; International Crisis Group, *Jonglei's Tribal Conflicts: Countering Insecurity in South Sudan* (Juba/Nairobi/Brussels: International Crisis Group, December 2009), p. 11; E. Ensign, 'Arms collection begins in Southern Sudan', *Arms Control Today*, 39:7 (2009), p. 28.

45   International Crisis Group, *Jonglei's Tribal Conflicts*, pp. 11–12.

46   Ensign, 'Arms collection begins in Southern Sudan', p. 29.

47   Minority Rights Group International, 'Press Release: Urgent measures needed to protect all ethnic groups after recent South Sudan attacks', 5 January 2012, available at: www.minorityrights.org/11147/press-releases/urgent-measures-needed-to-protect-all-ethnic-groups-after-recent-south-sudan-attacks-mrg.html (accessed 25 April 2014).

48   J. Gettleman, 'Born in Unity, South Sudan Is Torn Again', *New York Times* (12 January 2012), available at: www.nytimes.com/2012/01/13/world/africa/south-sudan-massacres-follow-independence.html?pagewanted=1&_r=1&ref=global-home.

49   Gettleman, 'Born in Unity, South Sudan Is Torn Again'.

50   J. Brethfeld, *Unrealistic Expectations: Current Challenges to Reintegration in Southern Sudan* (Geneva: Small Arms Survey, 2010), pp. 6–7.

51   Brethfeld, *Unrealistic Expectations*.

52   N. Kulish, 'New Estimate Sharply Raises Death Toll in South Sudan', *The New York Times* (9 January 2014), available at: www.nytimes.com/2014/01/10/world/africa/new-estimate-sharply-raises-death-toll-in-south-sudan.html (accessed 20 January 2014).

53   Lokuji, *Overview of the Challenges to the Comprehensive Peace Agreement*, p. 19.

54   Ensign, 'Arms Collection Begins in Southern Sudan', p. 29.

55   Paris, *At War's End*, p. 80; J. Schear, 'Riding the Tiger: The United Nations and Cambodia's Struggle for Peace', in W. Durch (ed.), *UN Peacekeeping, American Politics, and the Uncivil Wars of the 1990s* (New York: St. Martin's Press, 1996), p. 136.

56   Paris, *At War's End*, p. 80.

57   D. Pike, 'The Cambodian peace process: Summer of 1989', *Asian Survey*, 29:9 (1989), p. 845.

58   For a more detailed discussion of the lead-up to the peace settlement, see Schear, 'Riding the Tiger', pp. 137–9.

59   See 'Agreement on a Comprehensive Political Settlement of the Cambodia Conflict', 23 October 1991, para. 12, Annexes 1 & 3.

60   D. Ashley, 'The Undoing of UNTAC's Elections: No Mechanism for a Transfer of Power', in D. Hendrickson (ed.) *Safeguarding Peace: Cambodia's Constitutional Challenge* (London: Conciliation Resources, 1998), p. 61; D. Roberts, 'Finishing what UNTAC started: The political economy of peace in Cambodia', *Peacekeeping and International Relations*, 28:1 (1999), pp. 14–15.

61   Ashley, 'The Undoing of UNTAC's Elections', p. 23.

62   Uppsala Conflict Data Program, 'UCDP Database', n.d., available at: www.ucdp.uu.se/database (accessed 22 April 2014).

63   C. Bergquist, 'Chronology', in Hendrickson (ed.), *Safeguarding Peace: Cambodia's Constitutional Challenge*, p. 90.

64   Paris, *At War's End*, p. 85; United Nations Secretary General, *Report of the Secretary-*

General in Pursuance of Paragraph 6 of Security Council Resolution 810 (1993) on Preparations for the Election for the Constituent Assembly in Cambodia (New York: United Nations, 15 May 1995), p. 5.

65 United Nations, *The United Nations and Cambodia, 1991–1995* (New York: United Nations, 1995), p. 46.

66 Y. Akashi, 'The challenge of peacekeeping in Cambodia', *International Peacekeeping*, 1:2 (1994), p. 207.

67 Schear, 'Riding the Tiger', p. 170.

68 J. Sanderson and M. Maley, 'Elections and liberal democracy in Cambodia', *Australian Journal of International Affairs*, 52:3 (1998), p. 243.

69 Paris, *At War's End*, p. 86.

70 Roberts, 'Finishing what UNTAC started', p. 15; Paris, *At War's End*, p. 87; D. Ashley, 'Between War and Peace: Cambodia 1991–98', in Hendrickson (ed.), *Safeguarding Peace: Cambodia's Constitutional Challenge*, p. 24.

71 Sanderson and Maley, 'Elections and liberal democracy in Cambodia'.

72 E. Gottesman, *Cambodia After the Khmer Rouge: Inside the Politics of Nation Building* (New Haven: Yale University Press, 2003), pp. 353–4.

73 Ashley, 'Between War and Peace', p. 28.

74 Ashley, 'Between War and Peace', p. 28; S. Peou, 'Diplomatic Pragmatism: ASEAN's Response to the July 1997 Coup', in Hendrickson (ed.), *Safeguarding Peace: Cambodia's Constitutional Challenge*, p. 32.

75 Ashley, 'Between War and Peace', pp. 28–9.

76 Paris, *At War's End*, p. 89.

77 Paris, *At War's End*, p. 87.

78 Sanderson and Maley, 'Elections and liberal democracy in Cambodia', p. 244.

79 Ashley, 'Between War and Peace', p. 29.

80 Ashley, 'Between War and Peace', p. 29.

81 S. Downie, 'Cambodia's 1998 election: Understanding why it was not a "Miracle on the Mekong"', *Australian Journal of International Affairs*, 54:1 (2000), pp. 43–62; International Crisis Group, *Cambodia's Flawed Elections: Why Cambodia Will Not Be Ready for Free and Fair Elections on 26 July 1998* (Brussels: International Crisis Group, 1998); International Crisis Group, *Cambodia: The Elusive Peace Dividend* (Phnom Penh/ Brussels: International Crisis Group, 2000), p. 1.

82 Sanderson and Maley, 'Elections and liberal democracy in Cambodia', pp. 246–50.

83 Ashley, 'Between War and Peace', pp. 25–6.

84 S. Hameiri, *Regulating Statehood: State Building and the Transformation of the Global Order* (Basingstoke: Palgrave Macmillan, 2010), p. 183.

85 International Crisis Group, *Cambodia: The Elusive Peace Dividend*, p. 24. The establishment of a liberal democratic system was emphasised in the Paris Agreement, see 'Agreement on a Comprehensive Political Settlement of the Cambodia Conflict', Annex 5.

86 L. Mong Hay, 'Cambodia's Agonising Quest: Political Progress Amidst Institutional Backwardness', in Hendrickson (ed.), *Safeguarding Peace: Cambodia's Constitutional Challenge*, p. 39.

87 Mong Hay, 'Cambodia's Agonising Quest'.

88 Akashi recounts that he told colleagues within UNTAC that 'real democracy takes decades and even centuries to develop' and argues that UNTAC was just trying to sow 'some of the essential seeds for the growth of democracy which the Cambodian people themselves had to nurture after our departure'. Akashi, 'The Challenge of Peacekeeping in Cambodia', p. 206.

89   Schear, 'Riding the Tiger', p. 173.
90   S. R. Ratner, *The New UN Peacekeeping: Building Peace in Lands of Conflict After the Cold War* (New York: St. Martin's Press, 1995), p. 158.
91   For a discussion of the impact of injecting pluralism into the Cambodian system, see Schear, 'Riding the Tiger', p. 174.
92   C. Hughes, 'Transnational networks, international organizations and political participation in Cambodia: Human rights, labour rights and common rights', *Democratization*, 14:5 (2007), p. 836.
93   S. Peou, *Intervention and Change in Cambodia: Towards Democracy?* (Singapore: Institute of Southeast Asian Studies, 2000), p. 427.
94   D. Roberts, *Political Transition in Cambodia 1991–99: Power, Elitism and Democracy* (Surrey: Curzon Press, 2001), p. 171.
95   Roberts, *Political Transition in Cambodia 1991–99*, p. 171.
96   Peou, *Intervention and Change in Cambodia*, p. 429.
97   For a discussion of this 'deploring' and its consequences, see Roberts, *Political Transition in Cambodia 1991–99*, p. 204.
98   Roberts, *Political Transition in Cambodia 1991–99*, p. 205.
99   Roberts, *Political Transition in Cambodia 1991–99*, p. 210.
100 International Crisis Group, *Liberia: How Sustainable Is the Recovery?*
101 M. Bastick, K. Grimm, and R. Kunz, *Sexual Violence in Armed Conflict: Global Overview and Implications for the Security Sector* (Geneva: Geneva Center for the Democratic Control of Armed Forces, 2007), pp. 183–8; N. de Watteville, *Addressing Gender Issues in Demobilization and Reintegration Programs*, Africa Region Working Paper Series (New York: World Bank, 2002), p. 20.
102 M. Barron, *When the Soldiers Come Home: A Gender Analysis of the Reintegration of Demobilized Soldiers — Mozambique 1994–96* (UK: School of Development Studies of the University of East Anglia, 1996), p. 20.
103 Roberts, *Political Transition in Cambodia 1991–99*, p. 210.

7

Humanitarian intervention and the moral dimension of violence

Jannika Brostrom

T HIS CHAPTER EXAMINES the use of moral suasion in cases of violence, justified as humanitarian intervention. It argues that rather than this being reflective of normative shifts in world politics brought about by global civil society, it can be explained by referring to the role of power and interests. After an examination of how supporters of global civil society have argued for changing norms of sovereignty tied to greater acceptance of human rights, the chapter takes a critical view of the notion of the just use of force. Specifically I argue that where instances of humanitarian intervention have occurred, there have been particularistic national interests motivating elite decisions to use force. Thus, the chapter finds that normative perspectives misrepresent the moral considerations that justify the use of force. Instead I find that a focus on the interests relative to morality offers a more accurate understanding of what factors motivate a state's commitment to resort to violence in order to achieve 'humanitarian' objectives.

Moreover, the apparent selectivity of contemporary humanitarian interventions does much to counter arguments that the just use of force has evolved into a guiding norm of international society. Below I seek to address those arguments. Accordingly the chapter is organised into three parts. First I examine the interplay between morality and violence in the literature on international relations, and demonstrate that while Just War theory provides a partial explanation for humanitarian intervention, a more traditional focus on interests is arguably more useful in explaining why interventions occur at some times but not at others. Second, I go on to examine the normative case for understanding the use of force by charting the development of humanitarian intervention. This section pays particular attention to the role of global civil society (GCS) in pushing for a change to the concept of sovereignty, and in establishing a set of criteria for when it is appropriate for states to exercise the just use of force. The third section takes a critical view of this argument, demonstrating that in a number of cases of intervention, from Kosovo to Libya, there have been overriding national interests involved. The chapter concludes with some observations about the problems involved in viewing the just use of force as a way to operationalise responses to future human rights emergencies.

Interests, morality and violence: the 'humanitarian' use of force

The relationship between morality and violence in international politics is uneasy. For some, to act 'morally' denotes that states (and individuals) simply refrain from violence altogether.[1] This distinction has been the basis for arguments that when states choose to avoid violent means, they make room for 'peaceful' interaction in resolving issues of world affairs.[2] The recourse to violence is considered a last resort and against the civilised practice of everyday statehood. This line of thinking has also been at the forefront of perspectives that hold sovereignty as the primary ordering principle of the rules based international society, as the use of violence is seen to upset the moral laws governing state behaviour.[3] These two views have underpinned the perception that moral acts should be separate to acts of violence, and that sovereignty – determined by the right of the state to wield force – is central to maintaining the pluralist order of the modern international system.

The end of the Cold War challenged the accepted wisdom on this relationship, with the use of violence in pursuit of 'humanitarian' ends increasingly being seen as a moral act. This was reflected in the rise of humanitarian intervention, which showed that traditional notions of sovereignty could be overruled in favour of a moral claim about upholding human rights. In response, scholarly contributions sought to revitalise the principles of the Just War doctrine found in the writings of St Augustine, Thomas Aquinas and Hugo Grotius (amongst others) to argue that there were specific cases, such as genocide, crimes against humanity and ethnic cleansing, where the use of force was justified.[4] Specifically, scholars like Timothy Dunne, Nicholas Wheeler and Alex Bellamy have argued that a normative consensus on the rules governing humanitarian intervention has transformed the practice into a morally preferred policy option.[5] Here, elements of GCS are identified as having been important in facilitating a process of 'norm cascading' that has altered elite perceptions about the nature of sovereignty and the moral obligation of states to 'use all necessary means' to protect and uphold international peace and security.

Yet the connection between the moral consensus on the use of force and the motivation of states is not so clear. In their attempts to identify criteria for the just use of force, normative perspectives have tended to overlook the role of interests. The interests of states are important when considering the moral dimension of humanitarian intervention since international anarchy places a premium on the use of states' resources. In this environment, states are more likely to mobilise their forces when they see the potential for material benefits in return. Likewise, leaders in tune with the realities of power politics rarely put the interests of others above the responsibility they have to protect and pursue the interests of their own citizens. National interests can thus explain the often-puzzling situation whereby states will decide to intervene in some instances, while failing to do so in others.

From collective self-defence to the positive use of force

The end of the Cold War is a good starting-place to discuss the evolution of norms (relative to interests) in relation to the use of force. The collapse of bipolarity meant conventional concerns over nuclear and inter-state military conflict were replaced by more diffuse and multidimensional threats associated with civil war, transnational organised crime, oppression and underdevelopment.[6] Changes to how security was perceived corresponded with an increased role for the UN. Freed from the constraints of the bipolar power struggle, the UN could renew its efforts in acting as the principal agent for achieving peace and security. Indeed, in the period between 1991 and 1994, more peacekeeping missions were carried out than during the previous forty-five years. The UN-backed mission into Iraq-Kuwait in 1991, for instance, was the first example of collective self-defence since Korea, and signalled the beginning of what then-US President George H. W. Bush declared a 'New World Order' where cooperative security would become the norm in inter-state relations.[7] This was followed by a series of major UN peacekeeping operations that also marked a shift in perceptions about the threat (or use) of force to protect human rights. Peacekeeping efforts like those in Liberia in 1993 and the United Nations Transitional Authority in Cambodia (UNTAC), while still keeping within the self-defence framework, showed the growing preparedness of the international community to intervene to stop mass bloodshed, and in the case of Cambodia, acts of genocide.[8]

The demands on the UN in maintaining, observing and building peace culminated in the 1992 report by Secretary General Boutros Boutros-Ghali, *An Agenda for Peace: Preventive Diplomacy, Peacemaking and Peacekeeping*, which sought to outline specific decision-making criteria for the 'just' use of force.[9] Drawing on the principles of *jus in bello* and *jus ad bellum*, Boutros-Ghali argued that there must be a *just cause* whereby the primary objective is humanitarian; the action must be a *last resort* after all diplomatic measures have been exhausted; and that any mission must also have adequate resources to respond effectively to the threat in question. In other words, it must have both *proportional means* and *reasonable prospects for success*. Taken together, these criteria reflected a turn in how the international community responded to violations of human rights, viewing their role as both defender and enforcer of international peace and security. Widespread recognition of these principles was the starting point for the 'code of conduct' on the positive use of force and what is now classified as the established norm of humanitarian intervention: the 'Responsibility to Protect' (R2P).

Non-traditional security threats and the central role played by the UN in resolving them accounts for only half the story in explaining contemporary manifestations of humanitarian intervention. The remaining half, and what has contributed to debates on the legitimacy of the use of force, is the shift in how the norm of sovereignty has traditionally been perceived. Since the 1648 Peace of Westphalia, sovereignty had been defined as the state's claim to wield control over its territory and its citizens. Part of this control was also prefaced by the tacit assumption that the 'sovereign' would ensure the security of its citizens and defend the nation against any potential attack. The recognition of a state's 'right' to be sovereign had the effect of dividing each nation's jurisdictions along territorial lines, and corresponded with the attendant principle of non-interference. The principles of sovereignty and non-interference established the order of the international state system, which was later codified in Articles 2.1 and 2.4 of the UN Charter.[10]

During the 1990s, evidence that domestic populations were more often harmed by their own governments than external agents demonstrated that the state's apparent right to sovereignty (and with it the authority to use violence) was no longer an appropriate mechanism for maintaining international peace and security. The failure of the UN to respond to mass human rights abuses like those in Rwanda, Srebrenica, and Bosnia-Herzegovina also demonstrated that on its own, the institution was restricted in its capacity to intervene into the internal affairs of sovereign powers. Such restrictions brought attention to the problems of sovereignty determined as a right, and the new 'moral' duty of the international community to respond to large-scale atrocities.

The moral tension between sovereignty and human rights was first high-lighted by French physician and *Medicines Sans Frontiers* co-founder Bernard Kouchner, who argued that the triumph of liberal ideas of individual rights and democracy after the end of the Cold War reinforced a moral obligation of liberal democracies to intervene where violations of these rights were occurring. His 1992 article on the 'duty to interfere' drew on Immanuel Kant's notion of a categorical imperative that compelled individuals (and states) to treat others as ends.[11] As well as the moral obligation, Kouchner argued that states had the legal authority to disregard the principle of non-interference. Specifically, he claimed that since all states had signed the United Nations Declaration on Human Rights and yet clearly not all abided by it, the international community was justified in forcing them – sometimes with the use of violence – to honour their commitments.[12] From this perspective, the rights and duties tradition-ally attached to sovereignty were transferred to the international community, which then established the moral and legal frameworks for intervention into another state's territory.

Kouchner's right to intervene was extended by Sudanese diplomat Francis Deng's notion of 'sovereignty as responsibility'. Deng put forward a conception of sovereignty that incorporated the responsibility of the state to safeguard the individual rights and freedoms of their own citizens. He drew on the dual function of sovereignty to argue that if the state failed to protect its citizens from both internal and external threats, than the international community had a just cause to intervene.[13] Instead of turning to the obligations of the international community as a source for justifying intervention, Deng's sovereignty as responsibility targeted the action and conduct of the state itself.

Global civil society meets human security: norms as foreign policy drivers

These advocates were joined by a growing chorus of agents within GCS who demanded greater attention be paid to the protection of human rights. The lack of structural constraints opened space for a number of non-state actors to have a role in shaping international politics. Several think tanks, non-government organisations (NGOs) and commissions were established as key players in promoting the new 'humanitarianism'. With their ability to cut across state borders and create links at the national and trans-national level, these organisations influenced international perceptions about the use force. Supporters of GCS, such as Mary Kaldor, Martha Finnemore and Kathryn Sikkink, pointed towards institutions and NGOs such as the International Crisis Group (ICG), the Carnegie Endowment for Peace, *Medicines Sans Frontiers*, Human Rights Watch and the International Committee of the Red Cross as evidence that non-state actors had come to contribute to debates on the condition of human rights, as well as the measures taken to enforce them, to such an extent that they questioned the primacy of the state as the sole repository of sovereignty.[14]

Some, like Kaldor, went further and argued that a growing body of activism in international humanitarian law (IHL) and human rights law had started to combine to reflect a 'cosmopolitan law' that applied to both states and individuals.[15] This was evidenced by the creation of the International Criminal Court (ICC) and various special and *ad hoc* Tribunals, such as the International Criminal Tribunal for the former Yugoslavia (ICTY), the International Criminal Tribunal for Rwanda (ICTR), the Special Court in Sierra Leone, as well as the Special Tribunal for Cambodia. For advocates of this view, the rapidity with which these Tribunals were established demonstrated a growing acceptance that states (and more specifically, their leaders) could no longer shirk their sovereign responsibility to protect their own citizens.

The effects of globalisation in facilitating an increase in communication technology also allowed for real-time twenty-four-hour broadcasting of events. The ease with which this information could be accessed across state borders led to what some termed the 'CNN effect', where policy decisions were directly impacted by domestic responses to media images of ethnic cleansing and refugees fleeing persecution.[16] As Tony Blair commented when speaking about Kosovo: 'The mass expulsion of ethnic Albanians from Kosovo demanded the notice of the rest of the world'. Academic interest on the impact of media reporting on foreign policy largely came about during the First Gulf War where images of Kurdish refugees fleeing from the regime of Saddam Hussein were thought to have contributed to the unprecedented step of establishing Kurdish safe havens.[17] And despite it being widely acknowledged as both a foreign policy and a humanitarian failure, international and domestic media pressure also played a role in shaping the US decision to launch a mission into Somalia in 1992.

For many specialists, then, such developments represented a new 'epistemic community' governing the promotion of human rights and restricting the use of force. Directly related to this was growing support for the concept of 'human security'. Indeed, a human security network of NGOs, governments and institutions was established to promote recognition of the concept, which made its formal debut in the 1994 United Nations Development Programme (UNDP) *Human Development Report*. The UNDP described the concept as 'individual safety from such chronic threats as hunger, disease and repression', and 'protection from sudden and hurtful disruptions in the patterns of daily life – whether in homes, in jobs or in communities'.[18] Human security thus stressed the failure of traditional conceptualisations of security and foreign policy to prevent and respond to human suffering, and redefined the referent object to be protected (from the state to the individual) as well as the nature of threats faced (from military to non-military).[19]

At the time, the general consensus on the original UNDP definition was that it broadened and widened the scope of security a little too far to be of practical use. Yet over time it became more commonly accepted that security could be loosely translated as 'freedom from fear' and 'freedom from want'.[20] This had the benefit of providing a workable and recognisable framework for states to follow in policy practice, which bore fruit when these aspects of human security were incorporated into Japanese and Canadian approaches to foreign policy. For Canada, this was largely led by Foreign Minister Lloyd Axworthy, who later went on to act as co-chair for the International Commission on Intervention and State Sovereignty (ICISS). Axworthy saw human security as embodying the security of individuals from violent and non-violent threats. He invoked the concept during Canada's support for the campaign to ban anti-personnel landmines (the Ottawa Treaty), the trafficking of small arms and light weapons, and NATO's intervention into former Yugoslavia, which he described as the 'human security dynamic at work'.[21]

There is a natural connection between human security and humanitarian intervention. Indeed, the link between the freedom from fear (freedom from violent threats), and the use of force was the element of human security that most captured the interest of policy elites and campaigners. The freedom from want or basic human needs approach was not only popular within the Japanese diplomatic Bluebooks and amongst international aid and development circles.[22] Instances of civil war and state collapse demonstrated that issues of human security were more often the result of violent acts perpetrated by the state itself. In many cases, these acts were also in violation of established norms and conventions of international law such as the Refugee Convention and Protocols, the Universal Declaration of Human Rights and the Genocide Convention, which both enforced and empowered States Parties to utilise the appropriate means of resolving them. When it came to justifying the use of force, a greater amount of global interdependence made it clear that abuses of human security had transnational consequences and represented legitimate threats to international peace and security. Therefore, human security satisfied both the legal norms governing the use of force under Chapter VII of the UN Charter, and the just cause threshold of protecting the lives of persecuted individuals, as it expanded threats to international security to include threats to human rights.

From paper to practice? Humanitarian intervention, R2P and state sovereignty

In February 1999 US President Bill Clinton made a foreign policy speech that identified human rights, democracy promotion and respect for individual freedoms as key aspects of US internationalism in a post-Cold War environment. Coming off the back of its peacekeeping missions in Somalia and Srebrenica, as well as renewed efforts in negotiating peace in Dublin and Israel/Palestine, Clinton sought to frame US foreign policy in an era where a direct threat to US national interests was not immediately clear. Specifically, he stated:

> The question we must ask is, what are the consequences to our security of letting conflicts fester and spread? We cannot, indeed, we should not, do everything or be everywhere. But where our values and our interests are at stake, and where we can make a difference, we must be prepared to do so.[23]

In making the connection between US values and security, Clinton invoked the concept of human security to form the moral rationale behind the decision to use force against Serbia in March 1999. Two months later, British Prime Minister Tony Blair made a defining foreign policy speech that signalled more clearly than Clinton the new willingness of states to interfere where human rights abuses were occurring. Blair called on the support of the 'international community' in accepting responsibility for intervention, thrusting the decision-making criteria of humanitarian intervention identified several years earlier into the spotlight. And, in doing so, he laid out the justification for NATO's response to Serbia's treatment of Albanian Kosovars, noting that 'This is a just war, based not on any territorial ambitions but on values. We cannot let the evil of ethnic cleansing stand'.[24]

NATO's air campaign against Serbia was heralded as a new age of human-itarian intervention where the primary objective for the use of force against another sovereign was the achievement of humanitarian ends. It also cemented the code of conduct on how to intervene. The action was motivated by a just cause, was multilateral and was calculated to use proportional means with rea-sonable prospects for success. Indeed, after three months of NATO's intervention the Federal Republic of Yugoslavia's President, Slobodan Milošević, accepted the terms of a Russian–EU peace plan for a withdrawal of Serbian forces from Kosovo and for the presence of an international security mission to maintain peace.[25]

The success of Kosovo spurred elite support for humanitarian intervention in East Timor, which occurred in September 1999. The International Force for East Timor was a multi-nation humanitarian operation led by Australia and authorised under Chapter VII of the UN Charter. It was established in response to the 'scorched earth campaign' perpetrated by Indonesian-backed militia forces following East Timor's vote for independence. This campaign destroyed over 80 per cent of East Timorese infrastructure, caused the death of 200,000 and the displacement of 250,000 people in – and outside – East Timor.[26]

In a similar way to Kosovo, elements of GCS were viewed as central in pushing for intervention and particularly the diplomacy of Australia in leading the intervention. Indeed, Australia's Prime Minister John Howard echoed Tony Blair when he stated 'We have nightly viewed scenes of violence, death and destruction in East Timor' and witnessed the 'total failure of the Indonesian forces to control the violence and put an end to the killings that has greatly distressed the Australian people'.[27] International norms concerning torture, armed aggression, annexation and military occupation were major influences on Australia's decision to support the mandated use of force and lead the inter-vention. In fact, Australian Foreign Minister Alexander Downer even acknowl-edged the role of GCS as being fundamental to Australia's shift in policy, from pursuing a position of autonomy for East Timor, to actively supporting an act of self-determination.[28]

Growing acceptance that states must respond to threats to human rights reignited previous debates over the use of force and the changing nature of sov-ereignty. As noted above, sovereignty as the 'right to intervene' and 'sovereignty as responsibility' established separately the role of the international community and the role of the sovereign, but there had not yet been a characterisation that tied the two concepts together. This appeared in 2001 with the most recent var-iant of humanitarian intervention, the R2P, which was introduced through the ICISS-commissioned report co-chaired by Axworthy, Mohamed Sahnoun and Gareth Evans. It set out to gather a consensus on when it was appropriate to use force for humanitarian purposes.[29] The inspiration for the document was UN

Secretary General Kofi Annan's 2000 Millennium Address to the UN General Assembly, which called on the international community to develop a set of criteria for collective action against war crimes, genocide, crimes against humanity and ethnic cleansing.[30]

Broadly, the R2P attempted to bridge the right to intervene with sovereignty as responsibility as a means of transforming intervention into an inherently 'moral' act that must satisfy accepted norms of behaviour. It followed the principles established by Boutros-Ghali, but included the categories of *right intention* and *legitimate authority*. The emphasis on legitimate authority filled an important gap in determining what can be classified as the legitimate use of force, and distinguished humanitarian intervention from invasion or war. Questions over the legitimacy of humanitarian intervention were brought to attention after NATO's intervention into Kosovo, which did not explicitly have United Nations Security Council (UNSC) authorisation.[31]

The principle of right intention further strengthened the 'just cause' threshold by answering criticism that humanitarian intervention was not always performed for the purpose of upholding human rights. Right intention recognised that in most cases national interests such as halting the spread of refugees, countering the threat of terrorism and combating the spread of arms trafficking (not to mention other various sources of transnational organised crime) are involved in motivating the use of state resources. But as long as the overall purpose for military intervention was the reduction of human suffering, this satisfied the principle of right intention. In this regard, the R2P represented the bringing together of issues of human security and sovereignty. It acknowledged that in an interconnected global society states could no longer operate under the assumption that the security and wellbeing of other nations did not have a direct effect on their own interests.

But while the 1990s reflected the 'golden age' of human rights promotion where a groundswell of scholars, activists and leaders came to support the use of force for humanitarian ends, the events of the new millennium posed significant challenges to the legitimacy of humanitarian intervention.[32] The 9/11 attacks brought more global attention to the limited ability of states to control and enforce their own security, and pushed terrorism to the top of the list of potential threats to national and international security. The US's response in launching the 'war on terror' and its preference for 'coalitions of the willing' under its leadership, rather than UNSC-led operations, also demonstrated that human rights and the norms governing the use of force could easily be circumvented for material gain.

This was best illustrated through the adoption of the 'Bush Doctrine' in 2002. At the centre of this approach was the policy of pre-emption outlined in the National Security Strategy statement, which widened the scope of intervention to any instance where the US saw the potential for its interests to be threatened.[33] Such a policy provided the US *prime facie* justification to unilaterally decide when it could violate a state's sovereignty without concern for acquiring a UNSC resolution. Yet a UN resolution was important as it established the legal basis for the use of force, and distinguished humanitarian intervention from a declaration of war by committing the intervening forces to abide by mutually agreed-upon standards of conduct. For normative scholars, satisfying the requirements of Chapter VII of the UN Charter provided states with a stamp of legitimacy to violate the norm of non-interference, and to do so without upsetting the order of the international society. Hence when the US 'intervened' in Iraq in 2003 by claiming to protect the citizens of Iraq, and did so without the consent of the UN, it signalled to other nations that human rights norms were subject to the will of the great powers. By extension, the norms governing the use of force did not necessarily apply to those states with the capacity to work around them.[34] This was particularly damaging given that the US was part of the so-called group of 'norm entrepreneurs' whose leadership in response to Kosovo was seen as central to wider international acceptance for the principles guiding military intervention for humanitarian ends.

Doubts about the changing nature of sovereignty were also caused by the failed first test of the R2P in Darfur. By 2004, the crisis in Darfur had been declared a genocide by then-US Secretary of State Colin Powell, the first member of the US Executive to publically use the term.[35] At the time, the death-toll was estimated at around 400,000 with over four million displaced into refugee camps.[36] The government of Sudan had failed in its responsibility to protect civilians from the *Junjaweed* and was in some cases actively supporting them. Yet, despite Darfur appearing to satisfy the R2P's just cause threshold for trigging a forceful response, this did not occur. The African Union sent a small peacekeeping force of 9,000 which was under-funded and under-resourced, and lacked the legitimacy of a UN-backed blue-helmet mission. UN approval for a proposed peacekeeping mission in 2006 failed because of opposition from Sudan and China, the latter of which had interests in the oil-rich nation and immediately dismissed any notion of a forceful intervention.[37] Western nations in the midst of the 'war on terror' were also hesitant to spend the political capital needed to push for any agreement. The lack of international support for intervention in Darfur had many ready to declare support for the concept of R2P 'dead' – a year after it had been formally adopted by the General Assembly at the 2005 UN World Summit.[38]

The effects of the 'war on terror' and the failed first test of the R2P were severe blows to the momentum of the human rights regime, but there was still evidence that it had not faded completely. The 2005 World Summit Outcome Document demonstrated widespread recognition that sovereignty and human rights were wedded to a dual responsibility for the state to protect its citizens from external and internal threats, and for the international community to intervene when the state had failed in its sovereign responsibility. Specifically, the Summit concluded that states had an obligation to take 'timely and decisive action' against acts of genocide, war crimes, crimes against humanity and ethnic cleansing. The UNSC further endorsed the content of the document in 2006 with Resolution 1674.[39] Three years later, in 2009, the General Assembly and the UNSC both agreed to continue their consideration of the principle with A/63/308 and Resolution 1894 respectively.[40] In the same year, a Joint Office for the Prevention of Genocide and the Responsibility to Protect was established to consider potential cases where the R2P could be applied in practice.

A new dawn for R2P? The case of Libya

The campaign for the acceptance of the R2P appeared to receive a boost during NATO's intervention into Libya. It was the first case of the R2P being invoked as justification for the use of force against a sovereign nation, and was influenced by elements of GCS during the Arab Spring movement. The intervention into Libya was authorised by UNSC Resolutions 1970 and 1973, which called for the 'immediate establishment of a cease-fire', and authorised all Member States to employ 'all necessary measures ... to protect civilians and civilian populated areas under threat of attack'.[41] This included the establishment of a 'no-fly zone' over Libyan airspace and the authority to enforce it. The no-fly zone mandate was expansive and the first to be enacted solely for the protection of civilian populations. In previous examples, such as in Bosnia, the mandate was for the delivery of humanitarian aid and not explicitly for the protection of individuals.

The swiftness with which the international community responded to the crisis was also heralded as an endorsement of the 'responsibility to react' and the three pillars of the R2P outlined in the Outcome document. The responsibility to react, or pillar 3, emphasised the international community's obligation 'to respond to situations of compelling human need with appropriate measures, which may include ... in extreme cases military intervention'.[42] Indeed, the intervention was described as being unique in this regard as the primary moral justification was to prevent the Gaddafi regime from carrying out his threat to 'cleanse Libya house by house' and destroy the rebel-held Benghazi region where over 750,000 Libyans lived.[43] An estimated 8,000 had been killed by the regime when Resolution 1970 was passed in late February 2011, only two weeks after the initial fighting had broken out.[44] Resolution 1970 included an arms embargo and an asset freeze estimated to have resulted in the loss of US$32 billion, as well as international sanctions and a referral of Gaddafi to the ICC for crimes against humanity.[45] When this failed to deter the regime the UNSC passed Resolution 1973 on 17 March. Two days later NATO launched its air and missile campaign, as part of its mandate to use 'all necessary means' to enforce the no-fly zone and protect civilians; within seventy-two hours the

Libyan air defence system had been destroyed. By October 2011 the temporary representative of Libyan sovereignty, the Transitional National Council, had control over all territory and Operation Unified Protector withdrew all forces by the 31st of the same month.

Overall, the initial intervention in Libya satisfied the general criteria of the R2P. The international community was quick to mobilise military resources, but only after sanctions and diplomatic pressure had failed to deter Gaddafi and his regime. It was deemed proportional in that air strikes were largely launched against military targets that were a threat to civilians on the ground. The intervention was also calculated to have a reasonable prospect of success given the relative balance of capabilities between NATO and Gaddafi's forces. And, as mentioned above, the actions of the Gaddafi regime and the subsequent loss of life satisfied the just cause threshold, while the emphasis on the use of force for humanitarian purposes established the right intention. Finally, and most importantly, Libya demonstrated acceptance that sovereignty was conditional on the state's ability to fulfil its responsibility to protect (pillar one), and when it failed in this responsibility, then respect for sovereignty was no longer a defence to avoid foreign interference.

When intention meets reality: the foreign policy interest of appearing 'moral'

So far I have traced the evolution of humanitarian intervention in order to show how one might make the case for norms and ideas as forces shaping perceptions about the use of force for moral ends. This focused heavily on the influences of GCS in gathering international support for changing notions of sovereignty, as well as evidence where it appeared that the international community had been motivated by a just cause in militarily intervening into another state's sovereign territory. The centrality of establishing a just cause prior to intervention is rooted in a moral dilemma, which is naturally produced when one advocates the use of violence to stop or prevent violence. Normative scholars have argued that this can be overcome by demonstrating that the purpose for resorting to the use of violence has sufficient just cause so as to overrule the negative effects this usually engenders, and still be classified as a moral act. This is even the case for instances of humanitarian intervention, which produces a further dilemma about whether the pursuit of moral ends warrants a breach of the norms of mutual recognition of sovereignty and non-interference.

Yet as I demonstrate below, evidence of just cause does not present an accurate account of the factors that have motivated the use of force. Specifically, selectivity about when and where interventions occurred shows that the decision to intervene is contingent on time and context, and not guided by universal notions of duty and obligation. This calls into question the so-called 'international consensus' in support of changing norms of sovereignty, as well as the moral precepts involved in tying the use of violence to certain established codes of behaviour.

Indeed, it is entirely possible to give a more prosaic account of humanitarian intervention that is at least as persuasive as that given by human security advocates. It would run something like this: after decades of ignoring instances of mass atrocities in Africa, the Middle East and parts of Europe, the dominant West (rather than the 'international community'), determined that it was now time to devote serious attention to human rights. The end of the Cold War certainly made it easier for GCS to draw attention to these conflicts, and a weakened Russia and a still economically backward China meant traditional interpretations of international law in terms of state's rights were muted.

More importantly, there were specific geopolitical factors linked to traditional interests related to power and interests at play in the Kosovo conflict. These revolved around conflict spillover, and the possibility that cross-border security issues could spread through Western Europe. Tellingly, Blair alluded to as much in his Chicago speech, stating that 'it does make a difference that this is taking place in such a combustible part of Europe'.[46] Clinton expressed the same concerns when he argued that if the US did nothing then violence in Serbia would spread to Albania and Macedonia, potentially affecting its allies in Greece and Turkey.[47]

In this way, Clinton's rhetoric about the US being concerned with both achieving its interests and spreading its values of freedom and democracy was a convenient way to cement its claim as the world's indispensable nation. And its support for NATO's intervention into Kosovo was a means of committing hard power resources to maintain its policy of strategic primacy over Europe. As the dominant power in NATO, lack of US backing would have severely damaged its status in the eyes of its allies. As Clinton acknowledged, 'NATO itself would have been discredited for failing to defend the very values that give it meaning'.[48]

Blair's doctrine of the international community was probably subtler than Clinton's approach as a foreign policy strategy. To begin with, it was domestically important due to the need to pay lip service to a British 'Third Way' foreign policy that distinguished it from Tory *realpolitik*.[49] It was also a way of galvanising international support for NATO's intervention in the absence of a UNSC resolution, and to solidify US domestic resolve for the air campaign, which had started to waver after six weeks without Milošević capitulating. The lack of a UNSC resolution damaged the legal authority of the intervention and uncovered the moral relativism of NATO's selective intervention. And whereas NATO and its supporters preferred to reference the moral justification inherent in halting Milošević's forces, it promptly ignored the fact that Russia and China had vetoed a resolution designed to give the intervention legitimacy.

Likewise, even though it received less attention, the decision to use force in East Timor was also politically expedient. This was particularly so for Australia, which sought to gain materially from leading the mission. By accepting the responsibility of command in the first UN-mandated peace enforcement oper-ation outside of Africa and led by a country other than the US, Australia as a middle power was demonstrating a respectable degree of military and diplo-matic expertise. The geographic proximity between Australia and East Timor (it is 700km from Dili to Darwin), also meant that alongside the benefits to its international reputation, Australia had strategic interests in stopping the spill-over effects resulting from intrastate instability and prolonged political violence, which were also threating important trade routes and regional security.

The change in policy regarding Australia's decision to recognise East Timorese independence was also instructive. Since 1976 Australia had actu-ally supported Indonesia's annexation of East Timor. This was despite evidence of widespread human rights abuses being perpetrated by the *Tentara Nasional Indonesia* (Indonesian Army) and various efforts by GCS to rally support for self-determination. It was not until the situation deteriorated – to the extent that Australia's interests were being threatened – that Canberra signalled in September 1999 that it was willing to accept the Timorese claim to statehood.

Indeed, an independent East Timor was an advantage for Australia, as the threat of economic and military sanctions against Jakarta had the potential to severely affect trade relations. The economic motivation was visible in the fact that trade between the two nations markedly increased following interven-tion. In 1998 Australia's exports to Indonesia were worth A$2.2 billion and Australia's imports were valued at A$3.2 billion. Between 2000 and 2001 these figures increased to A$3.1 billion and A$4.5 billion respectively.[50] Not only were there trade benefits to be had with Indonesia, but there were also expec-tations that Australia could enact a more favourable energy deal with a new and oil-rich but underdeveloped East Timor, which would be in a comparatively weaker negotiating position to Australia than Indonesia. This expectation was realised when Australia and East Timor signed the Timor Sea Treaty on 20 May 2002 – the very first day of East Timor's independence.[51]

The reality behind the veil: R2P, Libya and the case for intervention

As discussed above, the introduction and adoption of the R2P doctrine was viewed by many as a watershed moment for the human rights campaign because it finally appeared that states were in agreement on their collective responsibility to respond to human suffering. But despite this, ambiguities over when the international community has a legal and moral authority to intervene have dogged the R2P since its formal articulation in 2001. The original thresh-old for intervention was described as too low as it pertained to any instance where a population was seen to be experiencing serious harm. Even Evans, a key supporter of the concept, admitted that this was too broad and left the norm open to manipulation by states seeking to pursue more self-interested ends.[52]

The UN World Summit sought to correct this by narrowing the focus to four specific crimes: genocide, war crimes, ethnic cleansing and crimes against humanity. While this may have, in theory, provided a clearer view of what acts trigger the just cause of the R2P, it had little effect on shaping the behaviour of states, as evidenced by the lack of support in operationalising the R2P in response to Darfur. This has much to do with the very nature of international law as well as the competing views of individual member states. The 2005 Outcome Document was tabled at a plenary meeting of the General Assembly, which (other than approving the UN budget) had no power to enforce its resolutions. Indeed, its resolutions are merely statements of common principles, are not formal treaties, and are not binding in international law. The document itself only listed the R2P in two of the 178 paragraphs, and failed to establish an agreed-upon set of criteria for the use of military force. This last point is crucial since this was one of the key sources of tension between sovereignty and the protection of human rights that ICISS was expected to resolve. Finally, governments in support of the concept were not compelled to reveal any concrete policy statements demonstrating their commitment to adopting the principles of the R2P, nor were they obliged to indicate its inclusion in any future policy proposals.

This meant that the norm was essentially open to a state's own interpretation, which was made apparent in 2008 when Russia invoked the language of the R2P to justify the use of force in South Ossetia under the guise of protecting ethnic Russians from persecution. For then-Russian President Dmitry Medvedev the decision to use force satisfied the principles of the R2P in that it was 'aimed at preventing the genocide, the elimination of a people, and helping them get on their feet'.[53] This action was widely criticised with claims that Russia was inappropriately using the principle to achieve its own territorial ambitions.[54] And yet Russia was effectively following precisely what Blair and Clinton had done in gathering international and domestic support for their policy choices by couching them in just terms. In fact, Medvedev said as much when he claimed that 'There is certainly no serious argument which would allow one to ... separate the process of the recognition of South Ossetia and Abkhazia from the decisions taken with regard to Kosovo'.[55]

Further evidence of the R2P's hollow nature was evident during the Libya crisis, where it was obvious that the moral pursuit of human rights was not the primary motivation of the intervening parties. In fact, in terms of invoking the principle of the R2P, UNSC Resolution 1973 only referred to the responsibility of the Libyan authorities, and particularly the opposition forces, to protect its citizens. It did not refer specifically to a resultant responsibility of the international community to intervene.

What then, was the purpose of the intervention? To begin with, France and Britain were almost unseemly in their haste to be the first nation to enforce the UNSC mandate. This was made obvious when France began its military involvement on 19 March, at the same time as Nicholas Sarkozy was still having discussions with British Prime Minister David Cameron about how best to coordinate the operation.[56] France had both domestic and international interests that made intervention logical. Domestically, with an approaching election, Sarkozy needed to solidify the perception of strong leadership by matching his high-sounding moral rhetoric on the conflict with a commitment to supplying resources to the military operation. France also had geographic links to the region and sought to strengthen its diplomatic support for democratic and economic reform in Northern Africa as part of its lead role in the Union for the Mediterranean.

Competing interests meant France and Britain responded differently to the crisis. France was consistent in its support for action against Libya. The UK was initially hesitant, and even refused to join EU sanctions. Britain's reluctance to use force in Libya can be linked to its relationship with Gaddafi after 9/11, when personal diplomacy by Blair had facilitated a warming in London–Tripoli relations, and also led to the UK winning a number of defence contracts.[57] But as the situation worsened in Libya and threats to regional security increased, the UK shifted its approach radically. In the words of Prime Minister David Cameron:

> We simply cannot have a situation where a failed pariah state festers on Europe's southern border. This would potentially threaten our security, push people across the Mediterranean and create a more dangerous and uncertain world for Britain and for all our allies as well as for the people of Libya.[58]

The lack of a coordinated response called into question the ability of the EU to act as an ethical agent capable of promoting collective security. Indeed, the European Common Foreign and Security Policy (CFSP) was famously criticised over its inaction in Libya with one diplomat declaring 'The CFSP died in Libya – we just have to pick a sand dune under which we can bury it'.[59] This is not that surprising given the different foreign policy goals being pursued between France and the UK on the one side, and Germany on the other, which abstained from voting on UNSC Resolution 1973.

As well as strategic and prestige interests, there were significant economic interests at stake in Libya. After NATO announced plans for its withdrawal, there was a rush to secure lucrative reconstruction contracts. The Transitional National Council that took over from Gaddafi had already indicated that it would preference those states that gave diplomatic and military support to the rebels, with Britain and France likely to achieve the most. This was a sizeable amount given the estimated US$166 billion in frozen assets that were set to be released. British Defence Minister Phillip Hammond highlighted the potential opportunities for Britain when he stated that 'I would expect British companies, even British sales directors, [to be] packing their suitcases and looking to get out to Libya and take part in the reconstruction of that country as soon as they can'.[60] The French Foreign Minister, Alain Juppe, also indicated that France was in a preferred position to benefit from reconstruction contracts. He claimed it was only 'fair and logical' for the new government of Tripoli to act favourably towards those that helped it the most during the crisis.[61] The expectation of material benefits in return for assisting the rebels demonstrates that this was not an act primarily motivated by moral considerations.

The supply of oil was also a factor motivating a quick resolution to the conflict. Italy relied on Libya for 20 per cent of its oil, while France, Switzerland, Austria and Ireland relied on the nation to provide 15 per cent of their energy needs. The oil company ENI in Italy was the largest producer, generating 273,000 barrels a day. ENI, along with BP of Britain, France's Total, YPF from Spain and OMV of Austria dominated the oil and gas sector before the intervention and were singled out by the Transitional National Council to benefit once relative stability was restored.[62] As a spokesman for the Libyan rebel oil company Agoca stated, 'We don't have a problem with Western countries like Italians, French and U.K. companies, but we have some political issues with Russia, China and Brazil'.[63] Gaddafi was seen as being notoriously difficult during negotiations for contracts, frequently forcing companies to renegotiate for 'bonus' payments and higher taxes, which further fuelled expectations that an alternative government would be better suited to the strategic and economic interests of the intervening powers.

In fact, the notion that the intervention was a cover for regime change clearly dispels any notion that Libya was a successful case of R2P. Those who were quick to label it as such even started to question the legitimacy of NATO's motives. The mandate provided under UNSC Resolution 1973 was to protect civilians, but the ambiguity of the Resolution allowed NATO to extend its air campaign to military targets where the threat to civilians was not entirely clear. The Resolution stipulated that NATO was authorised to use all necessary means 'to protect civilians and civilian populated areas under threat of attack in the Libyan Arab Jamahiriya'.[64] The use of 'under threat' and 'civilian populated areas' rather than 'protect civilians under imminent threat of *physical* [my emphasis] violence' allowed NATO to stretch the area of enforcement to suit its military aims. As Obama, Cameron and Sarkozy stated in a jointly written commentary justifying their decision to pursue the overthrow of Qaddafi: 'There is a pathway to peace that promises new hope for the people of Libya – a future without Qaddafi that preserves Libya's integrity and sovereignty, and restores her economy and the prosperity and security of her people.[65] Accusations of 'mission creep' were not helped by the violation of the UNSC's own arms embargo by the US and France when they supplied weapons and training to the opposition.[66] Together, these actions did much to demonstrate that the rules and laws governing the use of force ultimately rested on the preferences of major powers.

Humanitarian intervention: Syria and beyond

The international fallout from the NATO-led Libyan intervention was subsequently illustrated in Western dithering over responses to the civil war in Syria. From the time the conflict had begun in 2011, China and Russia had vetoed all proposed UN resolutions calling for action (including non-military intervention) against the Assad regime in Damascus.[67] The resistance of those nations can partly be explained by what they viewed as the West's deceit over the Libya mandate. As Russian Foreign Minister Sergei Lavrov stated, 'Russia will do everything it can to prevent a Libyan scenario happening in Syria'.[68] China's official newspaper, the *People's Daily*, stated a week after the airstrikes began that:

> The military attacks on Libya are, following on the Afghan and Iraq wars, the third time that some countries have launched armed action against sovereign countries. It should be seen that every time military means are used to address crises, that is a blow to the United Nations Charter and the rules of international relations.[69]

This has been made even clearer with international responses to Syria being increasingly dictated by competing US and Russian interests. The lack of support for intervention by Moscow is tied to its desire to maintain control of the naval base at Tartus, the only Russian military installation outside the former Soviet space. Russia also had significant economic interests in Syria and had counted on maintaining its diplomatic links with the Assad regime. It had arms contracts worth nearly US$5 billion and investments in infrastructure, energy and tourism worth over US$20 billion. Russia had legitimate fears that a change in the Syrian government would put these investments in jeopardy, as was the case in Libya when the new government failed to honour Russia's existing arms contracts.[70] When the initial violence broke out, Russian company Stroitansgaz was building a natural gas processing plant 200km east of Homs and was providing technical assistance to the Arab gas pipeline, which runs through Lebanon, Egypt, Jordan and Syria.[71]

For its part, Washington's approach to the crisis has also been revealing in showing how commitments to the use of force are still contingent on the rational calculation of material interests. Originally, the overall goal of the US was to find a negotiated settlement to the conflict out of concern that the situation would deteriorate into another protracted civil war in the Middle East, with potentially widespread regional security implications. In August 2011, Obama called for the resignation of President Assad, and implemented US sanctions. This was on top of the EU sanctions that had already been in place since May.

Over the next two years, the conflict in Syria fell off the US foreign policy radar. The provision of US aid to rebel forces (even non-lethal) was not agreed upon until February 2013.

By June 2013, nearly 100,000 Syrians had been killed and nearly two million had been displaced inside Syria or sought refuge in constructed camps on the borders with Turkey, Jordan and Lebanon, as well as in Iraq.[72] The poverty rate had increased to nearly 75 per cent of the population, with extreme poverty estimated at around 54 per cent.[73] A breakdown in access to government and social services meant disease spread across the country, which was exacerbated by the Assad regime's refusal to allow international humanitarian assistance to rebel-held areas. Towards the end of 2013 Syria recorded an outbreak of polio after having being previously cleared of the disease in 1999.[74] The complete collapse of the Syrian economy added another layer to the crisis. GDP fell by 31.4 per cent in 2012 and by 7.1 per cent in 2013. International sanctions put pressure on the domestic market and inflation rose 500 per cent. Conservative estimates on the overall cost of the conflict on Syria's economy were calculated at US$19.3 billion, or 91.3 per cent of Gross National Product.[75]

Apart from the dire humanitarian picture, Syria was also fast becoming a new breeding ground for terrorism and Islamic extremism. The best opposition fighters, such as those from *Jabhat al-Nursa*, were linked to Al Qaeda and the Islamic State of Iraq and Syria (ISIS) in Iraq as well as *Ahrar al-Sham*. These groups were well-organised and well-financed, and quickly established control over their own municipal territories, providing the basic human services the government and GCS were ill-equipped to deliver. Parallels to the mujahedeen in Afghanistan and sectarian violence in Iraq were made, with some claiming that the number of foreign jihadists in Syria surpassed the amount in Iraq during the peak of the insurgency.[76]

In terms of scale, the security and humanitarian situation had far exceeded what occurred in Libya but serious debate on the possibility of military involvement did not surface until September 2013 when US President Barack Obama famously made his 'red line' speech on what would warrant US support for the use of force in Syria. This had first appeared a year earlier when Obama hastily responded to a reporter's question on the topic: 'We have been very clear to the Assad regime, but also to other players on the ground, that a red line for us is [if] we start seeing a whole bunch of chemical weapons moving around or being utilized. That would change my calculus. That would change my equation'.[77] Besides raising a mixture of surprise and concern from political commentators for his heavy-handed approach, Obama's rhetoric had little effect on changing the dynamics of the situation on the ground. The civil war continued and the warring parties ignored the UN-brokered Geneva plan calling for an immediate ceasefire, the formation of a transitional government and the eventual holding of democratic elections. This changed after plausible evidence emerged that

Syria had used chemical weapons against its own citizens. Obama declared that the US would launch a limited airstrike with the aim of deterring Syria from using chemical weapons. In justifying his decision, Obama reiterated that this was a red line for the use of force. But he added one important caveat: it was not the US's red line, but the threshold set by the international community which had an important stake in stopping the use of chemical weapons. Yet Obama subsequently abandoned any airstrikes against Syria's air and defence forces, preferring instead to support a Russian initiative that outlined a timeline for monitored and safe disposal of the weapons.

There are two important points with respect to Just War and humanitarian intervention that arise from US strategy in Syria. The first is that it was not the failure of the Syrian government's responsibility to protect that prompted the US to consider changing its stance towards forcible intervention. Rather, it was the norm of non-use of chemical weapons. This questions the legitimacy of claims that force is used primarily for the protection of human life, and further demonstrates that norms are instruments of state power. If the pursuit of human rights was an overriding concern then justifications on the use of force would have referred to any of the number of humanitarian issues listed above and occurred well before over 100,000 lives were lost. Second, and with specific relevance to the moral justification for the use of force, is that states will choose whatever norm suits their political needs at the time. So, in a similar way to how Blair legitimated NATO's involvement in Kosovo in 'just' terms, and Russia used R2P to legitimise its actions in Georgia, Obama was selecting the norm that would best sell his foreign policy choices to international and domestic audiences.

Humanitarian intervention, R2P and the just use of force: a bleak future?

States routinely claim to be acting morally when using force. Yet as the analysis above suggests, their actual motives leave much to be desired with respect to the future prospects for the norm of humanitarian intervention. In the case of Libya, the lack of consensus on the parameters of the UNSC mandate uncovered the disconnect between the abstract morality informing the R2P, and the reality of external pressures, which are often seen to shape state responses to human rights issues. The actions of the major powers involved in the Libyan intervention – France, the UK and the US – showed that states still make decisions based on rational calculations of interests.

This also explains why, when debates on the use of force in response to Syria finally emerged, there was generally a lack of enthusiasm for action. Russia's geopolitical interests in keeping the Assad regime in power meant the issue would not pass the UNSC, and Obama's blundering over 'red lines' demonstrated a general reluctance by the US to commit military resources to resolve the crisis. At the time of writing, the conflict had reached its fourth year, with little evidence of any further decisive action being taken to reach a peaceful resolution between Assad and the rebel forces. Geneva II – the second round of UN-sponsored peace talks in January 2014 – broke down over disagreement between the opposition groups and the Assad government over who would be involved in a transitional government. This added weight to predictions that Syria is increasingly at risk of being fragmented along sectarian lines.[78]

The inconsistency of states' commitment to the just use of force also indicates that future invocations of the R2P are less likely. This has already been evident in the dwindling of the term's use during debates on how to respond to the crisis in Syria. US and EU norm entrepreneurs have signalled that in a changing international system, where the relative balance of power is not so clearly in the West's favour, foreign policy decisions will more often be based on calculations of hard power. This has led some, such as Ramesh Thakur, to argue that any prospects for the success of the R2P must be centred on accommodating a greater role for emerging powers.[79] On the surface, such observations have merit, particularly given the vocal scepticism of Brazil, Russia, India, China and South Africa (the BRICS), on the utility of the R2P. This hardened after it became clear that NATO's intention in Libya had shifted from civil protection to regime change. But evidence that these nations are willing (or in fact have the capacity) to fill any gaps in setting new standards of international rules and norms is uncertain, especially considering their preference for achieving their soft power goals through policies of foreign aid and development.

Conclusions

It seems obvious that moral considerations are present in the decision to use force for the achievement of humanitarian ends. But as this chapter has demonstrated, the relationship between morality and violence is more complex than a surface evaluation would suggest. This is particularly the case in an environment of international anarchy where universal notions of morality are a near impossibility. Normative perspectives on the use of force have tried to resolve this tension by pointing towards the activism of GCS in gathering support for changes to the norm of sovereignty. The current manifestation of humanitarian intervention – the R2P – was heralded as a success, merging sovereignty with the protection of human rights. But the lack of consensus on when the R2P should be operationalised and the inconsistency in which it has been used, highlights that sovereignty remains a form of 'organized hypocrisy'.[80]

Whether sovereignty is classified as a right, or a responsibility with strings attached, it will still be used by the powerful to pursue their own interests. This merely reflects the material hierarchy that characterises order in the international system. Yet it does not mean that states will entirely overlook moral considerations in their decisions to use force. Instead, it merely underscores that when humanitarian intervention does occur, the pursuit of human rights is frequently not the immediate objective. Since the end of the Cold War, in the few cases where states have claimed to be acting for the protection of others, there were clear material interests involved. In Kosovo and East Timor the states responsible for conducting the intervention had specific geopolitical, economic and prestige goals that informed their decision to commit state resources to physically perform each intervention. Interests were also the deciding factor in the cases where states arguably failed in their collective responsibility to intervene, as was seen in the lack of international action in Darfur and in Syria respectively.

NOTES

1   Defining morality is akin to describing the properties of mind, luck or culture; the varia-bility of it makes defining it very difficult. For the purposes of this chapter, I am primarily concerned with the effects of action claimed to be moral. Thus, morality is understood here as those acts perceived by agents to be just, right or good.

2   M. Doyle, 'Kant, liberal legacies, and foreign affairs', *Philosophy & Public Affairs*, 12:3 (1983), pp. 205–35.

3   This view was primarily held by the pluralist scholars of the English School of inter-national relations. See H. Bull, *The Anarchical Society: A Study of Order in World Politics* (Columbia: Columbia University Press, 1977); and R. Jackson, *The Global Covenant: Human Conduct in a World of States* (Oxford: Oxford University Press, 2000).

4   The classical principles of Just War were popularised by M. Walzer in *Just and Unjust Wars: A Moral Argument with Historical Illustrations* (New York: Basic Books, 1977). Modern scholars of the solidarist perspective have since incorporated them into their writings on humanitarian intervention. See J. Welsh (ed.), *Humanitarian Intervention and International Relations* (Oxford: Oxford University Press, 2002) and A. Bellamy, 'Motives, outcomes, intent, and the legitimacy of humanitarian intervention', *Journal of Military Ethics*, 3:3 (2004), pp. 216–32.

5   N. Wheeler, *Saving Strangers: Humanitarian Intervention in International Society* (New York: Oxford University Press, 2000); N. Wheeler, 'Legitimizing humanitarian interven-tion: Principles and procedures', *Melbourne Journal of International Law*, 2:2 (2001), pp. 375–8; T. Dunne and N. Wheeler, 'East Timor and the new humanitarian intervention-ism', *International Affairs*, 77:4 (2001), pp. 805–29; A. Bellamy, 'Humanitarian responsi-bilities and interventionist claims in international society', *Review of International Studies*, 29:3 (2003), pp. 321–41.

6   R. Ullman, 'Redefining security', *International Security*, 8 (1993), pp. 125–35.

7   George H. W. Bush made his 'Towards a New World Order' speech in front of a joint ses-sion of Congress in 1991. He argued that increased diplomacy and cooperation between the developed and developing world, Muslim and non-Muslim and Arab and non-Arab over condemnation of Iraq in Kuwait, as well as greater cooperation between himself and Gorbachev, demonstrated that 'a new world order – can emerge: a new era – freer from the threat of terror, stronger in the pursuit of justice, and more secure in the quest for peace'. G. Bush, 'Address Before a Joint Session of the Congress on the Persian Gulf Crisis and the Federal Budget Deficit', George Bush Presidential Library and Museum, Public Papers, 1990, available at: http://bushlibrary.tamu.edu/research/public_papers. php?id=2217&year=1990&month=9 (accessed 16 April 2014).

8   The UN peacekeeping mission into Liberia was the first joint international and regional mission that included the UN Observer Mission in Liberia and the Economic Community of West African States Ceasefire Monitoring Group . It was enacted in response to the long running civil war and was regarded as a success. For more see B. Nowrojee, 'Joining forces: United Nations and regional peacekeeping – lessons from Liberia', *Harvard Human Rights Journal*, 8 (1995), pp. 129–51. The mission into Cambodia was the first example of the UN adopting temporary administrative control of a nation. It was considered a relative success in that it included both an element of peacekeeping and peacebuilding with the UN overseeing free and fair elections. For more see M. Doyle and N. Suntharalingam, 'The UN in Cambodia: Lessons for complex peacekeeping', *International Peacekeeping*, 1:2 (1994), pp. 117–47.

9   B. Boutros-Ghali, *An Agenda for Peace: Preventative Diplomacy, Peacemaking and Peacekeeping*, Report of the Secretary-General pursuant to the statement adopted by the Summit Meeting of the Security Council on 31 January 1992, 17 June 1992, available at: www.unrol.org/files/A_47_277.pdf (accessed 16 April 2014).

10 According to Article 2.1, 'The Organization is based on the principle of the sovereign equality of all its Members and article 2.4 establishes non-interference, All Members shall refrain in their international relations from the threat or use of force against the territorial integrity or political independence of any state'. United Nations, 'Chapter 1: Purposes and Principles', in *The United Nations Charter*, 1945, available at: www.un.org/en/documents/charter/chapter1.shtml (accessed 15 April 2014).

11 Original text: B. Kouchner and M Bettati, *Le evoir d'ingerence: Peut-on les laiseer mourir?* [The Duty to Interfere: Can We Let them die?] (Paris: Noël, 1987). For more see T. Allen and D. Stayn, 'A Right to Interfere? Bernard Kouchner and the New Humanitarianism', *Journal of International Development*, 12:6 (2000), pp. 825–42.

12 Allen and Stayn, 'A Right to Interfere?', pp. 825–42.

13 F. M. Deng, S. Kimaro, T. Lyons, D. Rothchild and I. Zartman (eds), *Sovereignty as Responsibility: Conflict Management in Africa* (Washington DC: Brookings Institute Press, 1996).

14 M. Kaldor, 'The idea of global civil society', *International Affairs*, 79:3 (2003), pp. 583–93; M. Finnemore and K. Sikkink, 'International norm dynamics and political change', *International Organization*, 52:4 (1998), pp. 887–917; M. Finnemore and K. Sikkink, 'Taking stock: The constructivist research program in international relations and comparative politics', *Annual Review of Political Science*, 4 (2001), pp. 391–416.

15 M. Kaldor, 'Cosmopolitanism and Organized Violence', in S. Vertovic and R. Cohen (eds), *Conceiving Cosmopolitanism: Theory, Context and Practice* (New York: University of Oxford, 2002), pp. 271–7.

16 H. F. Carey, 'U.S. domestic politics and the emerging humanitarian intervention policy: Haiti, Bosnia and Kosovo', *World Affairs*, 164:2 (2001), pp. 72–82.

17 M. Shaw, *Civil Society and Media in Global Crisis* (London: St. Martin's Press, 1999), pp. 79–88.

18 UN Development Programme, *Human Development Report 1994* (New York: Oxford University Press, 1994), available at: http://hdr.undp.org/sites/default/files/reports/255/hdr_1994_en_complete_nostats.pdf (accessed 4 March 2014), p. 23; M. Ul Hag, *Reflections on Human Development* (Delhi: Oxford University Press, 1999).

19 G. King and C. Murray, 'Rethinking human security', *Political Science Quarterly*, 16:4 (2004), pp. 585–600; D. Henk, 'Human security: Relevance and implications', *Parameters*, 35:2 (2005), pp. 92–100; P. Ewan, 'Deepening the human security debate: Beyond the politics of conceptual clarification', *Politics*, 27:3 (2007), pp. 182–9.

20 UN Development Programme, *Human Development Report 1994* (New York: Oxford University Press, 1994), available at: http://hdr.undp.org/sites/default/files/reports /255/hdr_1994_en_complete_nostats.pdf (accessed 4 March 2014), p. 4.

21 L. Axworthy, 'NATO's new security vocation', *NATO Review*, 47:4 (1999).

22 Ministry of Foreign Affairs of Japan, 'Overview-Human Security', in *Diplomatic Bluebook Japan 2000*, available at: www.mofa.go.jp/policy/other/bluebook/2000/II-3–a.html#1 (accessed 15 April 2014).

23 W. Clinton, 'Remarks on US foreign policy at San Francisco', The American Presidency Project, 26 February 1999, available at: www.presidency.ucsb.edu/ws/index.php?pid= 57170 (accessed 15 April 2014).

24 PBS Newshour, 'The Blair Doctrine [transcript]' (22 April 1999), available at: www.pbs. org/newshour/bb/international-jan-june99-blair_doctrine4-23/ (accessed 10 March 2014).

25 BBC News, 'World: Europe Kosovo peace plan agreed' (4 June 1999), available at: http:// news.bbc.co.uk/2/hi/europe/359803.stm (accessed 23 March 2014).

26 J. Dunne, 'Crimes Against Humanity in East Timor, January to October 1999: Their Nature and Causes', UN-commissioned Report, 14 February 2001, available at: www. etan.org/news/2001a/dunn1.htm (accessed 26 August 2009).

27 J. Howard, 'Commonwealth Parliamentary Debates', House of Representatives, no. 14, 21 September 1999, pp. 8469–70.

28 A. Downer, 'Media release: Australian government historic policy-shift on East Timor', 12 January 1999.

29 'The Responsibility to Protect', Report of the International Commission on Intervention and State Sovereignty, 2001, available at: http://responsibilitytoprotect.org/ICISS per cent20Report.pdf (accessed 15 April 2014).

30 K. Annan, 'We the peoples: Role of the UN in the 21st Century', United Nations, 2000, available at: www.un.org/en/events/pastevents/pdfs/We_The_Peoples.pdf (accessed 15 April 2014).

31 The legitimacy of NATO's aerial campaign under international law remains contested. On 9 June NATO halted its bombing of Kosovo. A day later, the Security Council agreed to a plan for peace in Kosovo and authorised the international civil and military mission, the United Nations Interim Administration Mission in Kosovo. Resolution 1244 was passed with fourteen votes to none (China abstained largely as a symbol of dissatisfaction with NATO's accidental bombing of the Chinese embassy in Belgrade). The near unanimous approval of the mission has been taken as tacit approval of the outcome of NATO's action in Kosovo, which established post-facto legitimacy of the intervention.

32 J. Dunne, 'The rules of the game are changing: Human rights in crisis post-9/11', *International Politics*, 44:2 (2007), pp. 269–86.

33 US State Department, *The National Security Strategy of the United States of America*, 2002, available at: www.state.gov/documents/organization/63562.pdf (accessed 15 April 2015).

34 Alex Bellamy has made numerous contributions on this point. For more see A. Bellamy, 'Responsibility to protect or Trojan horse? The crisis in Darfur and humanitarian intervention after Iraq', *Ethics & International Affairs*, 19:2 (2005), pp. 31–54; A. Bellamy, 'Ethics and intervention: The "humanitarian exception", and the problem of abuse in the case of Iraq', *Journal of Peace Research*, 41:2 (2004), pp. 131–47; A. Bellamy, 'Wither the Responsibility to Protect? Humanitarian intervention and the 2005 World Summit', *Ethics & International Affairs*, 20:2 (2006), pp. 143–69.

35 BBC News, 'Powell declares genocide in Darfur' (9 September 2004), avail-

able at: http://news.bbc.co.uk/2/hi/3641820.stm (accessed 14 March 2014).

36 D. Gow, 'Death toll at 10,000 a month', *Guardian* (14 September 2004), available at: www.theguardian.com/society/2004/sep/14/internationalaidanddevelopment.sudan (accessed 15 April 2004).

37 D. C. Compert, 'China's responsibility to protect', *Washington Post*, 17 June 2008, available at: www.washingtonpost.com/wpdyn/content/article/2008/06/17/AR200806170 2017.html (accessed 15 April 2014).

38 C. G. Badescu and L. Bergholm, 'The Responsibility to Protect and the conflict in Darfur: The big let-down', *Security Dialogue*, 40:3 (2009), pp. 287–309.

39 United Nations, *Resolution 1674*, 28 April 2006, available at: http://daccess-dds-ny. un.org/doc/UNDOC/GEN/N06/331/99/PDF/N0633199.pdf?OpenElement (accessed 15 April 2014).

40 United Nations, *Resolution Adopted by the General Assembly on 14 September 2009: The Responsibility to Protect*, 14 September 2009, available at: www.un.org/en/ga/search/ view_doc.asp?symbol=A/RES/63/308&Lang=E (accessed 15 April 2014); United Nations, *Resolution 1894*, 11 November 2009, available at: http://daccess-dds-ny. un.org/doc/UNDOC/GEN/N09/602/45/PDF/N0960245.pdf?OpenElement (accessed 15 April 2014).

41 United Nations, *Resolution 1970*, 26 February 2011, available at: www.un.org/en/ga/ search/view_doc.asp?symbol=S/RES/1970(2011) (accessed 15 April 2014); United Nations, *Resolution 1973*, 17 March 2011, available at: www.un.org/en/ga/search/ view_doc.asp?symbol=S/RES/1973(2011) (accessed 15 April 2014).

42 United Nations, 'The Responsibility to Protect', Office of the Special Adviser to the Prevention of Genocide, available at: www.un.org/en/preventgenocide/adviser/respon sibility.shtml (accessed 15 April 2014).

43 BBC News, 'Libya protests: defiant Gaddafi refuses to quite' (22 February 2011), available at: www.bbc.com/news/world-middle-east-12544624 (accessed 15 April 2014).

44 D. Clarke, 'Libyan intervention was a success, despite the aftermath's atrocities', *Guardian* (29 October 2011), available at: www.theguardian.com/commentisfree/2011/oct/28/ intervention-libya-success (accessed 15 March 2014).

45 A. Hirsch, 'No Redness on Gaddafi asset seizure', *Guardian* (2 March 2011), available at: www.theguardian.com/law/afua-hirsch-law-blog/2011/mar/01/libya-international-criminal-court (accessed 15 April 2014).

46 PBS Newshour, 'The Blair Doctrine' (accessed 10 March 2014).

47 CNN, 'Clinton says US interests at stake in Kosovo' (29 February 1999), available at: http://edition.cnn.com/ALLPOLITICS/stories/1999/02/26/clinton.foreign.policy/ (accessed 24 March 2014).

48 W. Clinton, 'A Just and Necessary War', *New York Times* (23 May 1999), available at: www.nytimes.com/1999/05/23/opinion/a-just-and-necessary-war.html (accessed 15 April 2014).

49 R. Vickers, 'Labour's Search for a Third Way in Foreign Policy', in R. Little and M. Wickam-Jones (eds), *New Labour's Foreign Policy: A New Moral Crusade?* (Manchester: Manchester University Press, 2000), pp. 33–42.

50 Australian Bureau of Statistics, 'International merchandise trade Australia', 2001, available at: www.abs.gov.au/Ausstats/abs@.nsf/94713ad445ff1425ca2568200019 2af2/be75d8ff866cba97ca256aaa007fe175!OpenDocument (accessed 15 April 2014).

51 *The Age*, 'New Timor Gap treaty signed' (20 May 2002), available at: www.theage.com. au/articles/2002/05/20/1021801654981.html (accessed 15 April 2014).

52   G. Evans, 'From humanitarian intervention to the Responsibility to Protect', *Wisconsin International Law Journal*, 24 (2006), pp. 703–24.

53   C. J. Levy, 'Russia backs independence of Georgian enclaves', *New York Times* (26 August 2008), available at: www.nytimes.com/2008/08/27/world/europe/27russia.html?pagewanted=all&_r=0 (accessed 15 April 2014).

54   G. Evans, 'Russia and the Responsibility to Protect', *Los Angeles Times* (31 August 2008), available at: www.latimes.com/la-oe-evans31-2008aug31,0,1295318.story#axzz2z CE7laHZ (accessed 15 April 2014); G. Evans, 'Russia in Georgia: Not a case of the Responsibility to Protect', *New Studies Quarterly*, 25:4 (2008), pp. 53–5; C. G. Badescu and T. G. Weiss, 'Misrepresenting R2P and advancing norms: An alternative spiral?', *Review of International Studies*, 11:4 (2010), pp. 354–74.

55   J. P. Ruben, 'Russia's poor excuse for invading Georgia', *CBS News* (7 November 2008), available at: www.cbsnews.com/news/russias-poor-excuse-for-invading-georgia/ (accessed 15 April 2014).

56   BBC News, 'Libya: French plane fires on military vehicle' (19 March 2011), available at: www.bbc.co.uk/news/world-africa-12795971 (accessed 24 March 2014).

57   P. Beaumont and A. Clark, 'Britain's alliance with Libya turns sour as Gaddafi cracks down', *Guardian* (20 February 2011), available at: www.theguardian.com/world/2011/feb/19/britain-alliance-libya-gaddafi-crackdown (accessed 15 April 2014).

58   D. Cameron, 'Prime Minister statement on the UN Security Council Resolution on Libya', Foreign & Commonwealth Office, 18 March, 2011, available at: www.gov.uk/government/news/prime-minister-statement-on-the-un-security-council-resolution-on-libya (accessed 22 March 2014).

59   Atlantic Council, 'Diplomats "mourn" death of EU defence policy over Libya' (24 March 2011), available at: www.atlanticcouncil.org/blogs/natosource/diplomats-mourn-death-of-eu-defence-policy-over-libya (accessed 17 March 2014).

60   J. Adetunji, 'British firms urged to "pack suitcase" in rush for Libya Business', *Guardian* (22 October 2011), available at: www.theguardian.com/world/2011/oct/21/british-firms-libya-business (accessed 14 March 2014).

61   S. Erlanger, 'Libyan supporters gather in Paris to help ease new government's transition', *New York Times* (1 September 2011), available at: www.nytimes.com/2011/09/02/world/europe/02paris.html?pagewanted=all (accessed 15 April 2014).

62   J. Borger and T. Macalister, 'The race is on for Libya's oil, with Britain and France both staking a claim', *Guardian* (2 September 2011), available at: www.theguardian.com/world/2011/sep/01/libya-oil (accessed 15 April 2014).

63   R. Shabi, 'Nato nations set to reap spoils of Libya war', *Al Jazeera* (25 August 2011), available at: www.aljazeera.com/indepth/opinion/2011/08/201182511546451332.html (accessed 15 April 2014).

64   United Nations, *Resolution 1973* (accessed 15 April 2014).

65   B. Obama, D. Cameron and N. Sarkozy, 'Libya's pathway to peace', *New York Times* (14 April 2011), available at: www.nytimes.com/2011/04/15/opinion/15iht-edlibya15.html?_r=2&ref=global (accessed 24 March 2014).

66   There was considerable debate about whether France in particular broke the terms of Resolution 1970. On the one hand, Resolution 1973 authorised the Security Council to 'use all necessary means ... notwithstanding paragraph of Resolution 1970', which implemented the arms embargo. On the other, Resolution 1973 actually strengthened the commitment of the Security Council to enforce the embargo. L. Charbonneau and H. Hassan, 'France defends arms airlift to Libyan rebels', *Reuters* (29 June 2011), available at: www.reuters.com/article/2011/06/29/us-libya-idUSTRE7270JP20110629

(accessed 15 April 2014). In terms of the US, there was speculation that Barack Obama issued a presidential 'finding' authorising CIA operations to support the Libyan rebels. It was never fully confirmed that the US unilaterally supplied weapons to Libya like France. However, covert operations to support the rebels included arming and training rebels in coordination with Saudi Arabia and Qatar. For more see M. Hosenball, 'Obama authorizes secret help to Libyan rebels', *Reuters* (30 March 2011), available at: www.reuters. com/article/2011/03/30/us-libya-usa-order-idUSTRE72T6H220110330 (accessed 15 April 2014).

67   On 23 February 2014, the UN Security Council passed a non-binding resolution calling for the safe delivery of humanitarian aid to Syria. It did not place any obligation on the Security Council to ensure that this would occur; nor did it make any real threats that punitive action would be taken if the Assad regime failed to comply. Al Jazeera, 'UN unanimously adopts Syria aid resolution' (23 February 2014), available at: www.aljazeera.com/news/middleeast/2014/02/un-unanimously-adopts-syria-aid-resolution-2014222171953818913.html (accessed 14 April 2014).

68   D. Hearst, 'Why Russia is backing Syria', *Guardian* (2 December 2011), available at: www.theguardian.com/commentisfree/2011/dec/02/russia-syria-civil-war-dagestan (accessed 14 April 2014).

69   C. Buckley, 'China intensifies condemnation of Libyan airstrikes', *Reuters* (21 March 2011), available at: www.reuters.com/article/2011/03/21/us-china-libya-idUSTRE72K0LX20110321 (accessed 14 April 2014).

70   D. M. Herszenhorn, 'For Syria, reliant on Russia for weapons and food, old bonds run deep', *New York Times* (18 February 2012), available at: www.nytimes.com/2012/02 /19/world/middleeast/for-russia-and-syria-bonds-are-old-and-deep.html?pagewanted= all&_r=0 (accessed 25 March 2014).

71   Hearst, 'Why Russia is backing Syria' (accessed 25 March 2014).

72   M. Shalabi, 'Syrian refugees: How many are there and where are they?' *Guardian* (25 July 2013), available at: www.theguardian.com/news/datablog/2013/jul/25/syrian-refugee-crisis-in-numbers-updated (accessed 21 March 2014).

73   World Bank, 'Syria Overview', March 2014, available at: www.worldbank.org/en/coun try/syria/overview (accessed 21 March 2014).

74   BBC News, 'Polio outbreak in Syria as 10 cases confirmed' (5 November 2013), available at: www.bbc.com/news/world-middle-east-24815157 (accessed 21 March 2014).

75   S. Nadir, 'Syria's economic crisis magnifies human tragedy', *Almonitor* (14 August 2013), available at: www.al-monitor.com/pulse/originals/2013/08/syria-economy-suffers-war.html# (accessed 21 March 2014).

76   L. Morris, J. Warrick and S. Mekhennet, 'Rival Al-Qaeda linked groups fortifying in Syria with a mix of pragmatism and militarism', *Washington Post* (14 October 2013), available at: www.washingtonpost.com/world/national-security/al-qaeda-linked-groups-taking-root-in-syria/2013/10/13/11d01b12-334c-11e3-8627-c5d7de0a046b_story.html (accessed 16 April 2014).

77   G. Kessler, 'President Obama and the "red line" on Syria chemical weapons', *Washington Post* (6 September 2013), available at: www.washingtonpost.com/blogs/fact-checker/ wp/2013/09/06/president-obama-and-the-red-line-on-syrias-chemical-weapons/? clsrd (accessed 21 March 2014).

78   G. Baghahi, 'Syria peace talks end in violence', *CBS News* (14 February 2014), available at: www.cbsnews.com/news/syria-peace-talks-in-geneva-end-in-failure/ (accessed 15 April 2014).

79 R. Thakur, 'R2P after Libya: Engaging emerging powers', *The Washington Quarterly* 36:2 (2013), pp. 61–76.

80 S. Krasner, *Sovereignty: Organized Hypocrisy* (Princeton: Princeton University Press, 1999).

8

Limiting the use of force: the ICTY, ICTR and ICC

Matt Killingsworth

HROUGHOUT THE LONG history of organised violence, there have always existed some constraints on what was deemed acceptable behaviour during war. Yet until relatively recently, restraint during combat (so-called *jus in bello* – as opposed to *jus ad bellum* – restrictions) was primarily legitimated through appeals to *raison d'état*. Despite the evolution of international treaty law outlining what was not acceptable during war, for much of the modern period the sovereign state, with important exceptions like the Nuremburg and Tokyo war crime trials, remained the sole arbiter in determining who was guilty of violating these laws. This, in turn, raised questions as to the effect that *jus in bello* laws had on restraining the use of force.

In the immediate post-Cold War era, in response to violent wars in the Balkans and Rwanda, the UN Security Council established two *ad hoc* Tribunals; the International Criminal Tribunal for the former Yugoslavia (ICTY); and the International Criminal Tribunal for Rwanda (ICTR), which in turn paved the way for the subsequent establishment of the permanent International Criminal Court (ICC). As a challenge to long evolved norms of how the 'illegal' use of force is punished, the establishment of the ICTY, ICTR and ICC represent the most significant moments to date in the long evolution of attempts at restraining warfare.

This chapter sets out to explore the degree to which the two *ad hoc* Tribunals, and the ICC, can be understood within an environment where states are 'bound not only by rules of prudence or expediency, but also by imperatives of morality and law'.[1] In keeping with the themes of this volume, it offers an analysis of the degree to which these new mechanisms of international criminal justice serve to place limits on the way that states use force. The chapter challenges the idea that the *ad hoc* Tribunals and the ICC represent the '"progressive cosmopolitanisation" of international law'.[2] Instead, two interrelated arguments will be made: first, the extended reach of legality, as it concerns limitations on the use of force in the international system, remains restricted by factors explained by classic conceptions of state sovereignty and state interests; and second, while instituting legal mechanisms to punish individual violations of international humanitarian law (IHL) challenges historically established norms regarding the way that states use force, constraints on the use of violence are best understood through 'pluralist' interpretations of the sovereign right to use force and the sovereign right of non-interference. Thus, while it is clear that new mechanisms of justice have increased the efficacy of IHL, the state remains the primary arbiter with regards to punishing violations of the laws of war.

Beyond Nuremburg and Tokyo: responses to ethnic cleansing and genocide after the Cold War

The ICTY and the ICTR were the first mechanisms for international criminal justice since the post-World War II Nuremburg and Tokyo Tribunals. Although heavily criticised, both at the time and in later years, especially over allegations of so-called victor's justice, Timothy McCormack was correct to identify the Nuremburg and Tokyo Tribunals as constituting 'historic precedents for the now unassailable principle of individual criminal responsibility for violations of IHL'.[3] While the *realpolitik* that characterised Cold War-era interactions halted the post-Nuremburg and Tokyo impetus for a permanent international court,[4] two sets of events in particular provided renewed momentum for the establishment of what turned out to be a stepping stone towards the creation of the ICC.

The first of these was the implosion of the Soviet Union and the subsequent ending of the Cold War. A history of Security Council vetoes (and threats to veto) by the opposing superpowers provides compelling evidence that it is unlikely the *ad hoc* Tribunals would have been established had the Cold War not ended. The second set of events was the nature of the atrocities committed in the former Yugoslavia and Rwanda. The wars that resulted from the break-up of Yugoslavia in 1991–92 and the Rwandan Genocide in 1994 were characterised by a series of well-planned and executed programmes of ethnic cleansing and genocide. The two Tribunals were thus established in a particular historical milieu, when, according to Payam Akhavan, the barbarous acts that took place in the former Yugoslavia (in particular in Bosnia-Herzegovina) and Rwanda served to 'galvanise the collective will of the civilised world [into taking] decisive measures for the establishment of a just world order'.[5] While they were indeed representative of collective and decisive action, it will be argued here, contrary to Akhavan, that the UN-constituted Tribunals (and the ICC) contribute to a pluralist international order, as opposed to a cosmopolitan world order, where states remain the primary actors and international law, acknowledged as integral to maintaining order, remains informed by Vattelian interpretations of sovereignty.

The International Criminal Tribunal for the former Yugoslavia

In response to what the UN Security Council (UNSC) regarded as 'grave breaches of the Geneva Conventions and other violations of international humanitarian law committed in the territory of the former Yugoslavia', the ICTY was established through UNSC Resolution 827.[6] Specifically, the Tribunal was created 'for the sole purpose of prosecuting serious violations of international law committed on the territory of the former Yugoslavia between 1 January 1991 and a date to be determined by the Security Council upon the restoration of peace'.[7] More generally, its three main objectives were to deter further crimes, to do justice and to restore and maintain peace.

The Tribunal's Statute authorises the ICTY to prosecute four groups of crimes: grave breaches of the 1949 Geneva Conventions; violations of the laws or customs of war; genocide; and crimes against humanity.[8] Addressing the issue of responsibility, Article 7 of the Statute is designed primarily to challenge the long-established norm of sovereign impunity. Thus, Article 7.1 states that 'the official position of any accused person, whether as Head of State or Government or as a responsible Government official, shall not relieve such person of criminal responsibility nor mitigate punishment'. Furthermore, by announcing that acts committed 'by a subordinate does not relieve his superior of criminal responsibility if ... the superior failed to take the necessary and reasonable measures to prevent such acts or to punish the perpetrators thereof', the ICTY established its goal of prosecuting 'big fish'.[9]

With respect to the Tribunal's jurisdictional mandate, Article 9 of the Statute states that 'the International Tribunal shall have primacy over national courts. At any stage of the procedure, the International Tribunal may formally request national courts to defer to the competence of the International Tribunal in accordance with the present Statute'.[10] Importantly, Article 9 should not be interpreted as an attempt to supersede national judiciaries. Rather, it should be interpreted in two ways: first, the wording of the Article reflects both the inability and incapacity (and perhaps even the lack of desire) of domestic judiciaries to prosecute crimes that arose out of the wars in Yugoslavia; second, this Article articulates the idea of complementarity, one of the core foundational structures of international criminal legal mechanisms.[11]

Finally, Article 29 of the Statute obliges states to cooperate with the ICTY, 'without undue delay with any request for assistance or an order issued by a Trial Chamber, including, but not limited to: the identification and location of persons; the taking of testimony and the production of evidence; the service of documents; the arrest or detention of persons; and the surrender or the transfer of the accused to the International Tribunal'.[12] The principle jurisdictional purpose of the ICTY is thus to challenge impunity by identifying individuals and prosecuting them, thereby 'preventing the imposition of collective blame that often demonises groups and nations and fuels new cycles of violence'.[13] Politically, the Tribunal forms an intrinsic part of 'institutionalising strategies, along with peace negotiations [and] democratic elections that promote national reconstruction after mass atrocity'.[14]

The International Criminal Tribunal for Rwanda

While few modern acts of violence have shaken the collective conscience the way the 1994 Rwandan Genocide did, four aspects were especially confronting. The first was the speed with which the atrocities were carried out. While the exact number of deaths is debated, between 800,000 and a million people, mostly Tutsis, were murdered in 100 days. The second is that the killings were not carried out by weapons of mass destruction or technologically advanced means; rather, most of the victims were murdered with machetes or farming tools. Third, the nature of the violence, specifically the use of rape directed predominantly against Tutsi women, which came to be a central feature of the genocide. The fourth and final aspect of these events was the indifference exhibited by the UN and many of its member states. Not only did the UN ignore a number of warnings, but once it was clear what was happening in Rwanda, some countries (infamously, in the case of the US), went out of their way to avoid using the term 'genocide' to describe the events.[15]

The subsequent creation of the ICTR followed a similar pattern to that of the ICTY. Having formally established that genocide and systematic and widespread violations of humanitarian law had been committed in Rwanda,[16] and following a formal request by the Rwandan Government in 1994, the ICTR was established under UNSC Resolution 955.[17] The Tribunal's mandate was to 'prosecute persons responsible for genocide and other serious violations of international humanitarian law' both in Rwanda and on the territory of neighbouring states, between January and 31 December 1994.[18] Establishing its *raison d'être*, the ICTR was to 'contribute to ensuring that such violations [genocide, crimes against humanity and war crimes] are halted and effectively redressed' and that 'the prosecution of persons responsible for serious violations of international humanitarian law ... would contribute to the process of national reconciliation and to the restoration and maintenance of peace'.[19]

In an attempt to establish the optimal environment in which to achieve these aims, Article 28 of the Statute obliged all members of the UN to 'cooperate with the International Tribunal for Rwanda in the investigation and prosecution of persons accused of committing serious violations of international humanitarian law'. Further to this, the preamble of UNSC Resolution 955 stressed 'the need for international cooperation to strengthen the courts and judicial system of Rwanda'.[20] Therefore, although the Tribunal took 'primacy over the national courts of all States',[21] it was 'regarded by the Security Council as a complimentary institute to the Rwandese national judicial system and not as a substitute'.[22] Finally, the ICTR has financial primacy with regards to appropriating the necessary resources for prosecuting alleged mass atrocities.

The goals of the ICTR are thus threefold, all underpinned by the idea that 'politically, the recovery of the victim through international law represents the attempt to reverse victimisation produced by state violence'.[23] First, in the short and long term, it was devised to maintain peace and security in Rwanda and the immediate Great Lakes region. Second, in the long term, it was designed to provide justice to the victims of the genocide. Third, also in the long term, it was intended to act as an effective deterrent against future crimes.

Appraising the *ad hoc* Tribunals

As mechanisms of justice, the Tribunals have a mixed record. First, there is a reasonable expectation that justice be fair and even-handed. This was especially important for the two *ad hoc* Tribunals, operating as they were in the shadow of the justifiably criticised Nuremburg and Tokyo Trials. Recognising this, the Statutes of both Tribunals make reference only to spatial and temporal restrictions on their jurisdictional mandate. Even more specifically, the Commission of Experts' report that led to the establishment of the ICTR identified that 'Individuals from both sides to the armed conflict have perpetrated serious breaches of international humanitarian law' and 'Individuals from both sides to the armed conflict have perpetrated crimes against humanity in Rwanda'.[24] However, both Tribunals have been accused of institutionalising 'victor's justice'. For example, despite strong evidence of crimes committed during the Homeland War, the ICTY failed to indict Croatian President Franjo Tudjman, Defence Minister Gojko Susak and former Bosnian-Croat leader Mate Boban before their respective deaths.[25] The recent acquittal of Croatian Generals Ante Gotivina and Mladen Markač on appeal has served to reinforce the impression of an absence of even-handedness, especially among Serbs. But accusations of victor's justice are misplaced. Even if one conceived the actions the ICTY as directed against the Serbs, it is difficult to argue that they were vanquished.[26] Similarly, the ICTR has also struggled against claims of bias. Despite the recommendations of the Commission of Experts, and strong evidence pointing to serious violations of international humanitarian law by the Tutsi-dominated Rwandese Patriotic Front (RPF) and the Rwandese Patriotic Army, only one Tutsi has been a defendant at the Tribunal.[27] Defending the ICTR's prosecutorial record, Richard Goldstone, the first Prosecutor of the ICTR, argued that 'the magnitude of genocidal crimes wrought by the Hutu extremists so outweighed the RPF's massacres that the prosecutorial choice was clear'.[28] But while accusations of 'victor's justice' may be misconceived in this case as well, ignoring violations by non-Serbs and non-Hutus has nonetheless damaged the Tribunals' claim to be exercising impunity. This in turn compromises the very idea of international criminal justice.

There should also be a reasonable expectation that those accused are tried without undue delay, since a speedy trial is a prerequisite for justice. However, prosecutions at both the ICTY and ICTR have moved exceedingly slowly. Arguably the most infamous case of delayed justice was the death in custody of Slobodan Milošević, over four years after his trial had begun. Likewise, the completed trials at the ICTR have taken an average of four and a half years from arrest through to appeal.[29] While there are a number of mitigating factors, the most persuasive is offered by Erik Møse, who argues that not only were the ICTY and ICTR embarking upon uncharted waters, but that 'the trials conducted before the *ad hoc* Tribunals are legally and factually very complex'.[30] Nonetheless, the lack of a speedy trial is not only problematic for the defendant, it also undermines efforts to heal collective wounds and facilitate reconciliation.[31]

As noted above, central to both Tribunals was the aim that they would 'contribute to the restoration and maintenance of peace'. Rwanda's request and the UN's agreement to establish the ICTR represented an acknowledgment from all parties that while Rwanda had the desire to prosecute those responsible for the genocide, it lacked the capacity to do so.[32] Although established in a post-conflict environment, it is clear that all parties believed that, as a mechanism of justice, the Tribunal would simultaneously play a role in establishing and maintaining peace in Rwanda.[33]

However, while the Tribunal might have gone some way to facilitating peace and security in Rwanda, it has done little to stem Hutu–Tutsi related violence in the broader Great Lakes region.[34] Yet when exploring the degree to which the Tribunals might have contributed to the restoration and maintenance of peace and security, it is the ICTY's record that is the most unsettling. Admittedly, unlike the ICTR, the ICTY was set up while conflict still raged in the Balkans, and this hindered that aspect of its *raison d'être*. In fact, three of the worst atrocities (Srebrenica, the siege of Sarajevo and the crimes committed in Kosovo) had yet to occur. Even so, when one considers that the Tribunal began its operations in November 1993, and that the war in Bosnia continued until 1995, 'the existence of the Tribunal and the possibility of being indicted did not seem to encourage an ending of hostilities'.[35] Furthermore, and even more damning, the likelihood of indictment by the ICTY certainly did not restrain the conduct of Serbian political and military leaders in Kosovo in 1999. With this in mind, and despite the conviction that successful prosecutions by the Tribunals would contribute to the restoration and maintenance of peace, Janine Natalya Clark's observation that post-conflict societies cannot rely on retributive justice alone, and that they should be complemented by restorative justice initiatives, is especially salient.[36]

Hence as mechanisms of justice, the Tribunals are hindered, but not undermined, by slow trials, accusations of 'victor's justice' and general problems linked to their ability to contribute to the establishment and maintenance of peace and security. But the Tribunals are regularly undermined by their reliance on the cooperation of often-uncooperative states. In the case of the two *ad hoc* Tribunals state cooperation was both essential and expected. First, the general enthusiasm and support for the Tribunals from the UN and its constituent members, informed as much by the shocking nature of the conflicts as anything else, suggested that such cooperation would be forthcoming. Moreover, there was a general understanding, that, when called upon, member states of the UN would be legally obliged to cooperate without delay. Second, in both conflicts, the lack of central authority, inability to monopolise the security apparatuses and lack of control over borders (what Michael Humphrey refers to as 'fractured sovereignty')[37] meant that accused war criminals, especially alleged *génocidaire* in Rwanda, were able to quickly escape into neighbouring countries. Finally, when one considers the ethno-nationalist underpinnings of the conflicts in Yugoslavia in particular, and the degree to which those committing crimes were often regarded as ethno-national heroes, it was important that the new states that arose from the violent collapse of the Federation did not protect such individuals. To do so would further deepen the ethnic animosities that had catalysed the conflict in the first place. And to make matters worse, the failure to hand over indictees would serve to damage one of the Tribunals' primary goals: countering state-sponsored immunity and impunity.

In this way, while the Statutes obliged states to cooperate 'with undue delay' with the Tribunals, including, but not limited to, revealing knowledge of the whereabouts of persons, the arrest and detention of persons and their surrender to the appropriate international Tribunal, both Tribunals are replete with examples of states actively impeding their work. While the ICTY experienced problems extraditing indictees from a number of countries, its biggest problem was extraditing them from countries that were party to the conflict. In the 1995 Dayton Accords, Bosnia, Croatia and the Federal Republic of Yugoslavia all agreed to cooperate with and assist the Tribunal.[38] Yet despite the prolific issuing of indictments, between 1993 and 2002, only six individuals were transferred to the Tribunal from Serbia, two from Bosnia and three from Croatia.[39] While the Federal Republic of Yugoslavia (later Serbia), first under Milošević's leadership and later during its transition to democracy, used a number of methods to thwart the efforts of the ICTY,[40] Victor Peskin argues that it was the actions of Croatia under Tudjman's leadership that most damaged the operational capacity of the Tribunal. According to Peskin, 'under the authoritarian rule of President Franjo Tudjman, [the Homeland War] was effectively off limits to ICTY investigators', primarily because of the 'mythic status the independence struggle and the final victory ... acquired in Croatia. For Tudjman and his nationalist backers, the memorialization of the Homeland War became a cornerstone of the nation-building project as well as the font of the ruling party's legitimacy'.[41] Using a number of tactics to obstruct investigations, it was not until Tudjman's death in 1999 that Croatia increased its cooperation with the Tribunal. Nonetheless, successive governments, while cooperating on a functional level, continued to obstruct attempts to arrest and transfer high profile indictees, the most infamous example being that of Ante Gotovina.[42]

Similarly, the functioning of the ICTR has also been undermined by a lack of state cooperation. Large numbers of *génocidaires* escaped into neighbouring countries, specifically Zaire (now Democratic Republic of Congo (DRC)) and Kenya, which both refused requests to extradite suspects to Arusha. This was primarily due to regional geo-politics: Kenya and Zaire 'supported Rwanda's former rulers because they regarded the successor RPF-led government as a client of Uganda's President Yoweri Museveni, their rival for leadership in East and Central Africa'.[43] While the situation has improved somewhat, both the DRC and Kenya are thought to be knowingly harbouring indictees.[44] Further undermining the efforts of the ICTR have been the actions of the Rwandan government, especially regarding attempts by the Tribunal to investigate possible war crimes committed by the RPF. In response to the Chief Prosecutor's decision in 2002 to probe RPF atrocities, the Rwandan government instituted travel restrictions that blocked Tutsi genocide survivors nominated by the Tribunal as witnesses for the prosecution appearing in Arusha. The problem was exacerbated further when the UNSC, in response to a formal complaint from the Tribunal, declined to rebuke Rwanda, instead issuing them a reminder of their obligation to cooperate.[45]

Yet, in spite of all the obstacles discussed above, the *ad hoc* Tribunals serve as evidence of a subtle yet definitive shift in the way that states respond to violations of IHL. As discussed above, the very existence of the Tribunals is important, in that they represented a break from the long evolved, collectively assumed norm that the state was the sole arbiter in matters concerning the use of force. Their establishment not only represented a shared understanding that neither the former republics of Yugoslavia nor Rwanda had the capacity (or desire in the case of Yugoslavia) to prosecute violators of atrocities committed on these territories, but an acknowledgment that especially egregious violations were no longer afforded protection through purely statist interpretations of international law.

With regards to challenging long-established norms, the Tribunals achieved a number of important 'firsts'. The ICTY was responsible for the first indictment against a sitting head of state by an international court (Slobodan Milošević), while the ICTR was responsible for the first ever individual conviction for the crime of genocide (Jean Paul Akayesu), the first ever conviction of a former head of state for the crime of genocide (former Prime Minister of the Interim Government in Rwanda, Jean Kambanda), and the first judiciary to recognise rape and sexual violence as crimes of genocide.[46]

The Tribunals have succeeded in restoring dignity to victims who were degraded, demeaned and dehumanised.[47] Furthermore, as well as bringing high-ranking *génocidaires* to justice, the ICTR functioned to restrain post-genocide, anti-Hutu revenge killings.[48] Finally, by the very fact that they exist and function, the Tribunals have challenged long established norms of sovereign immunity and impunity. It is unlikely, for a variety of interrelated reasons, that high profile indictees such as Milošević, Radovan Karadžić and Ratko Mladić would ever have faced trial through domestic legal mechanisms. In serving as an avenue for justice where none otherwise existed, the Tribunals thus establish both a *de jure* and *de facto* limit to how belligerents should behave.

Peskin argues that 'at least in theory, the UN Tribunals possess a great deal of soft power because of their moral claim to being the ultimate judicial guardians of universal standards of human rights'.[49] Notwithstanding the limitations discussed above, the Tribunals demonstrated more than theoretical soft power. Indeed, their actions were reflective of a shift towards efforts that undermine the norm that violations of IHL can be tolerated as a legitimate tool of statecraft. Historically, the failure to hold such violators to account served chiefly to erode 'the inhibition and restraint against [genocide, war crimes and crimes against humanity], permitting an amoral account of *raison d'état*'.[50] As a response to crimes that the society of states designated as 'the worst of the worst', the ICTY and ICTR were the first important, albeit incremental, steps in subverting this entrenched practice of impunity.

A permanent international criminal court – the ICC

The next, and arguably most important, step in challenging the entrenched culture of impunity (and immunity) was the establishment of the ICC. Opened for signature in 1998, the *Rome Statute* received the required sixty ratifications in April 2002, entering into force on the first of July 2002 (at the time of writing, 121 countries had ratified the Statute). As outlined in Article 1, the ICC 'shall have the power to exercise its jurisdiction over persons for the most serious crimes of international concern [namely genocide, crimes against humanity, war crimes, and, since 2010 – following agreements made at the Review Conference of the Statute – crimes of aggression when committed after 1 July 2002] ... and shall be complementary to national criminal jurisdictions'. The Court's main objectives are to achieve justice for all; to end impunity; to help end conflicts; to remedy the deficiencies of *ad hoc* Tribunals; and to take over when national criminal justice institutions are unwilling or unable to act.[51]

The Court can exercise its jurisdiction over individuals who are nationals of a States Party to the Statute or have committed crimes on the Party's territory, when the case is referred to the Court by the UNSC or when initiated by the Office of the Prosecutor (OTP), although a Pre-Trial Chamber must approve any investigation initiated by the OTP. Article 14 of the Statute explains that cases can be referred to the Court either by the UNSC, or by States Parties. Finally, as outlined in Article 12, chapter 3 of the Statute, 'If the acceptance of a State which is not a Party to this Statute is required under paragraph 2, that State may, by declaration lodged with the Registrar, accept the exercise of jurisdiction by the Court with respect to the crime in question'.[52]

Cited as one of the main reasons behind the US's continued non-membership of the ICC, the UNSC cannot veto prosecutions by the Court. For a number of non-governmental organisations (NGOs) and smaller states involved at the 1998 Rome Conference, this decision represented a victory over power politics.[53] However, while the UNSC's power regarding the operation of the Court is limited (certainly more so than many of the permanent members wanted), specific state consent is not required in the case of UNSC referrals to the Court.

As outlined above, the *ad hoc* Tribunals were established and overseen by the UNSC. Hence all member states of the UN were obliged to act in accordance with their statutes, particularly as this related to arrests and access to information. The ICC, however, is established under treaty law, so no such obligation exists. Nonetheless, states party to the Statute 'shall, in accordance with the provisions of this Statute, cooperate fully with the Court in its investigation and prosecution of crimes within the jurisdiction of the Court'. While understandably more elaborate than the requirements of the *ad hoc* Tribunals, Articles 86–102 nonetheless make similar demands on states regarding cooperation with the ICC.[54]

Equally important with respect to the operational limitations of the Court are Articles 17–20 of the Statute, which articulate the principles of complementarity. As with the *ad hoc* Tribunals, the complementarity principle essentially holds that 'states are entitled *prima facie* to investigate and prosecute, but that the Prosecutor reserves the right to launch their own investigation if he or she determines that the national judiciary has not conducted a genuine investigation or trial'.[55] In this respect, the Prosecutor's determination on what constitutes unwillingness is guided by the Statute's provisions regarding inadmissibility.

We can thus draw two important conclusions about the capacity of the Court. First, it is clear that the Court is primarily interested in trying 'major' offences.[56] Second, while Kirsten Ainley claims that 'the Court has significant *actual* power over leaders and nationals of those states that have ratified its founding Statute, and significant *potential* power over leaders and nationals of those state that have not',[57] there is strong evidence to suggest otherwise. While the preamble to the Statute makes references to cosmopolitan ideals of common humanity and global justice, its most substantive articles make it clear that while making large inroads towards delegitimising sovereign impunity, the Court's capacity to operate is still heavily reliant on the cooperation of sovereign states.

Two examples in particular serve to highlight this: the case against Omar Al-Bashir, the President of Sudan, and the case against Saif Gaddafi, the former Prime Minister of Libya. Al-Bashir is charged with five counts of crimes against humanity, two counts of war crimes and three counts of genocide, all relating to the conflict in Darfur.[58] Sudan is not party to the Statute, and the Al-Bashir case was referred to the ICC by the UNSC, acting under the provisions outlined in Article 13. As a member of the UN, Sudan is thus obliged to honour the indictment. Yet, despite an arrest warrant being issued, Al-Bashir remains at large. More damning, however, is the behaviour of countries that *are* signatories to the Statute. When Al-Bashir was indicted, the neighbouring countries of Kenya and Chad, both States Parties to the *Rome Statute*, announced that they would arrest Al-Bashir if he were found on their territory. However, since the issuing of the arrest warrant, he has visited both Chad and Kenya, with neither state making any attempt to arrest him.[59] More recently, Bashir visited Nigeria, also a States Party to the Statute. Yet, as with the governments of Chad and Kenya, the Nigerian authorities refused to arrest Bashir, despite being reminded of their obligations by the OTP.[60]

The ICC's case against Saif Gaddafi also highlights the Court's reliance on state cooperation. Charged with two counts of crimes against humanity, he was captured in November 2011 while attempting to flee Libya and has been held in Zintan province since his arrest, despite regular missives from the ICC reminding Libya of their obligations to extradite Gaddafi to The Hague.[61] In May 2012, Libya challenged the admissibility of the case (as it is entitled to), arguing that its own investigation not only covered the same incidents as those outlined in the ICC arrest warrant, but was in fact broader than the ICC investigation. In finding that Libya was genuinely unable to carry out an investigation or prosecution, the Court rejected Libya's challenge of inadmissibility.[62] In defiance of this ruling, Libya announced in June 2013 that Gaddafi would be tried in Libya in August of the same year.

Yet as with the examples of the ICTY and ICTR, these two cases demonstrate the working limitations of the Court rather than serve as evidence of its insignificance. As a permanent legal mechanism for punishing individual violators of IHL, the ICC provides further evidence of an important shift in world politics. First, the existence of the Court serves to undermine traditional understandings of 'politics as power'. Despite vocal opposition from great powers (the US, Russia and China) and emerging powers (India), the resolution to adopt the Statute attracted 120 votes, with 20 abstentions and 7 votes against; furthermore, the 60 ratifications required to bring the Statute into effect were achieved in a remarkably short time frame.[63]

Second, the contemporary evolution of law beyond the domestic involves inevitable conflicts between international law and state power, or between international enforcement and the state's claim to the monopoly on the legitimate use of violence. The ICC provides evidence of an increasing delegation of state power to multilateral institutions premised on ethical norms. Furthermore, the existence of the Court provides an avenue for justice where, for a variety of reasons, none exists at the domestic level. Nowhere is this more evident than in the case of Bosco Ntaganda. In separate arrest warrants, Ntaganda was accused of seven counts of war crimes and three of crimes against humanity, allegedly committed first in north-eastern Congo in 2002 and 2003, and later as head of the rebel group M23 operating in the Kivu region of the DRC. His whereabouts was generally well known. Indeed, as part of a peace deal between the DRC and M23's predecessor, the National Congress for the Defence of the People, he and many of his fellow rebels were incorporated into the DRC army. But in March, 2013, following internal divisions in M23, Ntaganda handed himself to the US Embassy in Kigali, requesting that he be transferred to the ICC.[64] Again, without the Court, it is unlikely Ntaganda would ever have been held responsible for his crimes in a court of law.

Third, the Court has successfully diffused 'new norms arising from ICC jurisprudence into domestic laws'; there is compelling evidence to suggest that the organisational structure of the Court has had a positive effect on domestic efforts at prosecuting violations of IHL.[65] Finally, building on the precedent set by the two *ad hoc* Tribunals, the ICC serves as a counter to legitimating the use of force through appeals to *raison d'état* by extending legal and moral constraints to the realm of international affairs. In achieving this, the Court erodes the interlinked and equally long evolved practice of impunity, challenging deeply entrenched understandings of how violators of IHL might be held to account and, *post hoc*, providing alternative interpretations on how limitations to the use of force are understood in the international realm.

The ICTY, ICTR and the ICC: transcending sovereignty?

How, then, should we interpret the degree to which institutions of international criminal justice constrain the actions of sovereign states? Engaging with Hedley Bull's three 'traditions' (realism, internationalism and idealism/cosmopolitanism) and acknowledging that 'each of these traditional patterns of thought embodies a description of the *nature of international politics* and a set of prescriptions about international conduct',[66] it will be argued that the constraints imposed upon states by international criminal law are best understood as contributing to an emerging pluralist international society.

When grudgingly acknowledging its existence, realists argue that because international law's legislative, adjudicative and enforcement procedures operate without a central authority, it has limited effectiveness. For realists, the state and those acting on its behalf are the main determinants of justice in the international system. Thus, the laws of war, as a mechanism to limit the use of force in the international system, misunderstand the core characteristics of the system. Furthermore, because international law exists at the whim of states, and serves the interests of powerful ones, it has no independent agency. Hence any function of order it might provide is merely a reflection of pre-existing power configurations.[67]

But contrary to the arguments made by realists, the actions of these legal institutions cannot be condemned as redundant when considering contributions to limiting or restricting the use of force. The prosecution of high-ranking officials at the *ad hoc* Tribunals and self-referrals and surrendering to the ICC demonstrate that their activities are not entirely beholden to the national interest. Furthermore, while the *ad hoc* Tribunals are governed by the UN, the ICC is treaty-based, representing an institutional freedom from factors of *realpolitik*. Finally, despite the protestations of powerful states, the ICC continues to indict and prosecute war criminals.

For cosmopolitans, the *ad hoc* Tribunals and the ICC represent something utopian and indeed transformative. A number of arguments are made to this end. Most expansive are claims that law making has escaped the monopoly of states, with the Tribunals and the ICC part of a broader trend of events and movements that serve primarily to undermine Westphalian state sovereignty.[68] Proponents of these new legal institutions celebrate them as moral agents, able to rise above the petty squabbling that characterises power politics. Finally, they are seen as a component of what Marc Weller calls an emerging global constitutional system, which is constituted by universally acknowledged core values, increased rights for individuals under international law, and sanctions against individuals, including heads of state, for violating these rights.[69]

The degree to which the ICTY, ICTR and ICC are representative of a cosmopolitan order, however, is dubious. Such claims, closely associated with the supposed emergence of a 'global civil society', assume the gradual decline of state power. As highlighted throughout this chapter, it is clear from the complementarity principle that underpins the activities of the *ad hoc* Tribunals and the ICC that the judicial mechanisms of the state remain the primary focus in efforts to punish violators of IHL. Likewise, the lack of an enforcement mechanism means that these legal institutions continue to rely on the cooperation of states. As a result, the metaphorical tentacle of global justice does not exist, or is at least highly selective based on state preferences and/or their capacity to withstand it. Elaborating on this through focusing on the ICC, Gerry Simpson points out that it

envisages as its globalised legal order ... a matrix of increasingly active and resolute domestic courts ending the impunity afforded suspected war criminals ... Indeed, a perfectly functioning ICC would be one that did not function at all: all cases would be heard at the national level.[70]

Further to Simpson's point, IHL does not outlaw war. Instead, informed by the Just War tradition, it provides a set of criteria about what is legally acceptable during armed conflict. In the spirit of Immanuel Kant, cosmopolitans regard war as illegitimate under most circumstances. Hence, as legal mechanisms that moderate the use of force, rather than attempt to completely eradicate it, the *ad hoc* Tribunals and the ICC certainly do not contribute to cosmopolitan order.

The third alternative to understanding new mechanisms of international criminal justice is through the internationalist tradition. Engaging with Hugo Grotius, Bull, one of the more prominent English School theorists, suggested 'that states and the rulers of states in their dealings with one another were bound by rules and together formed a society'.[71] It is through the idea of international society that the role of international law – as a constraint on the behaviour of states – is best conceptualised. Within the internationalist tradition, international law is regarded as playing an integral role in determining behaviour among states, but the discipline divides itself over the degree to which international laws guide the actions of states, or even the degree to which states are obliged to obey these laws. Establishing the distinction between solidarists and pluralists, Bull argues that, according to the former, there is solidarity amongst the states that comprise international society sufficient to enforce the law, whereas pluralists 'do not exhibit solidarity of this kind, but are capable of agreeing only for certain minimum purposes which are short of that of the enforcement of the law'.[72] While solidarists and pluralists agree with Bull's dictum that in international society, 'states are bound not only by rules of prudence or expediency but also by the imperatives of morality and law',[73] they 'differ markedly over precisely how international society is to be further understood, with important implications for how they see international law'.[74]

In the Grotian tradition, a solidarist international society is one in which a sense of obligation to humanity as a whole transcends the society of states, and in which IHL evolves independently of states' consent and binds states, even those who withhold their consent, to the 'principles of humanity and the dictates of public conscience'.[75] As such, solidarists 'question the idea that international society should rightly be considered a society of states ... empirically and normatively it should be seen as a society of individuals and peoples'. Therefore, 'there is an ethical universe beyond the state that is, and ought to be, constitutive of international society and its law'.[76]

Engaging with the writing of Swiss jurist Emer de Vattel, pluralists identify the members of international society exclusively as states. But the state in a pluralist international society is not a Waltzian, atomistic unit. Rather, 'regulating states by international law to avert or reduce the incidence or extent of damaging collisions between them makes sense only if those entities are valuable in themselves'.[77] Within a pluralist conception of international society, international law consists of 'rules distilled by the common practices of the society of states, expressing more precisely and explicitly the terms of association embodied in them'.[78] Thus, international law is premised on the shared and mutually recognised right of non-interference and reciprocal recognition of sovereignty. However, in an important caveat, R. J. Vincent argues that the right to non-interference is not absolute. While Vincent emphasises the principle of non-intervention as integral to states' coexistence, exceptions to this norm may be provided when 'a state by its behaviour so outrages the conscience of mankind no doctrine can be deployed to defend it against intervention'.[79] Thus, for pluralists, international law exists primarily as positivist law (as opposed to natural law), and as something that states consent to, rather than have imposed upon them.

R. H. Jackson's insights into the nature and character of the state in international society, combined with Vincent's 'thick pluralism' – which acknowledges that agreement on human rights exists – provides a rationale for intervention in the most dire of circumstances. In turn, this qualified pluralism serves as a foundation on which to argue that the new mechanisms of international criminal justice, of which the ICTY, ICTR and ICC are examples, can be best understood as contributing to a pluralist international society, in which the state retains its primacy, but its activities are informed and constrained by its obligations to IHL.

A number of arguments can be made to this end with respect to the Tribunals and the ICC. First, and most importantly, the articles in each of the statutes relating to complementarity serve to highlight the ongoing primacy of the state. Not only does the complementarity principle cede first authority to national judiciaries, each of the legal institutions discussed here were established not to supersede domestic judiciaries, but rather to act where domestic judiciaries either could not or would not prosecute the worst violations of IHL. Therefore, while established on a foundation of humanitarian concern, the ICTY, ICTR and ICC nonetheless explicitly delegate judicial sovereignty to the nation-state. Second, as the obstructionist policies of Croatia and Rwanda, and the cases against Al-Bashir and Gaddafi demonstrate, attempts to prosecute violators and thus provide tangible restraints against the use of force are often impeded by the actions of uncooperative states. Hence, while there exists an acknowledged and shared perception of what cannot be done, informed primarily by the customary and treaty-based nature of IHL, punishment for violations of IHL are best understood with reference to pluralist interpretations of sovereignty and non-interference, where the state continues to reserve its historically established right to be the primary adjudicator about violations of IHL.

This is why the solidarist view of international criminal Tribunals and courts is fundamentally incorrect, at least at present. Certainly, English School theorists like Martin Wight and Bull both believed that as observers of international politics, we are best equipped to capture 'moments' in international relations.[80] However, when one considers that a solidarist international society is characterised foremost by the gradual decline of the capacity and efficacy of the nation-state, it becomes increasingly difficult to argue that the ICTY, ICTR and ICC are somehow reflective of justice beyond the state, and hence representative of a solidarist international or cosmopolitan world society. In this way, it is clear that the members of international society are not willing to relinquish their sovereign right of non-interference, even though there has been a shift in what constitutes such limits on sovereignty, underpinned by an expanding and shared understanding idea of humanitarianism and justice among states. But this remains a comparatively narrow conception. Thus, in practice, international mechanisms for punishing violators of IHL remain hindered by interpretations of sovereign non-interference that are premised on narrowly conceived perceptions of justice.

Conclusion

There have always existed rules that sought to restrain excessive conduct during warfare. The evolution of such rules into laws of war has largely coincided with the spread of the sovereign state as the primary political organising unit. However, for much of the modern period, such laws were primarily customary and existed generally as little more than tacit acknowledgements among European states. As such, violations of these laws were often legitimated through appeals to *raison d'état*, while sovereigns and heads of state were assumed immune from prosecution and the punishment of violators of these laws remained solely at the behest of the state.

While the evolution of attempts to limit the use of force during conflict did not remain entirely static during the modern period, the above description was generally accurate up until the period immediately following the end of World War II. The flaws of the Nuremburg and Tokyo trials are well documented, yet they were nonetheless harbingers of more concerted, collective efforts among states in the system at defining what was not permissible during war. However, while the momentum that emanated from the Nuremburg and Tokyo Tribunals for an international court that would further institutionalise such understandings was halted by the *realpolitik* of the Cold War, a combination of the implosion of the Soviet Union and especially violent conflicts in the former Yugoslavia and Rwanda served as the catalyst for the establishment of the two UN *ad hoc* Tribunals, and the subsequent establishment of the ICC.

The Tribunals and the ICC are international legal institutions that challenge deeply entrenched historical norms of sovereign immunity and impunity. Collectively, they represent the greatest advance in IHL since the end of World War II and are thus characteristic of something definitively different in international relations. There are now tangible consequences for violations of international law. States are no longer able to act primarily in the national interest and international politics can no longer exclusively be understood as a struggle for power.

However, while these new legal mechanisms are representative of an institutional rejection of *raison d'état* as legitimation for the use of force, they are not representative of a cosmopolitan realisation of global justice. Each of the statutes discussed here confirm this. They are all consistent, through the principle of complementarity, in their deference to (functioning) domestic judiciaries. In lacking an enforcement arm, the reach of global justice mechanisms remains limited. Therefore, the *ad hoc* Tribunals and the ICC are representative of a pluralist moment, where restrictions on the use of force are increasingly informed by obligations to international law, albeit reliant on relatively narrow conceptions of justice and humanitarianism. As such, these new legal institutions do not transcend sovereignty, but they do provide a medium beyond the self-interested space of the sovereign state to prosecute violators of IHL. They are thus representative of the latest shift that limits, without completely delegitimising, the state's right to use force.

NOTES

1 H. Bull, *The Anarchical Society: A Study of Order in World Politics* (Basingstoke: Palgrave MacMillan, 3rd edn, 2002), p. 25.
2 C. Reus-Smit, 'Introduction', in C. Reus-Smit (ed.), *The Politics of International Law* (Cambridge: Cambridge University Press, 2004), p. 7.
3 T. McCormack, 'The importance of effective international enforcement of international humanitarian law', *International Humanitarian Law Magazine*, Issue 1 (2011), p. 3.
4 See S. Roach, 'Introduction: Global Governance in Context', in S. Roach (ed.), *Governance, Order and the International Criminal Court: Between Realpolitik and a Cosmopolitan Court* (Oxford: Oxford University Press, 2009), pp. 7–8.
5 P. Akhavan, 'Punishing war-crimes in the Former Yugoslavia: A critical juncture for the New World Order', *Human Rights Quarterly*, 15:2 (1993), p. 265.
6 UN Security Council, Resolution 780, 6 October 1992, available at: www.ohr.int/otherdoc/un-res-bih/pdf/s92r780e.pdf (accessed 5 August 2013); UN Security Council, Resolution 827, 25 May 1993, available at: http://daccess-ods.un.org/access.nsf/Get?Open&DS=S/RES/827%20(1993)&Lang=E&Area=UNDOC (accessed 10 May 2013).
7 UN Security Council, *Resolution 827* (accessed 10 May 2013). Left open because of the continuing conflict in the region, the temporal mandate of the ICTY allowed for the investigation into crimes committed during the 1991–1992 Serbo-Croat War and the subsequent 1998–99 war in Kosovo.
8 United Nations, *Updated Statute of the International Criminal Tribunal for the Former Yugoslavia*, available at: www.icty.org/x/file/Legal%20Library/Statute/statute_sept09_en.pdf (accessed 16 May 2013).
9 United Nations, *Updated Statute of the International Criminal Tribunal for the Former Yugoslavia*.
10 United Nations, *Updated Statute of the International Criminal Tribunal for the Former Yugoslavia*.

11 See M. M. El Zeidy, *The Principle of Complementarity in International Criminal Law: Origin, Development and Practice* (Boston and Leiden: Martinus Nijhoff Publishers, 2008), pp. 143–5.

12 United Nations, *Updated Statute of the International Criminal Tribunal for the Former Yugoslavia* (accessed 16 May 2013).

13 V. Peskin, *International Justice in Rwanda and the Balkans: Virtual Trials and the Struggle for State Cooperation* (Cambridge: Cambridge University Press, 2008), p. 10.

14 M. Humphrey, 'International intervention, justice and national reconciliation: The role of the ICTR and ICTY in Rwanda and Bosnia', *Journal of Human Rights*, 2:4 (2003), p. 496.

15 See K. E. Smith, *Genocide and the Europeans* (Cambridge, Cambridge University Press, 2010).

16 See UN Security Council, *Report of the Secretary-General on Rwanda*, 4 October 1994, available at: http://daccess-ods.un.org/access.nsf/Get?Open&DS=S/1994/1125&Lang= E&Area=UNDOC (accessed 18 February 2013).

17 C. Cisse, 'The end of a culture of impunity in Rwanda? Prosecution of genocide and war crimes before Rwandan courts and the International Criminal Tribunal for Rwanda', *Yearbook of International Humanitarian Law*, 1 (1998), pp. 162–3.

18 UN Security Council, *Resolution 955*, 8 November 1994, available at: www.unhcr.org/ refworld/docid/3b00f2742c.html (accessed 14 February 2013). Somewhat ironically, Rwanda was the only member of the Security Council to vote against Resolution 955, citing three specific reservations about the proposed Tribunal: 1) UNSC Resolution 955 limits the maximum sentence to life imprisonment, while the Rwandan penal code provides for the death penalty. The Rwandan government was concerned about the tension it might create between Rwanda's national judiciary and the proposed Tribunal, arguing that the ICTR would be prosecuting those responsible for planning and carrying out the genocide, meaning those most culpable would not face the possibility of the death penalty; 2) arguing that the conflict covered by the Tribunal dated to before 1994, Rwanda argued that the temporal jurisdiction of the Tribunal should date back to 1990; and 3) Rwanda argued that the Tribunal should be based in Rwanda. P. Magnarella, *Justice in Africa: Rwanda's Genocide, its Courts, and the UN Criminal Tribunal* (Aldershot: Ashgate, 2000), p. 42. Under UNSC Resolution 977, Arusha was 'determined as the seat of the International Tribunal for Rwanda'. UN Security Council, *Resolution 977*, 22 February 1995, available at: http://www.unhcr.org/refworld/docid/3b00f1564f.html (accessed 14 February 2013).

19 UN Security Council, *Resolution 808*, 22 February 1993, available at: www.unhcr. org/refworld/docid/3b00f15d30.html (accessed 15 February 2013); and UN Security Council, *Resolution 955* (accessed 14 February 2013).

20 UN Security Council, *Resolution 955* (accessed 14 February 2013).

21 UN Security Council, *Resolution 955* (accessed 14 February 2013), Article 8.2.

22 Cisse, 'The end of a culture of impunity in Rwanda?', p. 165. At the adoption of Resolution 955, China stated that 'The establishment of an international tribunal for the prosecution of those who are responsible for crimes that gravely violate international humanitarian law is a special measure taken by the international community to handle certain special problems. It is only a supplement to domestic criminal jurisdiction and the current exercise of universal jurisdiction over certain international crimes' (cited in Cisse, 'The end of a culture of impunity in Rwanda?', p. 165). These sentiments echo those expressed by the British, who objected to the establishment of a Tribunal because 'the primary responsibility for bringing perpetrators to justice rests with national judicial systems' (cited in Smith, *Genocide and the Europeans*, p. 163).

23 Humphrey, 'International Intervention, justice and national reconciliation', p. 496.

24 UN Security Council, *Report of the Secretary-General on Rwanda* (accessed 18 February 2013).

25 See V. Peskin, 'Beyond victor's justice? The challenge of prosecuting the winners at the International Criminal Tribunals for the Former Yugoslavia and Rwanda, *Journal of Human Rights*, 4:2 (2005), pp. 213–31.

26 See G. Boas, *The Milošević Trial: Lessons for the Conduct of Complex International Criminal Proceedings* (Cambridge: Cambridge University Press, 2007), p. 38. See also G. Simpson, *Law, War and Crime: War Crimes Trials and the Reinvention of International Law* (Cambridge: Polity, 2007), pp. 16–17.

27 See L. Reydams, 'The ICTR ten years on: Back to the Nuremburg paradigm?', *Journal of International Criminal Justice*, 3 (2005), pp. 977–88.

28 Cited in Peskin, 'Beyond victor's justice?', p. 222.

29 L. Barria and S. Roper, 'How effective are international criminal tribunals? An analysis of the ICTY and ICTR', *The International Journal of Human Rights*, 9:3 (2005), p. 362.

30 E. Møse, 'Main achievements of the ICTR', *Journal of International Criminal Justice*, 3 (2005), pp. 927–8.

31 Barria and Roper, 'How effective are international criminal tribunals?', p. 362.

32 The Rwandan government's request was aimed at avoiding 'any suspicion of it wanting to organise speedy, vengeful justice' (see UN Security Council, *Letter dated 28 September 1994 from the Permanent Representative of Rwanda to the United Nations Addressed to the President of the Security Council*, 29 September 1994, available at: www.un.org/ga/search/view_doc.asp?symbol=S/1994/1115 (accessed 20 February 2013)).

33 See P. Akhavan, 'Beyond impunity: Can international criminal justice prevent further atrocities?', *American Journal of International Law*, 95:1 (2001), p. 23.

34 See A. Roberts, 'Implementation of the laws of war in late-20th century conflicts Part II', *Security Dialogue*, 29 (1998), pp. 137–50; and Peskin, *International Justice in Rwanda and the Balkans*, pp. 210–15. While it is not possible to demonstrate how the shortcomings of the ICTR might be to blame for the on-going violence in the Democratic Republic of Congo and neighbouring countries, it is not unreasonable to argue that increasing the Tribunal's mandate to include members of the Rwandese Patriotic Army and RPF might have had a positive impact on the on-going conflicts in the immediate area. See Reydams, 'The ICTR ten years on', pp. 981–7.

35 Barria and Roper, 'How effective are international criminal tribunals?', p. 362.

36 J. N. Clark, 'The limits of retributive justice: Findings of an empirical study in Bosnia and Hercegovina', *Journal of International Criminal Justice*, 7 (2009), pp. 463–87.

37 See Humphrey, 'International intervention, justice and national reconciliation', p. 501.

38 See 'Dayton Accords', United States Department of State, available at: www.state.gov/p/eur/rls/or/dayton/52578.htm (accessed 12 July 2013).

39 Barria and Roper, 'How effective are international criminal tribunals?', p. 359.

40 See Peskin, *International Justice in Rwanda and the Balkans*, pp. 29–91.

41 Peskin, 'Beyond victor's justice', p. 218.

42 It is generally agreed that Croatia only started to cooperate more proactively with the Tribunal once its cooperation was linked to its application for membership of the EU. For more, see V. Pavlakovi, 'Croatia, the International Criminal Tribunal for the former Yugoslavia, and General Gotovina as a political symbol', *Europe-Asia Studies*, 62:10 (2010), pp. 1707–40.

43 Magnarella, *Justice in Africa*, p. 51.

44 At the time of writing, Kenya has been implicated in the protection of Félicien Kabuga,

who is accused of bankrolling *Radio Télévision Libre des Mille Colline*, the radio station that broadcast anti-Tutsi propaganda leading up to and during the 1994 genocide. See United Nations, *Statement by Justice Hassan B. Jallow, Prosecutor of the ICTR, to the United Nations Security Council*, 4 June 2008, available at: www.unictr.org/Default. aspx?TabId=155&id=967&language=en-US&mid=560&SkinSrc=[G]Skins/UNICTR/ PrintSkin&ContainerSrc=[G]Containers/UNICTR/PrintContainer&dnnprintmode=true (accessed 22nd July, 2013).

45 Peskin, 'Beyond victor's justice', p. 225.
46 According to Nicola Henry, 'due to the general reluctance ... to call certain crimes 'genocide' or 'genocidal', the decision rendered in the *Akayesu* case has had enormous significance for the development of international humanitarian law, as various courts have considered genocidal sexual violence and/or upheld the *Akayesu* finding'. N. Henry, *War and Rape: Law, Memory and Justice* (London and New York: Routledge, 2011), p. 95.
47 See B. Nowrojee, '"Your Justice is Too Slow": Will the ICTR Fail Rwanda's Rape Victims', United Nations Research Institute for Social Development, *Occasional Paper 10*, November 2005, p. 20; N. Jones, *The Courts of Genocide: Politics and the Rule of Law in Rwanda and Arusha* (Oxford and New York: Routledge, 2010), p. 185.
48 Akhavan, 'Beyond impunity', p. 23.
49 Peskin, *International Justice in Rwanda and the Balkans*, p. 7.
50 Akhavan, 'Beyond impunity', p. 13.
51 See *The Rome Statute of the International Criminal Court*, available at: http://untreaty. un.org/cod/icc/statute/romefra.htm (accessed 23 July 2013). See also International Criminal Court, *Resolution RC/Res.6**, available at www.icc-cpi.int/iccdocs/asp_docs/ Resolutions/RC-Res.6–ENG.pdf (accessed 1 August 2012). When the Statute was first being negotiated, Parties could not agree on a definition of 'crime of aggression'. At the 2010 Review Conference of the Rome Statute, amendments to the Statute were adopted which include a definition of the crime of aggression and a regime establishing how the Court will exercise its jurisdiction over this crime. However, the Court will not be able to exercise its jurisdiction over the crime of aggression until (a) at least thirty States Parties have ratified or accepted the amendments; and (b) a decision is taken by two-thirds of States Parties to activate the jurisdiction at any time after 1 January 2017. For more See W. Schabas, *An Introduction to the International Criminal Court* (Cambridge: Cambridge University Press, 4th edn, 2011), pp. 11–16.
52 It was under this proviso that former President of Côte d'Ivoire, Laurent Gbagbo was indicted by the OTP.
53 See Schabas, *An Introduction to the International Criminal Court*, pp. 16–22.
54 *The Rome Statute of the International Criminal Court* (accessed 23 July 2013).
55 Roach, 'Introduction', p. 9.
56 T. McCormack, 'The importance of effective international enforcement of international humanitarian law', *International Humanitarian Law Magazine*, 1 (2011), p. 5.
57 K. Ainley, 'The International Criminal Court on trial', *Cambridge Review of International Affairs*, 24:3 (2011), p. 315 (emphasis in original).
58 See '*The Prosecutor v. Omar Hassan Ahmad Al Bashir*', International Criminal Court, available at: www.icc-cpi.int/en_menus/icc/situations%20and%20cases/situations/ situation%20icc%200205/related%20cases/icc02050109/Pages/icc02050109.aspx (accessed 25 July 2013).
59 The African Union defended the actions of Chad and Kenya through the following statement: 'both Chad and Kenya, being neighbours of Sudan, have an abiding interest in ensuring peace and stability in Sudan and in promoting peace, justice and reconciliation

which can only be achieved through continuous engagement with the elected govern-ment of Sudan'. African Union, *Press Release No. 119/2010* (29 August 2010).

60   See 'Decision Regarding Omar Al-Bashir's Visit to the Federal Republic of Nigeria', International Criminal Court, 15 July 2013, available at www.icc-cpi.int/iccdocs/doc/doc1619414.pdf (accessed 25 July 2013).

61   In March 2012, Pre-Trial Chamber 1 declared that 'although Libya is not a State Party to the Statute, it is under an obligation to cooperate with the Court ... Libya has therefore a general obligation to comply with the Surrender Request in accordance with Part IX of the Statute and, more specifically, with its article 89(1)'. See 'Situation in Libya – In the case of *The Prosecutor v. Saif al-Islam Gaddafi and Abdullah al-Senussi*, International Criminal Court, available at: www.icc-cpi.int/iccdocs/doc/doc1386229.pdf (accessed 19 December 2012).

62   See 'Situation in Libya, *The Prosecutor v. Saif Al-Islam Gaddafi'*, International Criminal Court, available at: www.icc-cpi.int/iccdocs/PIDS/publications/GaddafiEng.pdf (accessed 26 August 2014).

63   To date, three States Parties to the Statute – Uganda, the DRC and the Central African Republic – have referred situations occurring on their territories to the Court. In addition, the UNSC has referred the situation in Darfur, Sudan, and the situation in Libya – both non-States Parties. On 31 March 2010, Pre-Trial Chamber II granted the Prosecution author-isation to open an investigation *proprio motu* in the situation of Kenya. See 'Situation in Kenya -Decision Pursuant to Article 15 of the Rome Statute on the Authorization of an Investigation into the Situation in the Republic of Kenya', International Criminal Court, available at: www.icc-cpi.int/iccdocs/doc/doc854287.pdf (accessed 12 August 2012).

64   See P. Jones and D. Smith, 'Notorious warlord gives himself up to international criminal court', *Guardian* (19 March 2013), available at: www.theguardian.com/world/2013/mar/19/africa-congo?guni=Article:in%20body%20link (accessed 1August 2013).

65   L. Chappell, 'Women's Rights and Religious Opposition: The Politics of Gender at the International Criminal Court', in Y. Abu-Laban (ed.), *Gendering the Nation-State: Canadian and Comparative Perspectives* (Vancouver: UBC Press, 2008), p. 146.

66   Bull, *The Anarchical Society*, p. 23 (emphasis added).

67   J. Mearsheimer, 'The false promise of institutions', *International Security*, 19:5 (1994), pp. 5–49.

68   J. Cohen, 'Whose sovereignty? Empire versus international law', *Ethics & International Affairs*, 18:3 (2004), pp. 1–24.

69   M. Weller, 'The Struggle for an International Constitutional Order', in D. Armstrong (ed.), *Routledge Handbook of International Law* (London and New York: Routledge, 2009), pp. 179–94.

70   Simpson, *Law, War and Crime*, p. 36.

71   H. Bull, ' The Importance of Grotius', in H. Bull, B. Kingsbury and A. Roberts (eds), *Hugo Grotius and International Relations* (Oxford: Clarendon Press, 1990), p. 72.

72   H. Bull, 'The Grotian Conception of International Society', in H. Butterfield and M. Wight (eds), *Diplomatic Investigations: Essays in the Theory of International Politics* (London: Allen and Unwin, 1966), p. 52.

73   Bull, *The Anarchical Society*, p. 25.

74   C. Reus-Smit, 'Society, Power and Ethics', in Reus-Smit (ed.), *The Politics of International Law*, p. 275. For more on the distinction between solidarism and pluralism, see A. Linklater and H. Suganami, *The English School of International Relations: A Contemporary Reassessment* (Cambridge: Cambridge University Press, 2006).

75 J. Ralph, *Defending the Society of States: Why America Opposes the International Criminal Court and its Vision of World Society* (Oxford: Oxford University Press, 2007), p. 10.
76 Reus-Smit, 'Society, Power and Ethics', pp. 275–6.
77 R. H. Jackson, 'The Political Theory of International Society', in K. Booth and S. Smith (eds), *International Relations Theory Today* (Cambridge: Polity Press, 1995), p. 110.
78 T. Nardin, *Law, Morality and the Relations of States* (Princeton: Princeton University Press, 1983), p. 187.
79 R. J. Vincent, *Nonintervention and International Order* (Princeton: Princeton University Press, 1974), p. 347.
80 Likewise, Andrew Linklater and Hidemi Suganami point out that 'the degree of solidarity among states may be expected to vary from one set of states to another ... neither solidarism nor pluralism should be treated as stating a universal or timeless truth about international society'. Linklater and Suganami, *The English School of International Relations*, p. 66.

Conclusions:
violence and the state – past, present and future

Matt Killingsworth, Matthew Sussex and Gavin Daly

WHEN CONSIDERING THE relationship between the state and organised violence it is customary to first distinguish between violence as war (operating between states), and violence as a domestic instrument that operates within them. Clearly the establishment of a demarcated public and private realm is also important. But whether 'internal' or 'external', violence has typically been conducted for political ends, and has also consistently been justified as a legitimate means for the pursuit of state interests. In this respect, war can be differentiated from less organised violence. This is because it was defined as an activity 'carried out by a newly fashioned "public" entity which established the law and exceptions to the law'.[1] Through a centuries-long process, emerging European states assumed a monopoly on the use of violence through dual processes of internal pacification and international war making. Even allowing for contemporary trends towards asymmetric conflict, the state has proven itself as a potent war-fighting institution. Closely related to the demonstrated capacity of the state to conduct war was the emergence in the early modern period of the idea of *raison d'état*, informed by a core pillar of Westphalian sovereignty: the right of sovereigns (and later states) to make war in the pursuit of their interests. This allowed war to be understood – in Clausewitzian terms –as an 'act of policy ... [unable to] be divorced from political life'.[2] Moreover, the modern state was also able to successfully claim to represent the collective interest. As Max Weber famously claimed the state came to define the 'public', and the 'public arena' became that in which force was legitimate.[3] Thus, war fighting by agents of the state was understood as both legal and legitimate.

But during the last decade of the twentieth century, this state-centric understanding of organised violence has been challenged from a number of quarters. Violence as an expression of political ends is not just about war, and in fact has never simply been so. As the chapters in this book have demonstrated, violence has taken on a number of historical forms of state coercion (as well as resistance to it), and continues to do so in the contemporary era. Violence can be an instrument of elites undertaking national unification projects; used to decapitate rival elites; or employed at times of great weakness and fragility. Whether there are distinct patterns to be identified in the conduct and nature of violence, of course, remains a matter for debate. In this concluding chapter we therefore re-examine some of these claims in light of the findings contained in the main empirical contributions in this volume.

Before doing so, some qualifications are necessary. First, this book has sought to provide a number of 'snapshots' of violence in the modern period. We do not claim to have provided a linear history of violence, nor do we claim that it is possible to trace it in terms of an evolutionary arc. Second, the conclusions we draw are, by nature, broad. This is partly due to the interdisciplinary nature of the book's framework, encompassing assessments of violence from sociologists, historians and specialists in international relations. However, we do believe that the core finding of the book – that the role of the state as an agent of violence is significantly underestimated in contemporary scholarship – will serve both as a useful corrective, and as a platform for further debate between scholars with an interest in violence from an array of cognate research fields.

Violence and the state in the modern era

It is interesting that while contemporary violence tends to be theorised increasingly in ways that downplay the role of the state, the same tendency has not (yet) been as robustly manifested in historical studies. In particular, for historians examining war and violence in early modern Europe, it was unnecessary to 'bring the state back in' (to adopt Theda Skocpol's classic formulation of the 1980s). This is because for such scholars the state had never really left in the first place.[4] Yet in the thirty years since, a rich body of historical research has highlighted a more complex and nuanced relationship between violence and state formation than had initially been set out by the pioneering state-development theories of Weber and Otto Hintze, and those of later historical sociologists, most famously Charles Tilly.[5] While the state has remained central to this – meaning that it is well and truly 'back in' – it is not treated as simply as it has been in the past.

Within this body of scholarship, there is now a greater appreciation of national variations across states and how they functioned in practice.[6] Dovetailing with work from international relations on different historical 'societies' of states, this thinking now extends beyond Europe to Asia as well.[7] On the inter-state level of analysis there is a growing sensitivity to war making as a complex interaction between social, cultural, economic and technological forces operating in conjunction with the state.[8] And there is a growing sense of the degree to which successful fiscal-military states evolved in conjunction *with* rather than *against* prevailing elite interests and *ancien regime* power dynamics.[9] The recent work of David Parrott on the 'business of war' in early modern Europe, both in France and elsewhere, has stressed the importance and vitality of military enterprise and private contractors, operating in partnership with the state, all the way down to the French Revolutionary-Napoleonic epoch. Parrott placed privatisation and military outsourcing at the centre of the early modern European 'Military Revolution', with the 'Contractor State' at the heart of provisioning, clothing and arming the large standing armies of the eighteenth century.[10]

In all this, some of the most important historiographical developments have been in relation to the eighteenth-century British state. Traditional Whiggish notions of a 'weak' British state, together with the relatively small size of the domestic British army, never fitted into conventional development theories about state formation and war, or indeed the concept of the Military Revolution. Such was the conventional thinking until the appearance of John Brewer's *The Sinews of War*.[11] Brewer argued for a 'strong' British state emerging from the 1688 Glorious Revolution onwards and placed the pressures of war at the centre of this transformation. A British fiscal-military state emerged, whose sinews of war, according to Brewer, were just as extensive as those of continental absolutist states, including Prussia. This was a British fiscal-military state built, above all, on a highly successful and efficient revenue system of loans and taxes. In contrast to Tilly, who argued that state 'resource extraction' from agrarian societies was much more bureaucratic intensive than for commercial ones,[12] Brewer found that the British collection of indirect taxes required an ever-growing body of skilled professionals – in this case, the Excise Department, which became the largest government department. Brewer's work has subsequently generated a great deal of historical debate and scholarship.[13] Recent research trends include an increasing emphasis on the British state contracting out the business of war;[14] a sensitivity to the successful consensual 'partnership' that the state was able to cultivate with elites, financiers and private enterprise;[15] and a renewed focus on the importance of the Navy, prompting calls that the term 'fiscal-naval state' is a more appropriate one for Britain.[16]

Thus we now have, courtesy of historical research carried out since the 1980s, a plethora of terms for characterising the relationship between early modern European states and war: the 'fiscal-military state', the 'dynastic state', the 'contractor state', the 'enterprise state', the 'fiscal-naval state', and the 'caring fiscal-military state'[17] – all alongside the traditional 'absolutist state'. Yet what is apparent in all of this is that as international society expanded the paths led inexorably back to the 'state'. This has been the case whatever its diverse forms, mechanisms of reach and control, and interactions with other prevailing historical forces and actors. In other words:

> There is no necessary incompatibility between the growth of the power of the state and the development of a substantial sphere of private military activity. Indeed, the latter made possible a robustness and organizational 'reach' that would otherwise have been unattainable to government authority.[18]

Hence, notwithstanding variations across time and place, and acknowledging the importance of technological, social, cultural, ideological and economic forces in shaping war and violence, what we find across Europe between 1500 and 1800 is a broad trend of growing state power amidst the escalating demands of violent conflict. In its broadest sense, as this book has argued, the symbiotic relationship between war and the state remains a central framework for understanding the history of violence in the early modern and modern epochs.

These processes and dynamics, at least for the early modern period, culminated in the Revolutionary-Napoleonic era. Indeed, as Gavin Daly's chapter argued, such was both the quantitative and qualitative shift in the scale and nature of war during this epoch that it represents a watershed between the early modern period and the greater transformations of the modern era. The French Revolution was the epicentre of this transformative episode, with a new ideological, political and cultural dynamism interacting with the legacy of the Military Revolution. The defining moment was the 1793 *levée en masse*, with the Jacobin state fusing the traditional public–private divide, mobilising the entire French nation for war, and in the process prefiguring the modern 'total war' of the twentieth century. The French 'contract' or 'enterprise' fiscal-military state ended with the Jacobin 'totalisation' of war, with the mobilisation of military resources placed now directly in the hands of the state. The radical introduction of conscription in 1793, melding citizenship and soldiering, effectively ended the Old Regime practice of mercenary armies, heralding the 'nation-in-arms'. Napoleon inherited, harnessed and tamed this powerful legacy, turning the French state and its military machine into the most formidable in Europe. Domestically, the Napoleonic state regularised and normalised the new demands of war on French society. While abroad, the regime's armies and cadres of civil administrators brought both revolutionary reforms and new oppression and exploitation, extracting local resources to help sustain and expand French hegemony across the Continent, with war feeding off war.

But it took another hundred years (and World War I) before we could truly refer to 'total' war. By then states were operating within a crucible of technological and industrial revolution, amidst a new ideological landscape of mass politics, nationalism, imperialism, socialism and fascism, in a world convulsed by revolution, economic depression and the redrawing of political maps. It proved a lethal combination. The result was mass industrialised slaughter, both between and within states, with at least fifty million lives lost in Europe alone. In the words of Ian Kershaw, violence had '*epochal character, it determined the age*'.[19]

It was 'total war' that gave the age its violent character. Coined in France during World War I, the term later found its fullest and deepest realisation during World War II, most especially in the war of barbarisation waged on the Eastern Front between Nazi Germany and the Soviet Union. This 'totalisation' involved the full-scale mobilisation of entire societies and economies, the ideal of totally destroying the enemy and their way of life with various forms of violence, and the breaking down of traditional distinctions between combatants and non-combatants.[20] Totalisation dramatically enhanced the power of the state, whether liberal or authoritarian. Unprecedented state intervention ensued, from military conscription to news management, from industrial production to human reproduction. This was also marked by unprecedented levels of state violence directed against civilians across a broad spectrum of contexts, from conventional war to political violence against ethnic and class minorities.[21] Jan Pakulski's chapter has addressed one such case study – the fate of elites in Poland during World War II – from amidst the age's geographical epicentre of state violence against civilians – the 'Bloodlands' of Eastern Europe that lay between Nazi Germany and Stalinist Russia.[22]

The end of World War II brought a close to this era of total war. In the words of Michael Howard, the dropping of the atomic bombs on Hiroshima and Nagasaki 'marked the close of the age of mass-warfare, of conflicts in which the fully-mobilized populations of industrialized countries had devoted their full energies to overthrowing one another'.[23] But in representing the high water mark of state mobilised mass total war, it marked anything but the demise of the state as a central actor in organised violence. The Cold War that followed divided the globe into two poles of power, and in the process coined the new term 'superpower' to describe the respective capabilities of the Soviet Union and the US. Backed by the logics of deterrence and containment, and enacted through proxy wars and struggles for control of peripheral states, as well as intense ideological and economic competition, the Cold War was nonetheless largely stable at the global level.[24] It was certainly true that the overlaying narrative of bipolar rivalry meant that many powerful forces, linked to violence and operating within and between states, were under-evaluated as social and political phenomena. These included decolonisation movements in Africa and Asia, state weakness and fragility, and the emergence of transnational terrorism, amongst many other forces. They also incorporated the construction of a rudimentary form of global governance through (largely Western) frameworks of international law, as well as institutions to regulate regional economic and political orders. These produced great affluence in some cases, and a growing awareness for the plight of the disadvantaged in others. They also provided grounds for resentment, a rejection of homogeneity, and a push back against dominant norms. As a result, the twin themes of integration and fragmentation that we associate with contemporary globalisation had their roots in the Cold

War era, much of which was also associated with violence, both direct and indirect, as well as real and perceived.

Yet even so, the state remained the primary reference object of international politics, if not the sole one. Self-determination campaigns had – and continue to have – a territorial state as their intended end-point. Institutions and regimes, whether constructed to foster epistemic community or more targeted around single issues, also have states at the heart of decision-making processes. But the Cold War's unanticipated ending, brought about by the collapse of the USSR and its satellites in the Warsaw Pact, led to a new enthusiasm that untrammelled state power, and hence a potent source of violence, could be curbed. While the passage of events has proven this to be erroneous, it is instructive to now turn to examine the tendency of much optimistic scholarship to overstate the constraints on state behaviour, both internally and externally. Nowhere is this more apparent than in the immediate aftermath of the Cold War.

The state and violence after the Cold War: old wine in new bottles?

The end of the Cold War led to significant expectations that the conclusion of bipolar rivalry would produce not only a 'peace dividend', but also the chance for the enlargement of 'zones of peace' via democratisation.[25] Francis Fukuyama's influential 'end of history' thesis certainly reflected a mood of great optimism in the West that violence as a product of ideological competition had more or less concluded.[26] Thanks to a variety of factors, many also identified major interstate war as being virtually redundant. One of these factors was nuclear weapons, which for some scholars made conflict between nuclear-armed states a mutually suicidal proposition.[27] Another was the growth of interdependence, which for others represented a key means to shift competition between states from the geopolitical to the economic realm.[28] Still others pointed to the increasing efficacy of international law, growing faith in the UN, and the rise of regional security communities in Asia and elsewhere that prioritised cooperation over conflict.[29] For a great many analysts, then, the nature of violence as we knew it in the modern era – defined by, legitimised by, and monopolised by states – seemed to be over.

The overall frequency of violence certainly did decline in the first two decades of the twenty-first century, even though there were numerous examples of mass bloodletting. In an international system where interstate war had become scarcer, the genocides in Rwanda and Darfur, the brutal warlordism in Somalia, the Srebrenica massacre and the atrocities committed against the Kosovars came under close scholarly scrutiny. So did the knock-on effects of the US 'war on terror' in Afghanistan, Iraq and in tribal areas of Pakistan. Meanwhile, the attendant fear of a clash of civilisations, perhaps even by proxy, came to challenge the idea that violence as the product of competing ideologies had died.[30]

Nations experiencing an Islamic 'insurgency', however loosely defined, saw their conflicts become more prominently examined as a result. This was the case for Chechnya, for southern Thailand, for the Philippines and for Indonesia following the Bali bombings of 2002.

Beyond the 'war on terror', past atrocities committed in the name of the state, like the 'Killing Fields' of Cambodia under the Khmer Rouge during the 1970s, were also examined more closely.[31] But other crises that involved either the aftermath of state violence or state failure altogether – in Liberia and Sierra Leone, for instance – received rather less attention. In addition, the process by which various international criminal Tribunals emerged and then moved towards convictions was costly, painfully slow, and by nature highly selective and politicised.[32]

Yet claims about democracy's 'triumph', about the erosion of violence for political ends, about the severing of the link between violence and statehood, as well as the view that contemporary civil conflicts are a 'new' kind of violence, have all been greatly overstated. In fact, the reasons for violence in the twenty-first century have remained remarkably constant, even though the means may have changed to varying degrees. In fact, the main four varieties of state violence analysed in this book can be identified in numerous contemporary examples. First, violence continues to be waged within the state as a struggle for control between competing elites. Second, violence remains a potent means to *escape* the state, and yet at the same time to paradoxically seek the formation of new ones. This has been the case in numerous self-determination campaigns since the end of the Cold War, from those with a highly specific set of political objectives to those with seemingly much more vague rationales. Third, many states use violence as a means of national unification, particularly those that have eschewed the initial post-Cold War gravitation towards democratisation. Finally, states – both powerful ones and weak ones – continue to use violence to combat external threats to their interests, to project their power, and impose their dominance over others.

Even the most cursory reading of conflict in the post-Cold War era would have to conclude that the relationship between elites and violence remains a strong one. While there has by no means been a form of targeted and systematic 'national decapitation' by an external actor, as witnessed in Poland and other Eastern European states in the middle of the twentieth century, inter-elite clashes are still prominent sources of contemporary political violence. The 'Arab Spring' revolutions were, by and large, bloody affairs, as existing elites struggled to hold onto power against a series of popular uprisings. But rather than being connected to one another as a mass flowering of democracy across North Africa and the Middle East, each uprising occurred for a different reason. Just as a nuanced response to the frequently heard statement 'the Arab street' should be 'which Arab street?', the combination of local politics, ethno-religious resentment, and economic motivations that arose across the region were highly specific to each particular state, leading to sultanism in many cases.[33] Rather than ideology, the common theme was more often a struggle for power, and in particular a struggle between current, former and aspirant new elites. The campaign in Libya to unseat Gaddafi was at least in part a conflict between the old military and societal elites that had been left in the wilderness since the overthrow of King Idris.[34] So too was the conflict in Syria that remained ongoing at the time of writing. Democracy in Egypt was short-lived, as the old elite swiftly (and brutally) purged the Islamic Brotherhood. And beyond the Middle East, a series of 'coloured' revolutions in Georgia, Ukraine and Kyrgyzstan also had elite politics at their core.

In addition to elites, self-determination campaigns are a prominent source of contemporary violence. The state is central to such events since a movement for independence – whether sought on national, economic or ethnic lines – seeks as its ultimate objective the formation of a state. Sometimes self-determination movements that have used violence have seemingly quite murky aims. Yet even Al Qaeda had as its main objective a state in the form of a pan-Islamic Caliphate. This is also the goal of Abu Bakr al-Baghdadi, the leader of the brutal and repressive Islamic State of Iraq and Syria.[35] Meanwhile, more conventional self-determination campaigns using violence are also tied to notions of statehood. This was the case in former Yugoslavia, in FRETELIN's successful struggle in East Timor, and in Chechnya. On some occasions the search is not for independence but reintegration into an existing state, as in South Ossetia and parts of eastern Ukraine; and to an extent in southern Thailand and in Kashmir. On other occasions independence has led almost immediately to war, as occurred in the split between Sudan and South Sudan in 2011. And while the reasons for seeking independence through violence will always be couched in terms of identity politics, their end aim is essentially Westphalian in nature. In other words, such movements continue to seek a homeland that has its own territory, defensible borders and central form of ruling authority.

The third area in which violence and the state remain linked is through national unification projects. This has been the specific subject of two chapters in this volume. As Terry Narramore has demonstrated, the use of violence by the People's Republic of China against Muslims in its restive Xinjiang province has all the hallmarks of a campaign against an ethnic 'other' used to solidify the dominant Han group's support of the nation. The branding of separatists as terrorists, a national discourse that condemns 'splittism', and the use of at times disproportionate means to clamp down on dissent have been indistinguishable from similar historical examples in the past, and have been pursued for the same traditional political motives. Similarly, in post-communist Russia, national unification has been a powerful determinant of violence. According to Matthew Sussex, violence has been an enabler of a consolidation of state control, a movement away from democracy and a 'strengthening of the vertical' in Russia. This occurred at three specific points: at a time of national weakness shortly after independence, when rival power structures clashed; at a time of national consolidation when an internal threat was dealt with harshly; and at a time of expansion, when Russia used violence as a means to help maintain its primacy in the former Soviet space.

A fourth arena for state violence in the post-Cold War era has been via the employment of coercion to prevent threats to national interests. An excellent example here is the policy and posture of the US after the events of 11 September 2001. While there are many potential reasons for the US-led 'war on terror', it was ultimately a war on threats to American interests, either real or imaginary. The rise of asymmetric conflict by Al Qaeda may have looked like a new form of tactics by a non-state adversary (in that the use of civilian airliners has only comparatively recently been available), but it was not a conflict undertaken by either side for fundamentally new reasons. Although the mechanisms of the US response were different (as former Defence Secretary Donald Rumsfeld noted, 'banker's pinstripes' were just as important as 'desert camouflage'),[36] it was nonetheless responding to a direct threat against its homeland, and against its allies in the Middle East, Asia, Europe and Africa. The notion of a 'war on terror' also served as a powerful narrative to enlarge the pool of potential US alliance partners, giving rise to the possibility for the establishment of new US bases. It justified the continued development of the US National Missile Defence program to guard against 'rogue' states and the use of drones to target terrorists inside states that may even be US allies. It also justified the continued US reticence to sign and ratify the Rome Statute, on the grounds that since US servicemen were deployed overseas more than any other state, it was the job of the US to punish them if they misbehaved. It is instructive that under President Barack Obama the US position on each of these issues has remained unchanged, despite the ending of the war on terror.[37] If anything, following the US 're-balance' to counter a rising China in Asia, the maintenance of violent means by the state to protect its core interests is becoming more, rather than less, visible.

Below we address in more detail the prospects for violence in light of the development of norms and legal frameworks related to human rights, and the ways in which states might legitimately exercise violence. However, if the preceding analysis is accurate, one might expect the state to remain at the centre of violence for the foreseeable future. The reason for this is simple. Given current trends towards what might be called the 'new authoritarian-ism', addressed in several chapters in this volume, one must question whether the Western-dominated normative order is likely to be sustained in future, or whether it will endure at all. Moreover, this is occurring at a time of changing power dynamics, in which we are currently witnessing – in the words of the US National Intelligence Council itself – an 'unprecedented shift of relative wealth and power ... from West to East'.[38] This increases the likelihood that there will be many normative narratives in contestation in future, and more complex justifications for violence. Such is the sense of trepidation that the prominent essayist Michael Ignatieff recently posed the question: 'are the authoritarians winning?'[39] Whatever the answer, it is unlikely that past patterns of state violence will disappear. If anything, they are likely to become more evident.

Violence and the state: norms, laws and the future

Notwithstanding the premature identification of peace dividends, and hopes for democratic universalism that occurred after the end of the Cold War, contemporary scholarship on violence remains generally critical of state-centric approaches. This has been driven in part by poststructural and postpositivist scholarship, but also by writing from within the liberal tradition that stresses the evolutionary character of external and internal barriers to states seeking to engage in violence. Such critiques can be broadly (and rather crudely) collected within the overall rubric of norms, rights and international law. As such, they are informed by the growing reach and appeal of globalisation, the increasing 'thickness' of international law and the evolution in understandings of human rights and the protection of these rights in the shape of humanitarian intervention. The contributors to this collection do not question the existence of such norms. What we question is the degree to which such norms affect the way that states behave. Through identifying a number of continuities *vis-à-vis* the state's use of violence, we conclude that they have some, but limited, effect on what states do.

Underpinning these critiques is a particularistic reinterpretation of sovereignty. Under this interpretation, the long-understood and practised norm of sovereign immunity no longer affords protection to the most egregious violations of human rights, with national leaders now accountable to what Ruti Teital calls 'an emerging transnational legal order'.[40] Similarly, sovereignty is redefined as a responsibility, rather than a Hobbesian-informed right, which has in turn informed ideas pertaining to humanitarian intervention. Finally, a variety of factors all broadly related to the forces of globalisation have facilitated the dual-process of blurring the distinction between public and private and internal and external, and, through the emergence of competing actors, rendered the state's claim to the monopoly on the legitimate use of violence redundant. With respect to the second claim, the end result is the declining political significance of territorial boundaries and the advent of a range of conflicting authority types, described by John Keane as representing an 'emerging neo-medieval order'.[41]

Yet such critiques fail to appreciate the institutional resilience of the state and its capacity, in what remains an essentially anarchical order, to resist the encroachment of normative forms of authority. None of the contributors to this volume deny that ideas pertaining to human rights have evolved and spread in the international system. However, the degree to which the spread of such norms has limited or even restricted the state's use of organised violence is questionable. In their respective chapters, both Narramore and Sussex demonstrated that despite external and internal condemnation of their respective actions, the Chinese and Russian states regularly resort to violence in the protection of the 'national interest'. Likewise, providing examples where 'new war' advocates posit that violence is informed by a multitude of factors outside those elucidated by Clausewitz, Jasmine-Kim Westendorf demonstrated that post-conflict violence in Liberia, South Sudan and Cambodia were essentially Clausewitzian political conflicts, in that they are fundamentally contests about power and authority, and not simply a product of a culture of violence which facilitates the use of violence to pursue individuals. And as Graeme Herd argued in his chapter, structural imperatives linked to domestic ones can form 'trilemmas' that are fundamentally tied to notions of power and interest. In the absence of robust institutional structures to deal with such problems, the potential for strategic divorces increases in a nonpolar international order.

In light of these findings, any confident pronouncements about the decline of the state and its declining ability and capacity to utilise organised violence to serve material ends are hasty. So too are arguments that seek to link the rise in international law to the declining capacity of the state, especially as it relates to its use of organised violence. For argument's sake, had we been writing this conclusion in the middle of the previous decade, our conclusions might have been more circumspect. The Coalition of the Willing's war against Iraq had been largely discredited, a growing international consensus had developed around the Responsibility to Protect and the International Criminal Court (ICC) had begun indicting gross violators of international humanitarian law. Yet within a relatively short period, the enthusiasm that these occurrences offered proof of a definitive change in the way we view the state's use of violence had mostly dissipated. Here, legal claims about the diminishing of political violence are incorrect for three reasons. These are related to the invocation of law, the constraints of legal mechanisms, and distinctions between the private and public sphere.

The first claim we take issue with is that that the increasing reference by states to international law equates to *de facto* compliance with it. This view was espoused by Sir Arthur Watts when he noted that 'virtually without exception states seek always to offer a legal justification for their actions' which 'demonstrates the value attached by states to compliance with international law'.[42] Yet while the advent of new supra-national legal mechanisms (specifically, the post-conflict Tribunals for Rwanda, Yugoslavia and Sierra Leone and the ICC) suggest an intensification of international law, the story is much more complicated than this. As Sussex pointed out in Chapter 4, the uses of legal justifications are more often than not instrumentalised, rather than representing a genuine appreciation of attempts to limit the actions of states. Likewise, Jannika Brostrom demonstrated that instead of being bound by international laws underpinned by ideals pertaining to the 'moral good', 'traditional' thinking, informed by conventional notions of statism, continues to influence such behaviour.

The second argument about state capacity declining in respect to organised violence concerns the spread of norms and laws that prohibit violence and punish violators. Increased prosecutions of violations of international humanitarian law and international human rights law at multiple jurisdictional levels have notionally created what Kathryn Sikkink famously called a 'justice cascade'. Sikkink was careful to add that this does not mean that 'perfect justice has been done or will be done, or that most perpetrators of human rights violations will be held criminally accountable'. Rather, she argues that the 'justice cascade' reflects a 'shift in the *legitimacy of the norm* of individual criminal accountability for human rights violations and an increase in criminal prosecutions on behalf of that norm'.[43]

But even with Sikkink's qualifier, the idea of a 'cascade' is difficult to maintain when one looks not only at the example of Saif Gaddafi and Omar Al-Bashir (as discussed by Matt Killingsworth), but also at the failure to hold gross violators of international humanitarian law and human rights laws and norms in Sri Lanka and Syria to account at any jurisdictional level. As such, although Sikkink and her ilk are not necessarily incorrect in their observation about the development of these norms, their influence on the way that states use violence both internally and externally appears quite marginal.

Third, placing an emphasis on the breakdown between public and private, and the subsequent ramifications this has for understanding conflict, is also flawed. Arguing that 'public–private distinctions shift and change as an effect of political power', Patricia Owens points out that 'there is clear historical and sociological evidence to support the conceptual claim that a variety of public–private distinctions are made and remade during war'. Thus, debates about political violence are better understood 'historically as the transnational constitution and circulation of military and economic power'.[44] Indeed, as a number of contributors to this volume have identified, the concepts of sovereignty and the claim to the monopoly on the legitimate use of force, while mutually reinforcing, are essentially unrealised ideal-types.

The contributions to this edited collection have highlighted the significant historical continuity in patterns of violence from the formative era of the sovereign state to contemporary times. While aware that the nature of violence has certainly not remained static during this time, we have argued that the state remains central to any understanding of the use of violence, both internally and externally. This book also demonstrates that despite arguments to the contrary, the state continues to reserve the right to use violence when and where it sees fit. While perhaps no longer able to lay absolute claim to the monopoly on the legitimate use of violence, claims of a neo-medieval order remain specious.

Predictions about the future are infamously risky. It would be foolhardy to make sweeping forecasts about how the relationship between the state and violence is likely to play out. Nonetheless, the continuities identified in this volume, combined with the institutional resilience of the state, suggests that the conclusions offered here will remain valuable for at least the foreseeable future.

NOTES

1   P. Owens, 'Distinctions, distinctions: "Public" and "private" force?', *International Affairs*, 84:5 (2008), p. 983.

2   Carl von Clausewitz, *On War*, eds. Michael Howard and Peter Paret (New Jersey: Princeton University Press, 1984), pp. 605–7.

3   M. Weber, *From Max Weber: Essays in Sociology* (London: Routledge, 1991), p. 71.

4   P. Evans, D. Rueschemeyer and T. Skocpol (eds), *Bringing the State Back In* (Cambridge: Cambridge University Press, 1985).

5   For an overview of some of the key trends, see A. James, 'Warfare and the Rise of the State', in M. Hughes and W. J. Philpott (eds), *Palgrave Advances in Modern Military History* (Basingstoke: Palgrave Macmillan, 2006), pp. 23–41.

6   See for example, T. Ertman, *Birth of the Leviathan: Building States and Regimes in Medieval and Early Modern Europe* (Cambridge: Cambridge University Press, 1997).

7   See for instance A. Phillips, 'Saving civilization from Empire: Belligerency, pacifism, and the two faces of civilization during the Second Opium War', *European Journal of International Relations*, 18:1 (2012), pp. 5–27.

8   S. Gunn, D. Grummitt and H. Cool, 'War and the state in early modern Europe: Widening the debate', *War in History*, 15:4 (2008), pp. 371–88.

9   See for example, J. Glete, *War and the State in Early Modern Europe: Spain, the Dutch Republic and Sweden as Fiscal-Military Sates, 1500–1660* (London: Routledge, 2002); G. Rowlands, *The Dynastic State and the Army under Louis XIV: Royal Service and Private Interest 1661–1701* (Cambridge: Cambridge University Press, 2010).

10 D. Parrott, *The Business of War: Military Enterprise and Military Revolution in Early Modern Europe* (Cambridge: Cambridge University Press, 2012).

11 J. Brewer, *The Sinews of War: War, Money and the English State 1688–1783* (London: Unwin Hyman, 1989).

12 C. Tilly, 'War Making and State Making as Organised Crime', in Evans, Rueschemeyer and Skocpol (eds), *Bringing the State Back in*, p. 182.

13 See for example, L. Stone (ed.), *An Imperial State at War: Britain from 1689 to 1815* (London: Routledge, 1994); J. Brewer and E. Hellmuth (eds), *Rethinking Leviathan: The Eighteenth-Century State in Britain and Germany* (Oxford: Oxford University Press, 2004).

14 See for example, R. Knight and M. Wilcox, *Sustaining the Fleet, 1793–1815: War, the British Navy and the Contractor State* (Woodbridge: Boydell Press, 2010).

15 S. Conway, *War, State, and Society in Mid-Eighteenth-Century Britain and Ireland* (Oxford: Oxford University Press, 2006), pp. 33–55.

16 N. A. M. Rodger, 'From the "Military Revolution" to the "Fiscal-Naval State"', *Journal for Maritime Research*, 13 (2011), pp. 119–28; A. Page, *Britain and the Seventy Years War 1744–1815* (Basingstoke: Palgrave Macmillan, 2015), ch. 3.

17 E. Charters, 'The caring fiscal-military state during the Seven Years War, 1756–1763', *The Historical Journal*, 52 (2009), pp. 921–41.

18 Parrott, *The Business of War*, p. 8.

19 I. Kershaw, 'War and political violence in the twentieth century', *Contemporary European History*, 14:1 (2005), p. 108 (emphasis in original).

20 On these three classic characteristics of total war, see P. H. Wilson, 'Was the Thirty Years War a "Total War"?', in E. Charters, E. Rosenhaft and H. Smith (eds), *Civilians and War in Europe, 1618–1815* (Liverpool: Liverpool University Press, 2012), p. 24.

21 Kershaw, 'War and political violence', pp. 107–23.

22 T. Snyder, *Bloodlands: Europe between Hitler and Stalin* (London: Vintage Books, 2011).

23 M. Howard, *War in European History* (Oxford: Oxford University Press, 2009), p. 135.

24 J. L. Gaddis, 'The long peace: Elements of stability in the postwar international system', *International Security*, 10:4 (1986), pp. 99–142.

25 See for instance A. M. Kacowicz, 'Explaining zones of peace: Democracies as satisfied powers?', *Journal of Peace Research*, 32:3 (1995), pp. 265–76. For a more critical viewpoint see R. Cohen, 'Pacific unions? A reappraisal of the theory that democracies do not go to war with each other', *Review of International Studies*, 20:3 (1994), pp. 207–23.

26 F. Fukuyama, *The End of History and the Last Man* (New York: Free Press, 1992).

27 These views had been espoused during the Cold War. See K. Waltz, 'Nuclear weapons: More may be better', *Adelphi Papers*, 171 (1981). For a contrary view see N. Wheeler, 'Beyond Waltz's nuclear world: More trust may be better', *International Relations*, 23:3 (2009), pp. 428–45.

28 This literature is summarised in (for instance) in J. Sperling and E. Kircher, 'Economic security and the problem of cooperation in post-Cold War Europe', *Review of International Studies*, 24:2 (1998), pp. 221–37.

29 Much of this was based on liberal scholarship during the 1980s. See for instance M. Doyle, 'Kant, Liberal legacies and foreign affairs part 2', *Philosophy and Public Affairs*, 12:4 (1983), pp. 323–53. For enthusiastic liberal commentary after 1991 see for example D. Deudney and J. Ikenberry, 'The nature and sources of liberal international order', *Review of International* Studies, 25:2 (1999), pp. 179–96 and B. Russet, *Grasping the Democratic Peace: Principles for a Post-Cold War World* (New Jersey: Princeton University Press, 1994). On security communities, see A. Acharya, *Constructing a Security Community in Southeast Asia: ASEAN and the Problem of Regional Order* (New York: Taylor and Francis, 2nd edn, 2009).

30 S. Huntington, *The Clash of Civilisations and the Remaking of World Order* (New York: Simon Schuster, 1996).

31 See for instance W. Lambourne, 'Transitional justice and peacebuilding after mass killings', *International Journal of Transitional Justice*, 2:2 (2009), pp. 20–31.

32 J. Brinkly, 'Justice squandered: Cambodia's Khmer Rouge tribunal', *World Affairs Journal*, 2013, available at: www.worldaffairsjournal.org/article/justice-squandered-cambodia's-khmer-rouge-tribunal (accessed 19 August 2014).

33 A. Stepan and J. Linz, 'Democratization theory and the "Arab Spring"', *Journal of Democracy*, 25:2 (2013), pp. 15–30.

34 A. Pargeter, 'Localism and radicalisation in North Africa: Local factors and the development of political Islam in Morocco, Tunisia and Libya', *International Affairs*, 85:5 (2009), pp. 1031–44.

35 S. Clemons, 'Thank God for the Saudis: ISIS, Iraq, and the lessons of blowback', *Atlantic* (23 June 2014).

36 D. Rumsfeld, 'A new kind of war', *New York Times* (27 September 2001), available at: www.nytimes.com/2001/09/27/opinion/27RUMS.html (accessed 1 August 2014).

37 F. Zakaria, 'Obama the Realist', *Washington Post*, 21 July 2008, p. A15.

38 US Government National Intelligence Council, *Global Trends 2025: A Transformed World* (Washington DC: US Government Printing Office, 2008), p. iv.

39 M. Ignatieff, 'Are the authoritarians winning?', *New York Review of Books* (10 July 2014), available at: www.nybooks.com/articles/archives/2014/jul/10/are-authoritarians-winning/?insrc=hpma (accessed 30 July 2014).

40 R. Teital, *Humanity's Law* (Oxford: Oxford University Press, 2011).

41 See J. Keane, *Violence and Democracy* (Cambridge: Cambridge University Press, 2004,) pp. 19–20; P. Cerny, 'Neomedievalism, civil war and the new security dilemma: Globalisation as durable disorder', *Civil Wars*, 1:1 (1998), pp. 36–64.

42 A. Watts, 'The Importance of International Law', in M. Byers (ed.), *The Role of International Law in International Politics* (Oxford: Oxford University Press, 2001), p. 7.

43 K. Sikkink, *The Justice Cascade: How Human Rights Prosecutions are Changing the World* (New York and London: Norton, 2011), p. 5 (emphasis in original).

44 Owens, 'Distinctions, distinctions', p. 988.

INDEX